A H andbook for D... **STAND** ...
Sup ...rvisors ...

Historically, it has been presumed that being an experienced researcher was enough in itself to guarantee effective supervision. This has always been a dubious presumption, and it has become an untenable one in the light of global developments in the doctorate itself and in the candidate population which have transformed demands upon and expectations of supervisors.

This handbook will assist both new and experienced supervisors to respond to these changes. Divided into six parts the book looks at the following issues:

- the changing contexts of doctoral supervision;
- recruiting, selecting and working with doctoral candidates;
- supporting the research project;
- supporting candidates of all nationalities and academic backgrounds;
- supporting completion of projects and examination;
- evaluation and the dissemination of good practice.

A Handbook for Doctoral Supervisors focuses on the practical needs of supervisors, draws examples from a wide range of countries and uses self-interrogation as a means of encouraging readers to reflect upon their practice, making it an essential read for anyone involved in doctoral supervision.

Dr Stan Taylor is Academic Staff Development Officer at the University of Durham and has been involved in training doctoral supervisors for fifteen years at universities in the UK and overseas. **Dr Nigel Beasley** is now retired, but was previously Director of Staff Development at the University of Leicester.

A Handbook for Doctoral Supervisors

Stan Taylor and
Nigel Beasley

Routledge
Taylor & Francis Group

LONDON AND NEW YORK

Learning Resources
Centre

1272842X

First published 2005
by Routledge
2 Park Square, Milton Park, Abingdon, Oxon OX14 4RN

Simultaneously published in the USA and Canada
by Routledge
270 Madison Ave, New York, NY 10016

Routledge is an imprint of the Taylor & Francis Group

© 2005 Stan Taylor and Nigel Beasley

The right of Stan Taylor and Nigel Beasley to be identified as the
Authors of this Work has been asserted by them in accordance with
the Copyright, Designs and Patents Act 1988

Typeset in Goudy by
HWA Text and Data Management Ltd, Tunbridge Wells
Printed and bound in Great Britain by
MPG Books Ltd, Bodmin

All rights reserved. No part of this book may be reprinted or
reproduced or utilised in any form or by any electronic, mechanical,
or other means, now known or hereafter invented, including
photocopying and recording, or in any information storage or
retrieval system, without permission in writing from the publishers.

British Library Cataloguing in Publication Data
A catalogue record for this book is available from the British Library

Library of Congress Cataloging in Publication Data
A catalog record for this book has been requested

ISBN 0–415–33545–0

To Patricia and Vivienne with grateful thanks for their
support

Contents

Acknowledgements

The authors would like to thank the many – in all several hundred – doctoral supervisors with whom they have shared experiences and practice in workshops over the last decade or so, and who were the inspiration for this book.

We gratefully acknowledge permission to reproduce extracts from:

Association of American Universities for an extract from *Association of American Universities Committee on Graduate Education Report and Recommendations*, October 1998.

Biotechnology and Biological Sciences Research Council for an extract from Joint Statement of the Research Councils'/Arts and Humanities Research Board's Skills Training Requirements for Research Students.

The Centre for Educational Development and Academic Methods (CEDAM), The Australian National University, for extracts from Cullen *et al.* (1994) *Establishing Effective PhD Supervision*.

Charles Darwin University for reproduction of their questionnaire designed to facilitate discussion held by postgraduate research students and supervisors.

City University of London for extracts from their *Research Studies Handbook*.

Council of Graduate Schools [US] for use of extracts from Syverson (1996) 'Data sources: the new American graduate student – challenge or opportunity?', *The Communicator*, XXIX (8); Pruitt-Logan *et al.* (2002) *Preparing Future Faculty in the Sciences and Mathematics: A Guide for Change*; Council of Graduate Schools (1998) *Distance Graduate Education: Opportunities and Challenges for the 21st Century – A Policy Statement*.

Golde, Chris. M. (2000) '"Should I stay or should I go?" Student descriptions of the Doctoral Attrition Process', *The Review of Higher Education*, 23: 2, 199, 209, 216. Copyright The Association for the Study of Higher Education. Reprinted with permission of the Johns Hopkins University Press.

Jessica Kingsley Publishers for extracts from Becher *et al.* (1994) *Graduate Education in Britain*; Phillips (1994) 'The quality of the PhD', and an extract from Torrance and Thomas (1994) 'The development of writing skills in doctoral research students', both in Burgess (ed.) *Postgraduate Education and Training in the Social Sciences*.

M. Kiley and G. Mullins for an extract from Macauley, P. (2000) 'Pedagogic continuity in doctoral supervision: passing on, or passing by, of information skills', in M. Kiley and G. Mullins (eds) *Quality in Postgraduate Research: Making Ends Meet*. Adelaide: Advisory Centre for University Education, The University of Adelaide.

Oxford Centre for Staff and Learning Development for extracts from Ryan (2000) *A Guide to Teaching International Students*.

Professor Arthur Georges for use of material from his address to the University of Canberra Postgraduate Students Association in 1996.

Professor Peter P. C. Mertens and the Biotechnology and Biological Sciences Research Council (2000) Outcomes and Underlying Values for the BBSRC Training and Accreditation Programme for Postgraduate Supervisors. Biotechnology and Biological Sciences Research Council. Available online at http://www.iah. bbsrc.ac.uk/TAPPS/index.html.

Professor Stephen Rowland and the *Times Higher Education Supplement* for the use of extracts from his article 'Fuzzy skills agenda just dumbs down our PhDs', *Times Higher Education Supplement*, 17 January 2003.

Sage Publications, Inc. for an extract from Fitzpatrick *et al.* (1998) *Secrets for a Successful Dissertation*.

Taylor & Francis for extracts from Brown and Atkins (1988) *Effective Teaching in Higher Education*; and Delamont *et al.* (2000) *The Doctoral Experience: Success and Failure in Graduate School*, London: Falmer; Appel, L. and Dahlgren, L. (2003) 'Swedish doctoral students' experiences on their journey towards a PhD: obstacles and opportunities inside and outside the academic building', *Scandinavian Journal of Educational Research*, 47(1): 89–110; Dinham, S. and Scott, C. (2001) 'The experience of disseminating the results of doctoral research', *Journal of Further and Higher Education*, 25(1): 45–55; Evans, T. (2002) 'Part-time research students: are they producing knowledge where it counts?', *Higher Education Research and Development*, 21(2): 155–65; Gurr, G. (2001) 'Negotiating the "rackety bridge" – a dynamic model for aligning supervisory style with research student development', *Higher Education Research and Development*, 20(1): 81–92; Jackson, C. and Tinkler, P. (2001) 'Back to basics: a consideration of the purposes of the PhD viva', *Assessment and Evaluation in Higher Education*, 26(4): 355–66; Johnson, H. (2001) 'The PhD student as an adult learner: using reflective practice to find and speak in her own voice', *Reflective Practice*, 2(1): 51–63; Johnson, L., Alison, L. and Green, B. (2000) 'The PhD and the autonomous self; gender, rationality, and postgraduate pedagogy', *Studies in Higher Education*, 25 (2):135–47; McWilliam, E. and James, R. (2002) 'Doctoral education in a knowledge economy', *Higher Education Research and Development*, 21(2): 117; Morley, L., Leonard, D. and David, M. (2002) 'Variations in vivas; quality and equality in British PhD assessments', *Studies in Higher Education*, 27(3), 263–73; Smeby, J.-C. (2000) 'Disciplinary differences in Norwegian graduate education', *Studies in Higher Education*, 25(1):

54–67; Wu, S., Griffiths, S., Wisker, G., Waller, S. and Illes, K. (2001) 'The learning experience of postgraduate students: matching methods to aims', *Innovations in Education and Teaching International*, 38(3): 292–308. All of these are available through the Taylor & Francis journal web site at www.tandf.co.uk/journals.

The Australian for extracts from Massingham (1984) 'Pitfalls along the thesis approach to a higher degree', *The Australian*, 25 July 1984.

The authors and the Higher Education Research and Development Society of Australasia (HERDSA) for an extract from Gatfield, T. and Alpert, F. (2002) 'The supervisory management styles model', in A. Goody, J. Herrington and M. Northcote (eds) *Proceedings of the 2002 Annual International Conference of the HERDSA*. Perth: HERDSA.

The Controller of HMSO and the Queen's Printer for Scotland for permission for an extract from the Royal Society of Chemistry's Postgraduate Skills Record.

The Monash [University] Research Graduate School for extracts from their Supervisor Training Programme.

University of Birmingham for an extract from their Supervision Record.

University of Cambridge Computing Laboratory for an extract from its Advice to Research Students. Available online at http://www.cl.cam.ac.uk/ (accessed 18 May 2004).

Flinders University for a reproduction of their questionnaire on expectations of supervisor/student responsibilities.

University of Leicester for reproduction of their Code of Practice for the Employment of Part-Time Teaching Assistants.

University of South Australia for extracts from Code of Good Practice: Key Responsibilities in Research Degree Management and the Checklist for discussions with research degree candidates composed by Dr Sheila Scutter, School of Medical Radiation.

University of Washington and The Graduate School for use of the criteria for evaluating nominees for the Marsha L. Landolt Distinguished Graduate Mentor Awards, and Professors Tom Daniel, Judy Howard, David Notkin and Noel Weiss for reproduction of their Awardee's Statements.

Y. Ryan and O. Zuber-Skerritt for extracts from Aspland, T. (1999) '"You learn round and I learn square": Mei's story'; and Cryer, P. and Okorocha, E. (1999) 'Avoiding potential pitfalls in the supervision of NESB students', in Y. Ryan and O. Zuber-Skerritt (eds) *Supervising Postgraduates from Non-English Speaking Backgrounds*, Buckingham: Society for Research into Higher Education and Open University Press.

We would like to thank: Val Farrar of the HEFCE-funded Premia project on 'Making Research Education Accessible' for suggestions in relation to disability; fellow-participants in the European Universities Association Doctoral Programme Project Network 3 (Quality) for background information about their systems of doctoral education; and Greg Tunney for establishing the website to which readers are invited to contribute their views on the book and examples of good practice.

Introduction

Historically, the primary qualification for supervising doctoral candidates has been to hold the degree or to have equivalent research experience and to be active in scholarship or research. The logic underpinning this was summarised twenty years ago by Rudd (1985: 79–80) in that 'if one can do research then one presumably can supervise it'.

However, this presumption was widely questioned in the 1980s following global investigations which revealed that substantial numbers of candidates never completed their doctoral studies while those who did were taking up to twice as long as they should have done. While the causes of these disappointing findings were many and various, one was certainly perceived to be a lack of effectiveness on the part of supervisors (see Clark 1993; OECD 1995). The inference was drawn that, while being an active researcher was a necessary condition of being an effective supervisor, it was not a sufficient one. As Brown and Atkins (1988: 115) put the matter '… to be an effective research supervisor, you need to be an effective researcher *and* [italics added] an effective supervisor'.

The main response to this perceived need for additional knowledge and skills was the provision of opportunities for supervisors to undertake professional development. This probably went furthest in France where, since 1988, it has been necessary to gain the onerous and prestigious 'Habilitation à diriger des recherches' (HDR) before acting as a primary supervisor (see Conseil Scientifique de l'Université 1988). At this time or shortly thereafter, a few individual higher education institutions introduced formal awards for supervisors (see, for example, Clegg 1997; Pearson and Brew 2002).

But, as Neumann and Guthrie (2000) have pointed out, in the majority of institutions, initial professional development has taken the form of a day or two of initial training perhaps followed by a spell 'shadowing' an experienced supervisor. After that, it is assumed that the supervisor will be equipped to do the job for life, perhaps with the odd usually voluntary refresher session for those long in the tooth.

Between them the authors have extensive experience delivering both initial and continuing professional development workshops for supervisors, both in their own country of the UK and elsewhere in Europe and in the Far East. While we regard such workshops as useful and valuable, we are aware that they can only scratch the surface of what has become an increasingly complex and demanding area of academic practice. This has been evident not least from difficulties in shoehorning discussions into the limited time available, and from subsequent enquiries from supervisors about one aspect or another of their roles.

In order to respond to the needs of participants for greater depth or further information, we have referred colleagues to the literature on doctoral supervision which, in itself, is voluminous. Within this, however, there is, as Gatfield and Alpert (2002: 264) have pointed out a 'sparsity' of accounts aimed at potential or practising supervisors. Among these accounts there are some excellent ones (see, for example, Council of Graduate Schools 1990; Moses 1992; Cullen *et al.* 1994; Delamont *et al.* 1997), which we have drawn on extensively in writing this book. But these were published a few years ago and need updating in the light of what, as will be seen, are the momentous changes of the past decade or so in terms of the doctorate itself, the size and composition of the population of doctoral candidates, and of the additional demands made by these developments upon supervisors.

The present book was, then, conceived as an attempt to fill what the authors saw as a need in terms of an account aimed at the potential or established supervisor or advisor facing the changing world of doctoral supervision and considering what makes for effective supervision in their day to day practice.

We are aware that, while there is no hard and fast rule, the term 'supervisor' tends to be used in most of Europe, the UK, and countries where the system of doctoral education is based upon the UK model. Elsewhere, particularly in the United States and countries with systems based upon that model, the more common term is 'advisor'. We are also aware that this is not just a matter of style but also of substance; 'supervisor' implies a wider range of intervention with regard to the candidate and to the research project than 'advisor'. But, while we have written this book for supervisors (and used the term throughout) we believe that most, if not all, of it is also relevant to advisors, that is, that in covering the roles of the former we are also covering those of the latter.

With regard to 'supervision', it should be noted that our use of this term is primarily confined to the supervision of the candidate's research project. It does not include any taught components but we do think it is important that supervisors are aware of the whole doctoral programme in order that they can, where appropriate, advise students of opportunities to build upon their previous studies.

With regard to 'effective', this can be taken as meaning simply getting the candidate over the hurdle to a doctorate. But, as Phillips and Pugh (2000) have pointed out, there is more to it than that; effectiveness means a high-quality thesis, completion on time or as near as possible, dissemination to the subject community, and assisting in the preparation of the candidate for a career in research, in academia or, increasingly, elsewhere.

So, in our view, an effective supervisor is one who, alone or with an advisory committee or co-supervisor, enables the candidate:

- to, where appropriate, initiate and plan a research project;
- to acquire the research skills to undertake it and gain adequate access to resources;
- to complete it on time;
- to produce a high-quality thesis;
- to be successful in examination;
- to disseminate the results;
- to lay the basis for their future career.

Following Cryer (2004), we believe that, in order to be effective as defined above, supervisors need:

- to have a knowledge and understanding of the context within which they are supervising doctoral candidates;
- to be able to recruit and select candidates and establish working relationships with them and, where appropriate, with co-supervisors;
- to support candidates' research projects;
- to support the personal, professional, and career development of doctoral candidates;
- to support candidates through the processes of completion of their thesis and final examination;
- and to be able to evaluate their practice and, where appropriate, disseminate good practice.

In accordance with this model, we have divided the content of the book into six parts.

Part I deals with the context of supervision. Chapter 1 sets out the overall context in terms of the evolution and development of doctoral studies, particularly over the past two decades, while Chapter 2 considers the institutional context, and Chapter 3 the disciplinary one.

Part II is concerned with preparing the ground in terms of recruiting and selecting candidates (Chapter 4) and forming working relationships with them (Chapter 5) and, where appropriate, co-supervisors (Chapter 6).

Part III is devoted to supporting the research project. Chapter 7 deals with helping to get the project up and running and overcoming any initial academic problems. In Chapter 8, the focus is upon encouraging candidates to write up and giving them feedback. In Chapter 9, the focus is upon assisting candidates to keep the project on track and upon monitoring their progress.

Part IV is concerned with supporting the candidate. Chapter 10 is concerned with personal, academic, and support for candidates in general. In Chapter 11 and Chapter 12, these matters are looked at in the context of responding to diversity among the domestic and international candidate populations respectively.

Part V is devoted to completion and examination. After completing their research projects, candidates have to write up their theses and submit them for examination. Supervisors have a role to play in assisting candidates to complete, as outlined in Chapter 13, and may have a role helping them to prepare for examination, which is outlined in Chapter 14. Additionally, in many systems, supervisors also act as examiners, and this role is discussed in Chapter 15.

Part VI is concerned with how doctoral supervisors might go about evaluating their practice and disseminating good practice (Chapter 16).

As well as describing the content of the book, it is also appropriate to comment also upon the approach adopted in writing it. In order to illustrate effective practice, we have included numerous examples drawn mainly courtesy of the Web from higher education institutions virtually across the globe. In order to encourage readers to reflect upon their potential or actual practice as supervisors, we have followed what we believe to be the successful technique used in Fry *et al.* (1999, 2001) whereby prompts are supplied at key points in the narrative for readers to consider key issues or to interrogate their own practice. Such reflection is, as Brew and Pesata (2004) have shown, vital in the promotion of effective practice and our hope is that, through this process, readers will be able to personally engage with their own practice and, where appropriate, improve it.

Part I

The context

Chapter 1

The overall context

Supervisors tend to be immersed in their busy academic and/or professional lives, and seldom have the time to maintain an overview of developments in doctoral education. In consequence, many are experiencing new demands without understanding the wider context within which they arise. The purpose of the present chapter, then, is to try to set that wider context. The chapter begins with a brief summary of the historical origins and evolution of doctoral education from its modern origins through to the 1980s and then looks at subsequent developments that have transformed the doctorate itself, the population of candidates and expectations of doctoral supervisors.

The origins and evolution of doctoral education

While universities have awarded doctoral degrees since the twelfth century, these were not awards for research as such but primarily a licence to teach in a particular subject area (see, for example, Phillips 1994; Radford 2001; Noble 1994).

Modern research-based doctoral degrees have their origins in the introduction of the PhD in Berlin in the early years of the nineteenth century. The original intention of their progenitor, Von Humboldt, was to enhance the supply of scientists and other researchers by providing opportunities for promising students to undertake their first solo research project under the guidance of an experienced researcher (see, for example, Clark 1997). The intention was that students would devise a suitable research project and then find a senior professor (*Doktorvater*) who could offer initial support and guidance. Under their expert tuition, students would then begin to undertake their research project. As the latter progressed, the expectation was that students would rapidly outpace their supervisors as they become the experts in their topic of study and that, eventually, they would make their own independent contribution to knowledge and understanding in their subject. In this form, as the US Council of Graduate Schools (1998: 28–9) has put the matter '... the only requirements for the doctorate [are] independently completing an approved research project, submitting a dissertation and passing an oral examination'.

The new research degree made little headway during the rest of the nineteenth century in the European universities, which remained primarily concerned with undergraduate teaching. But if the universities of the Old World remained unimpressed by the doctorate, it was more rapidly embraced by those of the New World, by the United States. There, the first PhD was awarded by Yale in 1861 and the precedent was quickly followed by Harvard, Michigan and Pennsylvania.

But if Germany gave the PhD to the US, the latter developed it in a distinctive way. In Germany, in common with much of the rest of Europe, undergraduate education was an extended affair often lasting many years, at the end of which at least the brightest and best students could be regarded as emerging as research-capable.

The US, however, had adopted a system of short broad-based undergraduate degrees, which were not considered likely to take students to the frontiers of research. The implication was, then, that students required a further period of education and training at graduate level before they could successfully embark upon a research project.

So, in the US, the PhD took a different form, one beginning with a first requirement of budding researchers that they should undertake a programme of study to acquire leading-edge knowledge, understanding and skills. For those who attained this, there was then a second requirement that they undertook an appropriate training in the research skills pertaining to their area of interest. It was only when they had successfully completed such a training that they could be considered to be allowed to proceed to undertake a research project. As a result, PhD programmes developed in the US had, as Bowen and Rudenstein (1992: 251) have described it, three principal stages:

> The first comprises a period of formal course work that usually lasts two or three years. The second is a less defined interim period in which other stipulated requirements (and usually some teaching assignments) are completed. This stage may involve passing a general examination or qualifying exam and satisfying foreign language requirements as well as choosing a dissertation topic and, in some cases, submitting an approved prospectus. The last stage is one of intensive dissertation research and writing, including final defence of the dissertation.

So, in the United States, the PhD became an extended research training prog-ramme and, moreover, one conducted within a new form of institution, namely the graduate university or school. The latter was a recognition that graduate education was qualitatively different from undergraduate education and, as such, required a separate organisation. This, of course, was the distinction which gave rise to the founding in 1876 of Johns Hopkins University as a predominantly graduate institution and to the subsequent establishment of graduate schools in a number of other leading US universities in the late nineteenth century. In the latter, both the PhD and the graduate school became common in research universities in the US and by the turn of the century had been exported to Canada (see Noble 1994).

By the start of twentieth century, Germany and the US were the two biggest players in the market for doctoral education, with the consequence that they not only retained their own students looking to undertake research but attracted those from other countries. These included the UK which had, up until then, not only held on to its own domestic students but enrolled large numbers of international students both from its then Empire and other countries, particularly the US. So the UK began to suffer the defection of some of the brightest and best home students to undertake doctoral research in Germany as well as lose out on its traditional overseas market share to the United States. But, as Simpson (1983) has shown, universities in the UK remained unconcerned about these developments.

It was only when the First World War cut out Germany as a destination for overseas doctoral students and opened up the market that, under pressure from the government of the day, UK universities were persuaded to offer the PhD. The first (in fact a DPhil) was awarded by Oxford in 1920 and over the following decade all of the UK universities adopted the degree. But, in doing so, they adopted a somewhat different approach from that used in the US. While UK degrees were, like US ones, short in duration, they were narrowly specialised within subject areas. The view was taken that, because they were highly specialised, the best students at least should emerge with a leading-edge knowledge of their subject and hence that they should be able to proceed immediately to the research project. Subsequently, the PhD in this form was exported to other countries with higher education systems modelled on the UK, including Australia where the first doctoral programmes were offered in 1946 (see Williams 2000).

The 1950s and especially the 1960s saw research rise to the top of the political agenda in many countries as a key to both economic growth and defence capability and this was reflected in a rapid growth of PhD programmes and studentships in the Anglo-American democracies, particularly in the United States (see Bowen and Rudenstein 1992). Similar considerations led to the introduction of the PhD in the 1960s and 1970s in a number of other countries which had hitherto resisted it, particularly in Western Europe (see Oden 1997; Smeby 2000; Eurodoc 2003).

By the mid-1980s, the PhD had conquered Western Europe, but not Eastern Europe. In most of the so-called 'Soviet bloc', there were different arrangements based upon the USSR model of a two-step doctorate which could be taken inside or outside the universities, for example in the Academies of Sciences, and in either case was subject to state approval (see, for example, Connelly 2000). However, the 'velvet revolutions' at the end of the 1980s and start of the 1990s were followed by the re-organisation of graduate education and by the establishment of the PhD in the universities (see OECD 1998).

By the 1990s, then, the PhD had grown from its origins in Germany nearly two centuries earlier to become a qualification delivered over a large proportion of the globe. But, ironically, at the same time it became the subject of criticism in virtually all of the countries that had adopted it.

Criticisms of doctoral education

While, during the rapid growth of the PhD in the 1950s and 1960s, governments had funded an expansion of doctoral programmes, they had left their organisation and management to the universities. However, from the 1970s onwards governments across much of the globe were, for a variety of reasons, seeking retrenchment in public spending, which was subjected to intense scrutiny. This included scrutiny of spending on higher education and as such encompassed that on doctoral programmes. So, for the first time in history, PhD programmes became the subject of national investigation in many countries. This revealed what became a catalogue of criticisms of their fitness for purpose and of their fitness of purpose.

Fitness for purpose

While, as has been seen, there were different routes towards the PhD in different countries, in all the intention was that students would be funded for three or four years after which they would gain the award. But before the 1980s few, including governments, funding bodies and even institutions, had bothered to check whether, in fact, students were gaining the degree and, if so, how long they were taking.

When, from the 1980s, attention was turned to this matter, the findings of surveys (see, for example, Blaume and Amsterdamsaka 1987; Winfield 1987; Bowen and Rudenstein 1992; Leonard 2000; Colebatch 2002; McAlpine and Weiss 2000) indicated that only around half of the population of doctoral candidates actually graduated with a doctorate. So it became apparent that, as Golde (2000: 199) has put it:

> ... the most academically capable, most academically successful, most stringently evaluated and most carefully selected students in the entire higher education system – doctoral students – [were the] least likely to complete their chosen academic goals.

To make matters worse, the same studies found that, of those students who did gain the degree, relatively few completed within the allotted time. So, for example, an investigation of completion rates among social scientists in the UK (Winfield 1987) revealed that less than one-fifth of sponsored students completed within even four years. A similar study by Bowen and Rudenstein (1992) of the US revealed that successful students were taking, on average, eight years to do the degree, twice the time allotted. Even more damningly, their longitudinal evidence indicated that, over the previous 30 years, average completion times had increased by around 20 per cent.

Fitness of purpose

The purpose of the PhD had, as Leonard (2000) has pointed out, always been to give promising researchers the opportunity to undertake a piece of research on a topic of interest to themselves as a prelude to a university career as an academic subject specialist undertaking and disseminating research through publications and conferences. But, in the 1980s and 1990s, the appropriateness of this purpose came into question on four main grounds.

The first was the alleged disjuncture between curiosity-driven research and the utilitarian view, then gaining international currency, that the purpose of education was ultimately to further economic growth. In the PhD context, this was taken to mean that research topics should have relevance to 'real world needs', that is, be driven by the needs of stakeholders, including government, industry and commerce and not what were seen as the whims of research students or their supervisors.

The second was the disjuncture between the PhD as a piece of research conducted within a single discipline at a time when it was becoming increasingly evident that many research problems required interdisciplinary perspectives to be brought to bear to find a solution. So, for example, as Hagoel and Kalekin-Fishman (2002) have shown, solving pressing environmental problems such as the hydrologic cycle, ecosystems and sustainable development in general required wide-ranging expertise from agriculture, forestry, hydrology, marine resource management and law. The PhD was then, it was argued, failing to equip graduates to operate in this increasingly interdisciplinary world.

The third was the disjuncture between what PhD programmes were training students to be, namely academics, and what they were increasingly doing in a number of the leading providers of doctoral education, which was working in other forms of employment. For the most of the twentieth century, doctoral graduates did flow into academic posts and even the rapid growth in the numbers of PhDs in the 1960s and early 1970s was largely absorbed into tenure-track or tenured academic employment. However, particularly in the US and Western Europe, this was thrown into sharp reverse in the late 1970s and 1980s as governments cut back on spending on higher education. In consequence, the core of permanent tenure track and tenured jobs began to shrink and PhDs were effectively forced either into short-term research posts or to seek jobs outside academia. Evidence began to emerge in a number of countries (see, for example, Syverson 1997; Noble 1994) that, in some cases, PhDs were finding it difficult to find employment at all or, more commonly, were taking jobs that demanded lower qualifications and skills. This evidence of unemployment and under-employment among what should be the best qualified section of the workforce led to criticism of the PhD on the ground that it was failing to equip its holders for employment outside academia. As the matter was famously put in a UK Office of Science and Technology paper (1993: 3) '... the traditional PhD is not well matched to the needs of careers outside research in academia or an industrial research laboratory'.

The fourth was the disjuncture between what PhD programmes were training students to do and the likely demands upon them as key workers in the 'knowledge economies' of the future (see Usher 2002). The traditional PhD was, it was argued, aimed at producing researchers in the so-called Mode 1 of knowledge production, that is, academic subject specialists who would conduct the search for knowledge for its own sake in line with the traditional academic values of truth, objectivity and universality. But what was needed in the knowledge economies of the future was researchers trained in the so-called Mode 2 of knowledge production, that is, researchers inside or outside academia who were able to spot commercial opportunities for the application and exploitation of research, bring expertise to bear upon research problems, effectively manage research projects and place and market the final product. In a nutshell, the traditional PhD was about producing academics, but the new knowledge economy required research entrepreneurs.

The crisis of doctoral education

The criticisms above add up to a long list: the waste of funding and effort for the half of students who never completed their degree; the extra years of study, often self-funded, by students who did gain it; the alleged lack of relevance of research topics to national needs and priorities; the mis-match between the production of single subject specialists in a world in which research was increasingly interdisciplinary; the appearance of unemployment or under-employment among the most expensively trained and highest qualified of the workforce; and the lack of fostering of the entrepreneurial skills that would be needed by key workers in the knowledge economy. Small wonder then that, across the globe, doctoral education was seen as being in crisis (see Geiger 1997; LaPidus 1997; Kendall 2002).

Not surprisingly, the question arose as to who was responsible and should be held accountable: certainly not governments and other research sponsors who had provided massive funding for research studentships; certainly not the universities, who had received the funding but passed it on to their graduate schools and/or academic departments; and certainly not the latter, which had handed the matter over to PhD programme directors; and certainly not them, because they had handed it to advisory committees or supervisors; and certainly not them, because the whole rationale of the PhD was that students were required to undertake an independent piece of work and, ultimately, stand or fall by their own efforts and abilities; and certainly not the students, who had never received the guidance and support necessary for them to complete the degree on time and proceed to employment.

In short, everyone passed the buck and no one was willing to accept responsibility or be held accountable. This, on the one hand absolved all involved from blame and on the other pointed up the need to establish lines of responsibility and mechanisms for accountability in the future.

Responses to the crisis in doctoral education

Research sponsors, particularly of course governments and government-backed bodies, and higher education institutions responded to the crisis by a combination of structural reform of the doctorate, compulsion, measures to improve accountability and innovation.

Structural reform of the doctorate

With regard to tackling low completion rates and long completion times, at least outside the US these were blamed upon the fact that once accepted for doctoral study students were often left to get on with it with little or no support. In such circumstances and often with little or no previous experience of research, it was scarcely surprising that many students took a long time to find their feet, or never found them at all.

The solution to this in many countries was seen in terms of a re-structuring of doctoral education along the lines of the US model, including the introduction of formal research training requirements as part of the PhD. So, for example, as Huisman *et al.* (2002) have shown, governments, research funding bodies and institutions in the UK, the Netherlands, Germany and Sweden began to insist that students spent all or part of at least their first year or two of study undertaking a training in research and research management. Similarly, it was the US model which was used as the basis for establishing doctoral education in the newly liberated countries of central and eastern Europe.

In the same way and again clearly borrowing from the US model, graduate schools or similar began to spring up in a number of countries including the UK, where the first was established in 1989 at the University of Warwick, Germany, where Graduiertenkollegs began in 1990 (see Deutsche Forschingsgemeinshaft 2000) and France where the first écoles doctorales were established in 1992 and in 2000 became the sole institutions training research students and awarding doctoral degrees (see Voison-Demery 2001). This trend was also followed in the emerging systems of doctoral education in countries formerly in the Soviet bloc.

As again Huisman *et al.* (2002) have pointed out, these developments may be seen as part of a trend towards global convergence in the provision of doctoral education on the US model, although this trend is incomplete and, as Allen *et al.* (2002) have shown, by no means universal.

Compulsion

Many governments resorted to what amounted, in one form or another, to compulsion.

Examples

In Sweden, which was hitherto well-known for its *laisser-faire* attitude to PhD completion (see Frischer and Larsson 2000), the government passed a law in 1998 limiting the period of study for the PhD to four years, with no further opportunity for submission.

In the Netherlands, where PhD students are university employees, they had traditionally been entitled to four years' salary and then a year to write up during which they were entitled to unemployment benefit equivalent to 78 per cent of their salary. However, in 2001, this right was removed (see Tan and Meijer 2001).

In the UK, the government-funded research councils established steeply progressive annual targets for the proportions of students to complete within four years, backed in most cases by sanctions against under-performing departments in the form of the withdrawal of recognition for funding for research studentships (see Joint Funding Councils 2002).

In Australia in 1999 the federal government issued a white paper (Department of Education, Training and Youth Affairs 1999) deploring the wastage arising from low completion rates and high completion times and introduced target completion rates linked to the block grants to universities involving a re-distribution of funding for studentships towards those achieving the targets and away from the under-performers (see also Neumann 2002).

Accountability

In addition to coercion, there were also moves to impose systems for quality assurance upon institutions in a number of countries.

Examples

In Australia, in the mid-1990s the government 'invited' all universities to participate in a national Postgraduate Research Evaluation Questionnaire. This was administered to all students and, on the model of similar questionnaires on students on taught programmes, was intended to determine their overall satisfaction ratings and to rank institutions accordingly. While it proved an unsatisfactory ranking device (see Marsh et al. 2002), this measure served to focus the attention of the universities upon assuring and enhancing the quality of their doctoral degrees and many began to establish codes of practice for the conduct of research degrees and systems for candidate evaluation of the quality of their learning experiences.

In the same year, but in the UK, the Quality Assurance Agency for Higher Education (1999) produced a comprehensive code of practice against which institutions were asked to benchmark their research degree programmes and, where appropriate, take action to improve their provision. Subsequently, the Joint Funding Councils (2002) undertook a review which indicated that adherence was patchy and it was proposed that institutions should be required to set and monitor threshold standards for the conduct of their research degrees as a condition of continuing to receive funding for research students.

Innovation

In response to the criticisms of the fitness of purpose of the traditional PhD, there have been innovations designed to promote research which was deemed relevant to the 'real world', to promote interdisciplinary research, to incorporate employability and entrepreneurship as objectives of PhD programmes and finally to develop alternative modes of doctoral provision more suited to modern requirements.

With regard to relevance, research funding bodies, particularly public ones, began to take a tighter grip on the research topics which could be undertaken by students through identifying priority areas for research and then inviting research proposals from supervisors or students which fitted within these frameworks. Additionally, public funding bodies began actively seeking the involvement of industry and commerce in funding collaborative research ventures. These varied from the joint funding of single students to undertake research projects which would both benefit the non-academic sponsor and lead to a PhD through to the establishment of joint centres including the Network of Centres of Excellence in Canada, the National Science Foundation Industry–University Centres in the US and the Co-operative Research Centres in Australia (see Harman 2002).

With regard to interdisciplinarity, public funding bodies used similar strategies. Research funding was earmarked for topics requiring interdisciplinary expertise and in order to access this funding universities were effectively required to establish interdisciplinary research centres offering interdisciplinary research degrees. In addition, many of the collaborative research centres noted above were established on an interdisciplinary basis.

With regard to employability and entrepreneurship, in the United States there were calls in the mid-1990s from funding bodies and others for Graduate Schools to broaden doctoral programmes so that they, as Pruitt-Logan *et al.* (2002: v) have put it:

> ... cultivate a broader range of academic and career skills ... provide students with more knowledge about a wider variety of careers and foster a greater sense of entrepreneurship than is customary.

In the UK the initiative was taken by the government-backed Joint Research Councils and Arts and Humanities Research Board (2001) which agreed a set of key skills relating to employability and entrepreneurship. These included variously: generic research skills; generic knowledge and understanding of the research environment; the ability to manage research projects; personal effectiveness; communication skills, networking and team-working; and career management. In 2003, a requirement was laid on institutions to ensure that all doctoral training programmes included these components, with the prospect of research funding being withdrawn if they failed to do so. There were, as Leonard (2000) has noted, similar developments in Australia, New Zealand and a number of other countries.

All of the above involved, essentially, changing the purposes of the PhD to incorporate the new demands for relevance, interdisciplinarity, employability and entrepreneurship. But, in addition, attempts were made to promote alternatives to the PhD in the form of the so-called 'professional doctorates'.

Professional doctorates may be said to have four main characteristics distinguishing them from the traditional PhD. First, they are undertaken predominantly, if not exclusively, by practising professionals in a vocation relevant to the field of study. Second, they involve a significant taught component, which of course is a feature of the United States model of doctoral education, but an innovation in the European one. Third and crucially, the research project usually relates to the professional practice of the student and is undertaken in the workplace. Fourth, the thesis is normally shorter in length than that for a traditional PhD and expected to be useful as well as original, that is, address issues of professional practice and solve practical problems in ways that will benefit practitioners, clients and organisations.

Such doctorates are, in fact, hardly new: as Allen *et al.* (2000) have shown, Canada had one in 1894, while in the United States the first professional doctorates were established in the 1920s (see Bourner *et al.* 2001). But, for most of the twentieth century these degrees were far overshadowed by and in many cases regarded as inferior to, the traditional PhD (see, for example, Jablonski 2001).

However, in the late 1980s there was a re-evaluation of professional doctorates because, unlike the traditional PhD, they met the canons of relevance (research grounded in professional practice), interdisciplinarity (different disciplinary perspectives brought to bear on the research problem), employability (students were already in employment) and entrepreneurship (developing and marketing solutions to work-based and professional problems). In consequence, professional doctorates began to enjoy a new popularity in the United States, where there are now over 50 and as Bourner *et al.* (2001) have shown, in the 1990s they were introduced to the UK, Australia and a number of other parts of Western Europe.

Trends in the doctoral student population

If the doctorate was in crisis for much of the 1980s and 1990s, this did not appear to affect its popularity. On the contrary, the numbers registering for doctoral programmes in most countries increased very substantially over that period (see OECD 1998). The causes of this development probably lie in two main factors.

The first was the shift in many countries from an elite to a mass system of higher education at the undergraduate and taught postgraduate levels. On the one hand, the fact that there were many more people with undergraduate or master's degrees increased the numbers who were eligible to undertake doctoral programmes; on the other, the fact that these lower degrees had become relatively common increased the cachet associated with the doctorate and gave it an edge in terms of status and possibly qualifications in the labour market.

The second was the perceived need by governments virtually across the globe to ensure a flow of trained researchers to give their countries a competitive edge in the knowledge economies of the future. In many developed countries, this took the form of allowing or encouraging an expansion of doctoral places (albeit without increased public funding), whereas in many developing ones it took the form of increasing the opportunities for graduates to go abroad and study for their doctorates.

If these developments have led to larger numbers of doctoral students, they also led to changes in their social composition. Traditionally, doctoral candidates have come from elite institutions populated mainly by students from upper or middle class families and were disproportionately male and white (see, for example, Bowen and Rudenstein 1992; Conrad 1994; Humphrey and McCarthy 1999). But the new entrants to doctoral study came from a wider range of social backgrounds, a broader range of institutions, included many more women and more members of ethnic and racial groups, whether from within countries or from abroad.

Moreover, much of this expansion of numbers took the form of candidates who were older and studying part-time. Again, traditionally the route to a doctorate was through consecutive and full-time study for a bachelor's degree (or equivalent), a master's and then a PhD, by which time the successful candidate was in his or her mid- to late-20s. But this route was only possible because of wealthy parents and/or state support, which in many countries was generous until the 1990s. Then, governments began shifting the cost of undergraduate and taught postgraduate students leaving them deep in debt upon graduation while, at the same time, cutting back on research studentships and research stipends (see, for example, Cebrian 2001; Germano 2001; Tan and Meijer 2001; Voison-Demery 2001; Galanaki 2002; Neumann 2002).

Faced with debt arising from their previous education and the prospect of incurring significantly more as research students, many graduates have begun to delay entry to doctoral programmes until later in life and then studied part-time. As Syverson (1996) has put the matter:

> The traditional view of graduate students is of newly-minted Bachelor's degree recipients engaged in full-time study. However, the decided majority of students ... are quite different. They are older ... and have family and career responsibilities.

Conclusions

The effect of these developments has been to transform doctoral education virtually across the globe. As McWilliam and James (2002: 117) have written:

> Until relatively recent times, the achievement of a doctoral degree was a somewhat rarified and mysterious endeavour. Doctoral education was

conducted behind closed doors in spaces remote from either undergraduate teaching or the world of commerce and industry. Its pedagogy has been characterised by some – perhaps unfairly – as one in which the precocious few were called to emulate the master as scholar.

Much has changed. 'Doctoral education' is now a highly contested term and a highly populated and public domain of practice. We have seen in recent times the massification and diversification of postgraduate education in general and this has led, in turn, to an increase in the diversity of purposes and agendas that candidates bring to doctoral studies. Research training agendas are being affected by changes in university–industry–government relationships, adding to the diversity of outcomes that policy makers expect of the doctorate. All of this is being changed by and changing, modes of 'scientific' knowledge production.

So, over the past two decades or so, the precocious few doctoral candidates have become the diverse many; modes of doctoral education have begun to converge towards the model of research training conducted within a graduate school pioneered in the US; the purposes of doctoral education have been re-defined to embrace interdisciplinarity, economic relevance, employability and entrepreneurship; and doctoral education is now out of the closet and firmly in the public domain, with attendant pressures for responsibility and accountability.

Chapter 2

The institutional context

The developments in doctoral education described in the previous chapter are often only apparent to supervisors in their translation into the broad setting in which they work, namely their institutions. It is the latter, of course, that ultimately award doctoral degrees and which are responsible for defining the standards of awards, for setting expectations of supervisors and of candidates, and for providing the support necessary for both to meet them.

Institutions can, and do, vary in all of these matters and for this reason it is important that supervisors do not simply rely upon their own experience to inform their practice, especially if they are working in an institution other than the one in which they did their own doctorate and/or supervising a different kind of doctorate.

The present chapter, then, is concerned with the institutional context of doctoral supervision in terms of the standards of awards, the roles and responsibilities of supervisors and candidates, and the support available to both.

Definitions of the standards of doctoral awards

The ultimate object of the exercise is for the candidate to gain a doctorate, which involves them in meeting the standards set for the award. In order to supervise candidates to achieve standards, supervisors obviously need to know what they are.

If they do not then, as Phillips and Pugh (2000) have pointed out, it effectively means that both are operating in the dark, and this can be a recipe for disaster.

Of course, it is a requirement in many countries and/or institutions that supervisors have doctorates themselves, and on this basis most will have an understanding of the standards for the award. But, bearing in mind that there are differences between institutions in definitions of doctorates, as well as different types of doctorates, they still need to consult the institutional definition. This is usually set out in its regulations or ordinances.

Historically, these have not necessarily been the most enlightening sources of information. So, writing some time ago, Massingham (1984: 15) cited the example of one university with an institution definition which made it:

> ... almost impossible to get any clear information on what a thesis should be. Marvellously ambiguous phrases like 'a contribution to knowledge' are bandied around by the authorities ... the conditions for the award in the Calendar give more precise information on the size of the paper and the margins ... than on the university's understanding of what a thesis is.

But in recent years, institutions have been moved by external factors, including in some cases the imposition of national qualifications frameworks (see, for example, Quality Assurance Agency for Higher Education 2001) to define explicit standards for their doctoral awards.

In the case of the traditional PhD, the definition will normally include, where appropriate, successful completion of any taught components, undertaking a research project, writing up the latter in the form of a thesis or dissertation (the terms are used interchangeably in this book), and being judged by examiners to have made an independent and original contribution to knowledge and understanding in their academic discipline. But, beyond these fundamentals, institutions can and do vary in their requirements. So, for example, in the UK as Tinkler and Jackson (2000) and Powell and McCauley (2002) have shown, some universities insisted that candidates were able to relate their findings to the wider subject while others did not, and there was a similar variation in whether or not the material in the thesis should be worthy of publication.

More recent forms of PhDs include PhDs by publication and practice-based PhDs. The former is normally available only to members of staff of institutions and involves submitting a portfolio of publications along with a linking commentary. But, if the form of submission of evidence is different, institutional requirements are usually the same as for the traditional PhD, that is, that the publications make an original contribution to knowledge and understanding in the discipline (see, for example, Wilson 2002)

However, in the case of practice-based PhDs, there are differences both in the form of submission and institutional requirements. So the evidence submitted includes an artefact or artefacts (physical and/or artistic expression) usually accompanied by a critical commentary about how it was created which relates both the product and the process to the wider context of practice and theory in the discipline. In order to accommodate this somewhat different beast institutions have, as Bourner *et al.* (1999) have shown, added regulations which permit a PhD to be awarded for 'an independent and original contribution to practice in a discipline'.

As well as the PhD, traditional or otherwise, the main growth area in doctoral studies over the past two decades has been in professional doctorates. While, as noted in the introduction, these have a long history in some disciplines, they are much more recent in others, and institutions have found it necessary to define requirements for them. Research (see, for example, Bourner *et al.* 1999, 2001, 2002; Hoddell *et al.* 2001) suggests that, in most institutions, the starting point has been requirements for the traditional PhD, which have been modified in three main ways.

First, at least outside higher education systems with a US-style PhD, requirements have been added in the form of the completion of coursework, usually covering between a third and two-thirds of doctoral studies. Second, and reflecting the fact that candidates have less time to spend on their research projects compared to their counterparts undertaking traditional PhDs, the scale of the thesis has been shortened or replaced with other forms of evidence, for example, multiple short project reports. Third, to reflect the professional basis of such doctorates, the PhD requirement to undertake a research project which makes an original contribution to knowledge in an academic discipline has been substituted by a requirement to undertake a research project (or projects) which make an original contribution to improving practice in a professional discipline.

Interrogating practice

On the basis of your own experience as a doctoral candidate, what do you think the standards are for the award?

How does your institution define the standards for awards, including where appropriate the traditional PhD, practice-based PhDs, and professional doctorates?

Are you confident that you know the institutional standards of the award which you are supervising?

Institutional expectations of supervisors and candidates

Once supervisors have a firm grip on the standards for the award, they also need to know what their institution expects of them and their candidates. Institutional expectations will usually be set out in handbooks and/or codes of practice or conduct.

Institutional expectations of supervisors may include:

- familiarity with formal institutional regulations or ordinances governing research degrees;
- ensuring that recruitment and selection processes are conducted in accordance with institutional policies for widening participation and equal opportunities;
- selecting students who are appropriately qualified and with a clear potential to gain the award;
- ensuring that the supervisory team has the expertise to supervise in the candidate's area of study;
- ensuring that there are adequate resources to support the research project and reviewing this regularly;

- establishing, monitoring and maintaining a professional relationship with the student;
- establishing, monitoring and maintaining professional relationships with others in the supervisory team or advisory committee;
- in the event of absence for a given period of time, informing the appropriate person so that alternative arrangements can be made for supervision;
- meeting regularly with the student in accordance with at least a minimum schedule determined by the institution for formal and other meetings;
- where students are absent from the institution while undertaking their research, establishing and maintaining regular contact;
- ensuring that records are kept of formal meetings;
- being accessible at other appropriate times, which may be subject to an institutionally-defined maximum period from a student request for a meeting to be arranged;
- inducting students into relevant university policies, including those relating to equal opportunities, intellectual property rights, plagiarism, and ethical issues;
- inducting students into their research degrees and making sure that they have understood the institutional regulations relating to the award, including arrangements for progression;
- ensuring that students understand what the institution will provide and what their own obligations are, often signified by the main supervisor and student signing a learning contract or agreement;
- ensuring that students understand the importance of and attend relevant university, faculty, graduate school or departmental training programmes;
- where appropriate, assisting with the creation of the research project, which may be subject to an institutional deadline, for example, six months from registration;
- where appropriate, assisting in gaining any ethical clearances or access to sources or resources;
- assisting students to devise a realistic research proposal and plan and reviewing them with them regularly;
- supporting them in the initial stages of the research project, in particular in relation to the literature review and the choice of methodology and/or methods;
- agreeing a schedule for students to produce written work on a regular basis and motivating them to stick to it;
- giving constructive feedback on work in progress within an institutionally or personally defined period;
- assisting with academic problems with the research;
- assisting with keeping the research on track;
- in institutions where the supervisory team has a pastoral role, assisting with personal and social problems affecting the research or, where there isn't such a team, referring the student to a mentor or other pastoral advisor;

- assisting students to prepare for formal progress reviews;
- reporting formally on their progress at specified intervals to stakeholders, including the institution and research sponsors;
- collecting and responding to student feedback on the quality of their learning experiences;
- assisting students to write up and complete;
- advising them on submission or, where appropriate, signing off the thesis as worthy of defence;
- advising on the choice of examiners;
- where appropriate, assisting the student with preparation for oral examination;
- where appropriate, arranging the examination;
- in many countries, acting as an examiner;
- in cases where theses are referred for further work, assisting students to complete it within an institutionally defined time period;
- assisting students to develop appropriate networks;
- encouraging students to publish and advising on appropriate outlets;
- where publication is joint, establishing appropriate means for crediting the contributions made by supervisor(s) and students;
- assisting students to acquire the skills which will assist them to develop careers, either inside or outside academia.

Within this overall set of expectations, institutions which have supervisory teams may distinguish between their expectations of 'main' and 'secondary' supervisors or 'internal 'and 'external' supervisors, and these are considered in Chapter 6.

As well, of course, as being clear about what exactly the institution expects of supervisors in whatever capacity they are supervising, it is also important to know what is expected of candidates. This is usually contained in the Student Handbook or Code of Conduct which, with obvious exceptions and additions, are often the mirror image of those for supervisors.

In addition, of course, there are some responsibilities which are joint, with both the supervisor and the student having key roles to play.

Information on what is expected of supervisors, what is expected of candidates, and what is expected of both is vital, and it is very useful for supervisors to go through supervisor and candidate handbooks matching the topics and comparing their respective roles and responsibilities.

Example

Charles Darwin University in Australia has a Code of Conduct for Supervision which sets out the responsibilities of staff and students side by side so that their respective and joint responsibilities are clear, as in the short extract below.

Supervisor's responsibilities	*Candidate's responsibilities*
• fulfil the requirements of the Rules for Supervision.	• comply with the rules that govern the award of their degree.
• act in accordance with the general principles of the Student Charter.	• act in accordance with the general principles of the Student Charter.
• be aware of the ethical implications of all research and advise candidates accordingly.	• be aware of the ethical implications of all research and consult with their supervisor accordingly.
• encourage candidates to be aware of good conduct in research and data retention.	• be aware of issues associated with conduct of research and data retention.
• contribute to a learning environment which includes encouraging discussion and debate within the university and amongst external peers.	• participate actively and become involved in discussion and debate within the university and amongst external peers.
• complete the Research Degree Supervision Agreement where possible within the first month of supervision and review annually.	• complete the Research Degree Supervision Agreement where possible within the first month of supervision and review annually.

Source: http://www.cdu.edu.au/research/attachments/code_conduct_04.rtf

---

Interrogating practice

What are your institution's expectations of doctoral supervisors?

What are your institution's expectations of doctoral candidates?

What areas are you and the candidate jointly responsible for?

Support for supervisors and students

As well as providing descriptions of roles and responsibilities, most institutions now provide support for those of their staff involved in supervision. Such support may take the forms of initial professional development for new supervisors, apprenticeship or mentoring schemes, and opportunities for continuing professional development for established ones. Supervisors need to be aware of these sources of support, as well of course sources of support for candidates so that they can advise them where to seek assistance. Finally, they also need to be aware of the support for both in the event of problems in their relationship.

Initial professional development for supervisors

On p. 1, it was noted that one of the key institutional responses to the realisation that there was more to being a supervisor than being a researcher was the establishment of requirements or opportunities for them to undertake initial professional development.

Clearly, it is important for prospective supervisors to find out what is available in their institution, and whether it is a requirement that they attend before, for example, being placed on the register of prospective supervisors.

But it is also important that they consider whether the professional development on offer will be adequate to prepare them to supervise. In an ideal world, as Pearson and Brew (2002) have suggested, the outcomes of professional development programmes would include:

- self-awareness of own conceptions of research and supervisory practice;
- understanding of what constitutes a productive research learning environment;
- appreciation of good practice in approaches to supervision;
- a repertoire of supervisory strategies;
- knowledge of institutional requirements;
- practice in self-evaluating their efficacy and competence as supervisors;
- competency in interactional and communication skills;
- understanding of how to facilitate learning in one-to-one and group settings;
- experience of and familiarity with IT-mediated strategies for communication with research students;
- knowledge of the scholarly literature on research supervision;
- up-to-date knowledge of the expectations of stakeholder groups.

In the real world, there are, as Clegg (1997) has shown, certainly some institutions which offer programmes which cover all of these dimensions.

Example

The Monash Research Graduate School in Australia runs a nine module Supervisor Training Programme, which includes:

1 An introduction to postgraduate research training at Monash University – which covers such items as regulations and codes of practice.
2 First meetings – discussion with two experienced supervisors on such items as refining research topic and diagnosing students' skills and knowledge.

3   Initial three-to-four month period (full-time equivalent) – discussion with two experienced supervisors on guiding the student through the development of both the literature review and research methodology.

4   Monitoring student progress as candidate pursues research plan – discussion with two experienced supervisors on evaluating progress, progress reports and follow-up action, identifying skills required for successful completion of research project and identifying opportunities for a student to expose their work to peer review.

5   Reading and providing feedback on student's work especially during writing-up stage – discussion with at least one supervisor on providing feedback and constructive criticism.

6   Problem solving – discussion with at least two experienced supervisors on identifying difficulties that hinder progress.

7   Producing the thesis – discussion with an experienced supervisor (and possibly, his/her student) on such things as content, structure and style of the thesis.

8   Examination process – discussion with an experienced supervisor on selecting appropriate examiners and responding to examiners' reports.

9   Final debriefing – a debriefing with mentor to overview entire training programme.

Source: http://www.monash.edu.au/phdschol/forms/academic/trainmod.rtf

But, equally, it is clear that many institutions only offer a day, or even a half-day, often involving little more than a canter through the rules and regulations governing research degrees and supervision. In such cases, supervisors may wish to consider alternative sources of initial training and development.

Example

In the UK, the Biotechnology and Biological Sciences Research Council (BBSRC) has established a Training and Accreditation Programme for Postgraduate Supervisors (TAPPS). This was originally designed for staff working in the biological sciences but has since been made available to supervisors in all disciplines. The TAPPS scheme involves supervisors in attending a range of workshops and providing evidence that they have met six objectives, namely:

* designing a research project appropriate for a research degree;
* recruiting and selecting an appropriate student for the project;

- planning, agreeing and monitoring an appropriate research supervisory process and team;
- making a personal contribution to the promotion of the development of students as scholars and researchers;
- using an appropriate range of methods to monitor, assess and examine student progress and attainment.
- reflecting on their own practice and assessing their future needs as research supervisors and planning to meet them.

and adhere to six values, namely:

- an understanding of how to support student development and achievement in their research projects;
- a concern for student progression towards independence;
- a personal commitment to student scholarship, academic excellence and integrity;
- a commitment to work with, and learn from, colleagues;
- a commitment to and practice of equal opportunities;
- continuing reflection on professional practice.

Evidence relating to this is submitted in a portfolio which is assessed and, if passed, leads to accredited status.

Source: http://www.iah.bbsrc.ac.uk/TAPPS/index.html

Interrogating practice

What initial development and training does your institution offer to new doctoral supervisors?

Is it a requirement to complete it?

Will it equip you with the knowledge and skills to successfully supervise doctoral students?

If not, are there alternatives which will enable you to acquire the necessary knowledge and skills?

Apprenticeship/mentoring

A further response to the perceived skills gap between researchers and supervisors is that, as well as undertaking training, staff new to doctoral supervision may be required to undertake an apprenticeship by acting as a junior member of a supervisory team usually for one successful cycle of a doctorate. Alternatively, if they successfully bid for funding for a studentship as a named main supervisor, institutions may require that they have an experienced colleague as a co-supervisor and mentor during their first supervision.

If institutions do this then, as with other forms of apprenticeship and/or mentoring, there should be clear definitions of the roles and responsibilities of the participants and statements of the desired outcomes of the process. If not, it may be appropriate to negotiate them, perhaps using the institution's list of expectations of supervisors as a check-list.

In addition, it can be helpful for the apprentice or mentee to maintain a record of what he or she has learned, that is, a reflective log. This will stand them in good stead when they become a senior supervisor in their own right, provide a basis for continuing development over their careers as supervisors, and enable them to evaluate their practice and, where appropriate, disseminate it (see Chapter 16).

Interrogating practice

Does your institution have any requirements that you serve an apprenticeship or are mentored during the first cycle of doctoral supervision?

Does it have a formal definition of the roles and responsibilities of the participants and the desired outcomes of the process?

If not, can you negotiate them with your co-supervisor?

Would it be worth recording your learning in a reflective log?

Continuing professional development

In what has been, and continues to be, a turbulent environment, there is a need for even experienced supervisors periodically to update their knowledge and skills. So, for example, the skills learned by supervisors even a decade ago may need honing to cope with the rapidly changing world of doctoral students and doctoral studies outlined in Chapter 1.

In a few institutions the need for supervisors to regularly update their knowledge and skills has been recognised. So, for example, in 2003, the University of Edinburgh in Scotland introduced a requirement that staff had to undertake at least one day of continuing professional development every five years in order to remain in good standing as a supervisor.

But, in most institutions, it is left up to established supervisors whether or not to attend continuing professional development workshops. Such workshops can be a valuable opportunity for old dogs to learn new tricks, particularly in relation to responding to the larger numbers of students, the increased diversity of the student population, the pre-dominance of part-timers and the changes in the doctorate itself designed to improve the employability of graduates both generally and specifically in relation to the knowledge economy.

In addition to old dogs learning new tricks, it should be noted that combining initial and continuing professional development workshops may offer opportunities not only for old dogs to learn new tricks but for them to pass on old tricks to the new dogs.

Example

Newcastle University in the UK, where one of the authors has worked, offers both initial and continuing professional development to doctoral supervisors. For a number of years it had organised separate workshops for the two groups, but on one occasion circumstances forced both to be accommodated within a single workshop. The result was a highly successful session in which new staff discussed their recent experiences as doctoral students and established staff their experience as doctoral supervisors, to the mutual benefit of both groups. Subsequently, all workshops have been run with a mixture of experienced and inexperienced staff.

Interrogating practice

Does your institution have a continuing professional development programme for doctoral supervisors?

Are there any workshops on new developments which could benefit your practice?

Are there any aspects of your practice or experience that could benefit colleagues and that you could share with them at a workshop?

Support for doctoral candidates

As well as providing support for supervisors, institutions also provide support for doctoral candidates, and supervisors need to be aware of what is available so that students can be directed towards them. Such support may include induction, training and development opportunities, the provision of study facilities, the provision of funding for attendance at conferences, etc., and the provision of services particularly in relation to welfare, employability, and careers. Again, a good source for information about these matters is, or should be, the student handbook, and supervisors need to look at it and be familiar with what is available.

Interrogating practice

Does your institution provide an induction programme for doctoral candidates?

What arrangements does it have for training and development in research?

What does it provide in the way of study facilities?

Does it offer funding for students to attend conferences etc.?

What arrangements does it make for the welfare of doctoral students?

How does it seek to enhance the employability of doctoral students?

What arrangements does it make for career development?

Support for supervisors and candidates in the event of the breakdown of their relationship

While institutions can and do provide support for supervisors and candidates to meet expectations they cannot, of course, guarantee that there will be a smooth relationship between them. At the end of the day, supervisors and students are human beings who, for one reason or another, may fail to get on leading to a potential or actual breakdown in their relationship.

In such situations it has, in the past, often been the candidate who has come off the worst because the odds are stacked against them if they take matters further. The options available to them have included variously: informing the programme leader or Head of the School or Department (both academic colleagues of the supervisor(s)); invoking the institution's formal complaint procedures (and thereby risking the irretrievable breakdown of their relationship with their supervisor(s)) or asking for a change of supervisor(s) (and running the risk that there may be no one competent and willing to supervise their research project).

There is anecdotal evidence (see, for example, Wakeford 2001; Peters 1997) that, faced with this choice, many students have chosen to suffer in silence, often to the detriment of gaining their degree.

However, in recent years a number of institutions have recognised that this situation is unsatisfactory and have put mechanisms in place which provide for arbitration and conciliation by a third party outside the supervisory relationship or the academic unit in which the research project is being conducted. This may be the head of the graduate school, a senior academic from another faculty, a faculty mentor, or other designated person.

> **Example**
>
> The University of Bath in the UK has established a postgraduate ombudsman to deal with problems relating to supervision. Candidates who feel that consultation with their supervisor or other staff had been ineffective or that such consultation is inappropriate or inadvisable are able to take issues to the ombudsman, who will try and deal with them in strict confidence and only contact staff at the request of the research student.
>
> http://www.bath.ac.uk/postgrads/pg-ombudsman.html

If supervisors are unfortunate enough to experience a breakdown in their relationship with a candidate, it is important that they should be able to direct the latter towards an independent source of advice and, potentially, of mediation. It may be difficult, but it can be better than losing a candidate who has the potential to make the grade, or risking a formal complaint or even legal action.

Of course, this presumes that, in the event of breakdown, it is only the candidate who needs support, and this may not be the case. It can be very distressing for supervisors, particularly those relatively new to supervision, to find themselves at loggerheads with a candidate. There is at least an argument that, in the event of a difficult relationship with a candidate, supervisors should also have a designated source of support from a person independent of their school or department to whom they can turn for advice and guidance. This seems to be relatively rare in practice, but may be an innovation worthy of consideration.

> **Interrogating practice**
>
> What policies and procedures does your institution have in cases where the relationship between supervisor and candidates breaks down?
>
> Does it offer support to the supervisor in such circumstances?

Conclusions

Hopefully, the present chapter has indicated the importance of supervisors being aware of the institutional framework within which they are operating in terms of expectations, standards, and support. Often, these matters are covered in induction or initial professional development workshops for new supervisors who are thereby made aware of them at the time that they begin their supervisory careers. But it is worth noting that, as doctoral studies themselves are changing, institutions are having to follow suit, with the result that frameworks are constantly being modified and updated.

So, for example, in many countries, two decades or so ago there were no time limits on the period taken to complete a doctorate; because it involved the creation of new knowledge, it took as long as it took. However, and reflecting the pressures from stakeholders described on pp. 12–16, many institutions have been driven to define a doctorate in temporal terms, that is as what can be expected of a candidate in three or four years of full-time study. This clearly has implications for the scope of the research projects which candidates can be encouraged to undertake, and supervisors need to be aware of such limitations.

A further example concerns expectations of supervisors in terms of the development of generic skills. Again, historically, this has not been seen as part of the function of the supervisor. But, reflecting the emergence of the employability agenda described on pp. 11–12, in a number of countries supervisors have in recent times been asked to do this, as discussed in Chapter 10.

The point here is that it is not enough for supervisors to be aware of the institutional framework at whatever time they were taken through it in the past; they need to keep up to date on current developments and, where appropriate, embody them in their practice.

Chapter 3

The disciplinary context

While institutions set the framework for doctoral studies, they have historically usually been undertaken within a single academic discipline. Indeed part of the definition of the doctorate has of course been to make an original contribution to knowledge and understanding within the candidate's discipline. But different disciplines have different paradigms of research, which in turn are reflected in different conceptions of what constitutes an original contribution and in different ways of organising and conducting doctoral studies. So supervisors have always needed to be aware of the disciplinary context, particularly in so far as it relates to the criteria for what is appropriate as a research project and to their roles and responsibilities and those of candidates.

However, as noted on p. 15, increasingly doctoral studies are being undertaken across two or more academic disciplines (multi-disciplinary doctorates) or across academic and professional disciplines (professional doctorates) or academic and practical disciplines (practice-based doctorates). Supervisors of such doctorates need not only to be aware of the context of their own discipline, but also of those within the other disciplines, academic, professional, and practical, to which the research seeks to contribute.

The purpose of the present chapter is, then, to look at the disciplinary contexts for single, multi-disciplinary, professional doctorates and practice-based doctorates respectively.

Single-discipline doctorates

As Becher *et al.* (1994: 108) have written, there is '... no consistent view ... across disciplines ... about what constitutes an acceptable PhD'. So, as Delamont *et al.* (2000) have shown, in some disciplines, particularly those in the arts and humanities, PhDs are seen as acceptable only if they make a major original contribution to knowledge and understanding which opens up a new field of study in the subject. In other disciplines, particularly those in the sciences, PhDs are primarily expected to add to an established body of knowledge by the publication of new results, which may well be superseded within a short time of the completion of the research.

Historically, the expectation has been that supervisors would, during their own experience as a doctoral student, have been socialised into the relevant values and norms of their discipline, including those relating to expectations of the doctorate itself. So it can be a useful start for supervisors to begin by reflecting upon what they had learned during their own studies and what made their own doctorate meet disciplinary expectations for the award.

This is a valuable exercise, but it can be limited in so far as socialisation may have been implicit (or incomplete) and difficult to explicate. In any case, reflection is limited to a sample of one which may or may not be typical. In such cases, supervisors may wish to go further and find out more.

A further source of information is disciplinary colleagues who have been examiners of doctorates. It is, of course, precisely because doctorates are awarded for an original contribution to knowledge and understanding in a particular discipline that institutions appoint discipline experts as examiners to advise them as to whether candidates have met this requirement. So it may be worth talking to colleagues within the discipline who have substantial experience of examining and asking them about expectations for the doctorate. That said, evidence from interviews with examiners (see, for example, Delamont *et al.* 2000) suggests that the answers might be indeterminate, that is that many know it when they see it but are unable to explicate the criteria. In such cases it might be helpful to take theses examined by colleagues out of the library and discuss with them what, in their view, made them qualify for the award.

Finally, supervisors may be able to glean expectations from the publications of disciplinary or disciplinary related bodies. So, for example, in the UK bodies such as the Royal Economic Society (1992), the British Psychological Society and Universities and Colleges Staff Development Agency (1996) and the Royal Society of Chemistry (1995) have all published guidelines on what a PhD should consist of in their respective disciplines, which are a valuable source of information to supervisors. Additionally, guidelines may be available from bodies sponsoring research in the discipline. So, for example, the Economic and Social Research Council (2001) has published Postgraduate Training Guidelines in the UK which include generic outcomes for research training in the social sciences and specific ones for the domains of each of the disciplines covered by the council's remit.

In the same way that disciplinary paradigms influence what is acceptable for the doctorate, they also influence the organisation and conduct of research generally and of doctoral studies in particular. At their broadest, these distinctions are summarised by Becher *et al.* (1994: 87–8) in that:

> Research education in science is closely enmeshed with research organisation and the work of the specialist research group. The education of the individual research student is shaped by these conditions, which are designed to optimise the production of new knowledge.
>
> In the social sciences and humanities, the research enterprise is essentially individualist, and research education is therefore held to be distinct from the work of the established members of the disciplinary community. The

expectations of research students are higher than those entertained in respect of their scientific contemporaries.

These differences are, as Delamont *et al.* (2000) have shown, reflected in distinctive frameworks for doctoral education between disciplines, the extremes of which they define in terms of two 'ideal types', the 'positional' and the 'personal' respectively.

The 'positional' framework essentially refers to the first case set out above. Here, research in the discipline is characterised by:

- organisation in large, specialist, research groups that include academic staff, post-doctoral researchers, and doctoral students;
- leadership by a senior member of the academic staff, who on his or her own or with colleagues determines the research agenda for the group;
- dependence on research grants for the continuation of the group and its work;
- submission of research proposals by the leader and/or members of the group including details of the substance of the project, a timetable, theoretical framework, experimental framework, experimental equipment, and experimental design;
- if successful, recruitment of doctoral students who are assigned to undertake particular experiments identified in the proposal under a designated supervisor or supervisors;
- daily attendance by the student at the laboratory;
- contact and support on a day by day basis by the supervisor and/or other members of the research group;
- immersion in the research group and its professional activities, including dissemination and publication, and where appropriate its social life.

The doctoral student is thus within a formal group that has a clear authority structure and division of labour between its members and is 'positioned' in terms of status as an 'apprentice' or 'junior colleague' of the group.

The 'personal' framework refers to the second case, where research in the discipline is essentially individualist. This is characterised by:

- student determination of the broad area within which they would like to undertake research;
- student search for an appropriate supervisor or supervisors;
- acceptance of student by supervisor(s) with expertise in the proposed area of study, but not necessarily in the specific topic;
- guidance from the supervisor(s) but ultimately student responsibility for the creation of the research project, including choice of topic, research plan, theoretical framework, methodology, methods, and research design;
- research undertaken independently by the student, usually in isolation;
- student responsible for keeping the project on track;
- contact with the supervisor or team regular but infrequent and concentrated at the start of the project and during the period of writing up.

The doctoral student is thus primarily an autonomous researcher following their own path with guidance from the supervisor or supervisory team, and has personal status as a potential intellectual equal.

These are 'ideal types' and, in practice, matters are much less clear cut. So, students in large research groups may have a greater degree of autonomy, for example, if experiments lead to unexpected but promising results, while 'lone scholars' may be subject to a high degree of control by their supervisor over their choice of topic and the execution of their research project particularly if target times for completion are to be met. Again, in some disciplines doctoral studies may have elements of both, with an initial period spent in a large research group getting their head round a problem followed by a further period of independent study. Moreover, there is not an exact fit between science disciplines and a 'positional' model of doctoral education or non-science ones and a 'personal' model; in some science disciplines, for example, pure mathematics, the personal model may be followed (see, for example, Morton and Thornley 2001), while research teams are not unknown in the social sciences (see, for example, University of Essex: Institute for Economic and Social Research 2004).

But, with these caveats, the models do offer insights into differences in disciplinary patterns of doctoral education and into disciplinary expectations of the roles and responsibilities of students and supervisors. So within disciplines with at least a predominantly 'positional' framework, students may be expected:

- to do experiments as directed and in accordance with the protocols laid down in the research project;
- to report the results to their supervisor and, in cases where experiments do not work or yield negative results, to develop alternatives;
- when advised by their supervisor that they have 'enough' results, to write them up as their thesis;
- to participate in the research group by means including publication and attendance at conferences.

Supervisors may be expected:

- to determine appropriate projects for doctoral students which will enhance the work of their research group;
- to prepare research proposals and grant applications and secure funding;
- to secure any ethical approvals;
- to determine the timetable;
- to determine the theoretical framework, experimental framework, and experimental design;
- to ensure that appropriate equipment is available;
- to recruit and select research students for the specific project;
- to induct the student into the research group;
- to direct the research project on a day-to-day basis;

- to advise candidates when they have 'enough' results to gain the doctorate.

With disciplines with a predominantly 'personal' framework for doctoral studies, students may be expected:

- to develop their own research proposals and plans;
- to choose appropriate theoretical frameworks and methodologies and research methods;
- to undertake the research on their own;
- to keep the project on track;
- to decide when the project is complete;
- to write it.

Supervisors may be expected:

- to recruit students with promising ideas for research;
- to assist them in creating the research project, including research proposals and plans, theoretical frameworks and methodologies, research methods and data collection and analysis;
- to assist them in keeping the project on track;
- to provide regular but infrequent academic and social support while the student is working independently;
- to provide intense support towards the conclusion of the project as the student is writing up and finalising his or her thesis.

Interrogating practice

What made your own doctorate original, feasible and do-able?

Are there colleagues in your department and/or research group who have acted as examiners and who might be prepared to discuss disciplinary expectations with you?

Are there any publications by discipline-specific bodies or research sponsors which offer definitions of the outcomes of doctorates in your discipline?

How are doctoral studies conducted and organised in your discipline?

Do they correspond to a 'positional' or a 'personal model' or are they a mixture?

What discipline-specific roles and responsibilities have to be met by students?

What discipline-specific roles and responsibilities have to be met by you as the supervisor?

Multi-disciplinary doctorates

If expectations of doctorates and patterns of doctoral studies vary between disciplines, the question then arises about what should be expected of doctorates on subjects that are multi-disciplinary?

Clearly if supervisors have themselves undertaken multi-disciplinary doctorates and have examined them (or have colleagues who have examined them) then information is available from these sources.

Additionally, many institutions locate multi-disciplinary doctorates within research centres or units that bring together staff from a range of disciplines in the expectation that there will be cross-fertilisation and the emergence of synergies in the content of research and in the paradigms in which they are conducted. Such synergies should result in harmonisation of the expectations of doctorates and patterns of doctoral studies, and be a source of information for supervisors, inside or outside the unit.

That said, the evidence from the study by Delamont *et al.* (2000) of multi-disciplinary environments for doctoral studies is not encouraging. They found that such environments were characterised by the lack of a well-defined collective group structure, by the fragmentation of individual staff interests around their disciplines, and by a sense of isolation on the part of both staff and students. They (ibid.: 170) concluded that:

> Academic staff and doctoral students in the multi-disciplinary settings therefore tend to remain loyal to their primary discipline and maintain the boundaries which defined the constituent subject areas.

So assistance from that source may be limited.

In terms of other sources, in some well-established areas of multi-disciplinary research, there is a literature on the doctorate and on expectations of supervisors and students. So, for example, in women's studies there are a number of papers on these matters (see, for example, Boxer 1998; Friedman 1998; May 2002), and additional guidance may be available from research sponsors.

Example

The UK Economic and Social Research Council sponsors doctorates in women and gender studies. Its expectations include:

- that students acquire knowledge of approaches to and analysis of:

  - the epistemological and ontological questions and debates that underpin research in these areas
  - the range of theories within the social sciences and humanities that have shaped, and continue to shape research into questions of women and

gender studies and the practical and methodological implications of such theories for research

- the interrelation between individuals as gendered actors and societies and between history, biography and social change
- social diversity, social division and social inequality, and particularly the gendered forms and expressions associated with these facets of social life

- that students also

  - have knowledge of the use and value of comparative research both within and across societies
  - become competent in the rigorous formulation of research questions and their translation into practical research designs.

Source:http://www.esrc.ac.uk/esrccontent/postgradfunding/2000_Guidelines_f16.asp

But it would be fair to say that such published guidance is available only in a few areas of multi-disciplinary doctoral studies, and not across the board. Further, where guidance does exist, it tends to relate to multi-disciplinary studies in cognate disciplines which share similar research paradigms and hence a degree of common ground in definitions of the doctorate and frameworks for doctoral supervision, and not studies in diverse disciplines with contrasting frameworks.

At the present time, then, there seems to be a lack of guidance for supervisors, students, and, for that matter, examiners about expectations of multi-disciplinary doctorates and about appropriate frameworks for supervision. Given the drive to increase multi-disciplinary doctorates, we regard this as posing a potentially serious problem, and in Chapter 6 we suggest ways in which it might be addressed in the context of co-supervision.

Professional doctorates

As noted earlier, the main distinguishing characteristic of professional doctorates is that they are normally awarded for completion of a taught programme and for undertaking a research project or projects, usually in the workplace, which make an original contribution to improving practice in a professional discipline. But, in the same way as academic disciplines are distinguished by different paradigms of research and scholarship, professional ones have different notions of practice and its improvement. There is thus a need for supervisors to know what is an appropriate research project and know what constitutes an original contribution to improving practice in the relevant professional discipline.

In cases where academic and practitioner communities are co-extensive, for example education, nursing, and social work, the likelihood is that academic supervisors will have past or current experience of professional practice, which affords a basis upon which to explicate the professional criteria. The latter may also be reasonably well understood by practitioners within the field who, where appropriate, act as additional professional supervisors, although these will not necessarily be fully aware of the academic criteria governing the research project.

As in the case of other doctorates, further information can be gleaned from reading successful submissions, discussions with other supervisors and examiners and, in some cases, looking at the publications of professional bodies. So, for example, in the UK the Association of Business Schools (1997) has produced *Guidelines for the Doctorate of Business Administration* which yield at least some insights into professional requirements.

If expectations of what is a successful research project differ between traditional PhDs and professional doctorates, so do expectations of supervisors and students. These partly stem from the fact that students taking professional doctorates are likely to be mature professionals who are studying for the degree around the day job, matters which are dealt with in Chapter 11.

But they also stem from the fact that the research is being conducted off-campus and in the workplace. This can, of course, lead to academic isolation and increase the need for supervisors to ensure that contact is maintained and to provide additional support for students.

It is, of course, in part to counter such isolation that, in a number of professional doctorates, students have both an academic supervisor and a practitioner one in the workplace, often the candidate's line manager. This can be highly effective in ensuring that students have both academic and day to day support, but it can also potentially lead to problems, as discussed in Chapter 6.

Interrogating practice

Do you have experience as a practitioner, and what does this indicate about professional requirements?

Is there a course handbook that sets out the requirements for the award?

Can you consult successful theses and other supervisors and examiners?

Are there any professional guidelines in your field of study?

Practice-based doctorates

As has already been noted, practice-based doctorates have been introduced in a number of academic disciplines, principally in the arts, as a way of recognising originality in making a contribution to practice. While this is a welcome development, it leaves supervisors with what Winter *et al.* (2000) have shown to be the difficult task of determining what is to be expected for a project to make an original and independent contribution to practice. Despite international efforts in some disciplines (see, for example, Durling 2002) published guidance is lacking reflecting the fact that, as the matter was put by a study group established by the UK Council for Graduate Education (2001: 17), 'How the originality in creative work might be tested, measured or demonstrated in the different artistic fields gave rise to broad debate'.

In this case, in order to understand what is required, it may be possible to review successful doctorates – there is usually a requirement that the artefact is permanent or that there is a permanent record – or to seek guidance from experienced colleagues and/or examiners.

With regard to expectations of supervisors and students in practice-based doctorates, these clearly will conform in many respects to those arising from the 'personal' framework and set out on pp. 35–6 above, but clearly with adjustments to take account of the need to create artefacts and then provide a commentary. While research is lacking in this area, it may be worth noting that students under-taking practice-based doctorates may be more prone to isolation than their colleagues taking traditional ones, reflecting the very personal nature of their studies and the fact that they may be undertaken virtually entirely off-campus, for example, the creative writing student who writes his or her novel in a garret or the music student who composes their *magnum opus* at home. Supervisors may need to be aware of this and provide more in the way of support for such students.

Interrogating practice

Is it possible to review examples of successful practice-based doctorates?

Are there colleagues, possibly in other institutions, who have experience of supervising or examining practice-based work?

Do students taking practice-based doctorates have any special support needs?

Conclusions

For traditional PhDs conducted within single academic disciplines, there are fairly well-documented expectations of what is appropriate as a research project and of the roles and responsibilities of supervisors and students. For other forms of doctoral studies, particularly those introduced relatively recently, the position is much less clear cut. For multi-disciplinary PhDs the responsibility for defining what is acceptable and for determining supervisor and student roles seems to rest very much with the actors involved in the project. Similarly in professional doctorates, much seems to be left up for academic and practitioner supervisors to sort out on the hoof. The problem may be even worse with hybrids not considered above, for example, professional doctorates that are also multi-disciplinary. Finally, in the case of practice-based PhDs there seems to be little guidance in relation to the standards to be applied to artefacts, which puts supervisors and candidates, not to mention examiners, in a very difficult position.

Part II

Preparing the ground

Chapter 4

Recruitment and selection

Prospective supervisors have, traditionally, played a personal role in the recruitment of applicants for doctoral programmes within their own institutions and academic networks. But, increasingly, they are becoming involved in institutional strategies to recruit good doctoral students in a competitive market and, particularly in the United States, to increase applications from under-represented groups.

As well as being involved in recruitment, prospective supervisors are, or should be, involved in the process of selecting those whom they will be expected to supervise as doctoral candidates. In this regard, they of course need to be satisfied that applicants have the knowledge, skills and experience to enable them to undertake their research projects.

But, even if the applicant is satisfactory in terms of their experience and knowledge and skills levels, prospective supervisors also need to be satisfied on the one hand that they are competent to supervise in the proposed area of study and on the other that adequate resources will be provided to support the candidate and the research project and in the right place and at the right time.

The present chapter is then concerned with the roles of supervisors in recruitment and selection including in the latter case achieving a match between the candidate, the expertise of the supervisor, and the resources available to support the research project.

Recruitment

Traditionally, one of the major sources of recruits for doctoral programmes has been students who are already studying at institutions for undergraduate or master's degrees. Prospective supervisors who are also teaching students at these levels have often acted as talent-spotters in identifying students with the potential to succeed at the doctoral level and in encouraging them to apply for doctoral programmes.

Such internal recruitment has advantages to supervisors in so far as they are dealing with a known quality in terms of applicants. It can also be advantageous to the latter as well in so far as they are also dealing with a known quantity in terms of the supervisor and the institution. Additionally, they do not have to change location, which as Kiley and Austin (2000) have shown, can be a major factor in persuading students to apply for doctoral studies at their *alma mater*.

But it is important to note that staying on in the same institution may have the disadvantage for the candidate that it is intellectually incestuous and restricts opportunities for them to be exposed to the influences and ideas prevalent at other institutions. For this reason, prospective supervisors may need to balance the temptation to try to retain their best home students for doctoral work against the best environment for their research area and their needs in terms of a fresh stimulus elsewhere.

As well as fulfilling an internal recruitment role, many prospective supervisors have traditionally filled an external one as well. So, for example, they have used attendance at scholarly events, for example, research trips and conferences, as an opportunity to network with colleagues in other institutions who might be in a position to advise their own students about doctoral study or indeed to influence potential applicants directly.

In addition, recently many prospective supervisors have established personal web-sites, usually indicating the areas of research within which they can offer supervision and listing previous successful students and their thesis titles. If supervisors do this, it is clearly helpful to have a link to the graduate school and programme web-sites which give potential applicants full details of the programme, how to apply, and of any scholarships which are available.

In addition to these means of recruiting applicants, increased competition between institutions has led to greater efforts to attract doctoral applicants through, for example, recruitment fairs, teams of recruiters travelling to talk to potential applicants at their home institutions, and the holding of open days to enable interested students to tour the campus and see what is on offer. Prospective supervisors may be involved in any or all of these activities, especially open days which seem to be among the fastest-growing of activities (see, for example, Sheridan 2002), possibly because they seem to be a highly effective means of attracting applications (see, for example, Goodstein 2003).

As well as attracting applicants generally, a central thread running through all of these recruitment activities in recent years has been the need to recruit applicants from groups which are under-represented at the doctoral level, including women, members of ethnic and racial minorities, and disabled students. Such activities have been particularly apparent in the United States.

Example

In its *Report on Graduate Education*, the Association of American Universities Committee on Graduate Education (1998) recommended that:

Departmental recruitment and admissions policies should include provisions designed to increase the participation of talented students from groups underrepresented in their graduate programs. To make significant progress, universities will need to work with undergraduate institutions and K-12 schools to reach minority students as early as possible in their educational lives and encourage them to prepare for and pursue postgraduate study.

Substantial funding has been made available for doctoral candidates from such groups both by institutions and the government, for example, the US Department of Education Graduate Assistance in Areas of National Need programme designed to increase the numbers of African-American, Hispanic, and Native American doctoral candidates in engineering, mathematics, and chemistry (see US Department of Education 2003). But, of course, there is a need to attract under-represented groups to apply for doctoral studies in the first place. Members of such groups may not, as is argued in Chapter 11, have the same confidence as others in their abilities, particularly at doctoral level, and hence may be less willing to apply.

Here supervisors can have a role in encouraging students from such groups studying at undergraduate and master's levels in their own institutions to consider applying for doctoral programmes, and bear this dimension in mind in their external recruitment activities. Additionally, in many universities in the US, supervisors can participate in activities designed to give such students a taste of life as doctoral students and to whet their appetites for further study.

Example

The Graduate School of Louisiana State University (LSU) runs a Pre-Doctoral Scholar's Institute, a four-week programme aiming to prepare outstanding African-American undergraduates for doctoral study. The programme includes an introduction to doctoral education, an analytical writing seminar, and an opportunity to conduct research in a prospective field of study with a member of the LSU faculty acting as a research advisor. At the end of the Institute, candidates are invited to make an oral presentation of their research and to participate in a poster session.

http://appl003.lsu.edu/grad/gradschool.nsf/$Content/PreDoctoral+ Scholars+ Institute?OpenDocument

---

Interrogating practice

Do you have a role in identifying potential applicants for doctoral programmes at your institution?

Is it always in the interests of the student to continue to study for their doctorate at the same institution?

Do you play a role in recruiting external doctoral students?

Do you have a personal web site as a supervisor and is it linked to others in the institution?

What other recruitment activities does your institution organise to attract applicants for doctoral programmes?

Does it have any initiatives intended to recruit under-represented groups to its doctoral programmes?

Candidate selection

Whether or not supervisors have a role in the initial selection of candidates for doctoral programmes will depend upon the system of doctoral education and/or the type of doctorate. In the US or US-style doctorate, as well as professional doctorates, entry is initially to the taught part of the programme, which has to be passed before the candidate can proceed to the research one. Here initial selection is usually undertaken by the dean, the graduate school, the departmental committee, or the departmental admissions tutors and it is only when the candidate has made substantial progress with the taught part of the programme and begun to shape their research project that he or she will begin to look for a prospective supervisor. The latter then is not involved in initial selection, although as will be seen they will be involved in self-selection.

But in the Western European, UK or UK-style doctorate, entry is direct into the research part of the programme, and candidates will be expected to begin work on their research projects virtually immediately. This of course means that they will need to be supervised from Day 1, and hence a supervisor has to be identified who is willing to take them on and work with them for the period necessary for them to complete their doctorates. For this reason, it is then normal for prospective supervisors to be involved in the initial selection of candidates. Sadly, this is not always the case; as Phillips and Pugh (2000) have pointed out, pressure by institutions for graduate schools or departments to take on larger numbers of doctoral candidates has led to the latter being admitted and then allocated later to a supervisor. At best, this removes any ownership by the supervisor of the candidate or the research project; at worst, it can result in a mismatch with potentially disastrous consequences for all concerned.

However, in most cases, prospective supervisors are involved in the selection process. Usually, the latter is set out in the form of institutional and graduate school or departmental policies and procedures, which involve a number of stages.

Checking that applications are complete

Institutions will normally require that applicants: complete an application form setting out their personal details and in most cases naming referees; where appropriate provide evidence of competence in the language in which they will be studying; indicate their proposed area of research (or their suitability for an already established project); and provide information about financial support. Normally, once applications are received, they will be checked centrally or by the graduate school to ensure that all of the relevant information has been provided before being passed on to selectors, but it is not unknown for the latter to have to check this as well.

Checking that applicants meet the minimum academic criteria

Usually institutions will have minimum academic criteria for applicants to be admitted to a doctoral programme in the form of an undergraduate degree gained at a particular standard or, in a number of countries, a master's degree. In addition, graduate schools and departments may also have minimum criteria in the form of the subjects previously studied by the candidate, that is that they have a suitable background from which to commence their doctoral studies.

While these criteria are usually straightforward to apply, institutions may also have alternative arrangements whereby applicants who cannot meet them through formal qualifications may do so through the accreditation of prior learning and/ or experience (APL/E). In such cases, institutions and/or graduate schools may require that applicants are interviewed before decisions are taken whether to admit them to the programme.

Checking that applicants meet the criteria necessary to undertake the research project

Where, as is often the case in the sciences and engineering, the research project has been designed by the prospective supervisor, then he or she should have a clear idea of what is required to undertake it in terms of knowledge, skills and, where appropriate, experience, against which to judge the basic potential of applicants to undertake it.

Where, as is often the case in the social sciences, arts, and humanities, applicants produce their own research proposals, more work may be involved. Prospective supervisors will need to review whether the research proposal is, in itself, suitable as a doctoral project, and whether it is doable and viable within the time frame allowed. Assuming that it is, or can be amended to be so (in which case it may be necessary to negotiate with the applicant), prospective supervisors then need to establish what knowledge and skills etc. will be required to undertake the project, and assess from the applicant's CV whether he or she meets these criteria (or could do so with additional training).

Where applicants are applying for, or proposing research projects which are multi-disciplinary, there may well be a need for prospective supervisors from all of the disciplines involved to collectively determine criteria and collectively discuss how far these are met by applicants.

Contacting referees

Institutions vary considerably in whether they ask applicants to nominate referees and, if they do so, at what stage in the proceedings selectors are asked to contact them. This may be routinely undertaken at the start for all applicants who meet the minimum academic criteria (or who are being considered through the APL/E route), or it may be left to a later stage when selectors are satisfied that applicants are capable of undertaking research projects and need external confirmation of their qualifications and abilities before making an offer. Selectors need to be aware of when referees need to be approached, and of any institutional requirements for the number of references which need to have been received and considered prior to reaching a decision.

Reaching a preliminary decision about the application

On the basis of the documentary evidence submitted by the candidate, the review of their potential to undertake the research project, and possibly the reports of the referees, selectors can reach a preliminary decision about whether to proceed with the application. Where the applicant meets the criteria and this is confirmed by referees, normally the decision will be to proceed. Where they do not, applicants may be offered a qualifying programme to enable them to meet the criteria, or rejected. Where candidates are rejected at this (or earlier) stages, this must be on academic grounds.

Example

A professor at a university in the UK received an application to study under him from an Israeli student at Tel Aviv University. The professor had strong views on the Israeli–Palestine conflict and it was reported (Oliver 2003) that he wrote back to the applicant:

> I have a huge problem with the way that the Israelis take the high moral ground from their appalling treatment in the Holocaust and then inflict gross human rights on the Palestinians because they [the Palestinians] wish to live in their own country.

I am sure that you are perfectly nice at a personal level but no way would I take on someone who had served in the Israeli army.

The applicant made the email public, and the professor was obliged to apologise and was suspended for a period by the institution.

Interviewing the applicant

In the same way that institutions have varying policies on references, they have varying policies on whether a preliminary decision about an applicant needs to be confirmed by an interview. In some cases, this is mandatory before an applicant can be finally accepted or rejected, while in others it is not, that is, the preliminary decision taken on the basis of documentary evidence becomes the final one.

From the standpoint of the prospective supervisor, interviewing has the considerable advantages of enabling them to personally assess the candidate, their academic ability, and their suitability for the research project. This makes it considerably easier to determine whether the applicant is likely to succeed and if so whether, in principle, they will be able to work with them. Similarly, interviewing is, of course, a two-way process, and it also enables the applicant to get the measure of their prospective supervisor and determine whether they would want to study under him or her.

The downside of interviewing, of course, is that it can lead to abuse by selectors in so far as favoured internal candidates are nodded through while external ones are grilled and/or there is direct or indirect discrimination against applicants on grounds of gender, age, race, ethnicity, or disability.

In order to preserve the advantages and minimise the disadvantages of interviewing, many institutions now insist that selectors undergo appropriate training and provide guidelines on the conduct of interviews. Prospective supervisors who are involved in selection need to be aware of any training requirements and guidelines and to follow the latter as far as possible to the letter (see, for example, Becher *et al.* 1994).

Of course, face-to-face interviewing is not always possible, especially for obvious reasons with applicants from other countries. In the past, many prospective supervisors have had no alternative but to accept such applicants on a paper basis, and by the same token applicants have accepted places without contacting their prospective supervisors. In some cases this has, as Okorocha (2000) has shown, led to inappropriate selection with the results variously of over-stressed supervisors coping with candidates who are finding it difficult to undertake their research, expensive remedial action often in the forms of language and/or research training, international students coping with personal failure, and institutional reputations damaged by dissatisfied students returning home and informing others of their experiences.

In an era before instant electronic communication, this was difficult to remedy, but it is less so today with the possibility of video links, email, or the phone covering much, if by no means all, of the globe. While these may not be comparable to a face-to-face interview, they are better than nothing, and supervisors should, if at all possible, use them both for their own benefit and for that of the applicant.

Making a decision about the applicant

Finally, with the documentary evidence, reports from referees, and wherever possible personal contact through interview or other means, it is possible for prospective supervisors to make a decision about the suitability of the applicant for the programme.

Interrogating practice

Does your institution involve prospective supervisors in selecting applicants for doctoral programmes?

What are the minimum academic criteria for admission?

Does the institution and/or school have an APL/E policy for admissions to doctoral programmes?

What is the policy on references and their use by selectors?

What is the policy on interviewing?

Are selectors involved in interviewing required to undertake training?

Are there institutional or school guidelines on interviewing?

Are facilities available to conduct distance interviews with applicants from other countries?

Supervisor self-selection

But, as well as the initial selection of applicants, prospective supervisors also have to assess their own suitability to supervise their research before agreeing to act as supervisors. Similar decisions have to be made by prospective supervisors who were not involved in initial selection when they are approached by candidates to act as chairs or members of their advisory committee.

In terms of self-assessing their ability to supervise, perhaps the most obvious decision for a potential supervisor is about whether they are competent to supervise in the area of the topic of the research project.

Again, this is less likely to be an issue in the sciences and engineering as it is usually the supervisor who designs the research project in their own specialist field and gains the funding to support doctoral candidates to carry out the research, so they are normally qualified to supervise it in terms of research expertise.

But it may be an issue particularly in the arts, humanities, and social sciences, where Becher *et al.* (1994) have pointed out, the tradition is for research proposals to be individual and, in consequence, for them to be related but peripheral to the prospective supervisor's own area of expertise. Similar considerations may well apply also to non-traditional types of doctorates, including multi-disciplinary, professional, and practice-based ones where supervisors have to ask themselves whether they have the disciplinary breadth, the professional expertise and experience, or the practical experience respectively to offer adequate supervision.

If, on balance, the prospective supervisor feels that he or she may not be fully competent to supervise the research project, then the first step is to see if any deficiencies can be remedied, for example, by the appointment of another member or members of the supervisory team with the relevant expertise, possibly from another school or department within the institution or even from external institutions and organisations.

If this is not possible, then the second step may be to contact the applicant, explain the problem, and see whether it is possible to change or to modify the topic, that is reduce the risk to an acceptable level.

If further support cannot be identified and/or the candidate refuses to play ball, then the best course of action may be to decline to act as the supervisor. Otherwise, candidates can be penalised because of lack of supervisor expertise.

Example

Macauley (2000) conducted a survey of doctoral candidates from which it emerged that a number had been selected despite a lack of supervisory expertise and were experiencing problems in consequence. Responses included:

It has gradually dawned on me that my supervisor knows very little about my topic.

I am the sole researcher in the particular field that I am working in within my department, and in addition I almost never communicate in any meaningful way with researchers from other departments.

My supervisor has never contributed much to my literature review/data acquisition, as he is not particularly expert in my field of research.

I have had two 'nominal' supervisors – neither with significant experience in my field of study.

I'm involved in a newish field with no expertise in department.

But, even where prospective supervisors are confident of their expertise in the area of the topic they also need to think about whether they have the time to supervise the candidate and the research project. This will depend, of course, upon their other commitments, including how many other doctoral candidates they are already supervising. This can, as Graham and Grant (1997) have shown, be a particular problem in areas such as feminist research where there are relatively few supervisors and large numbers of interested candidates leading to the former being overloaded to the detriment of the quality of the learning experiences of the latter.

This is less likely to be a problem if institutions, graduate schools or departments have standard allowances for supervising doctoral candidates, for example, a set number of hours per student per week that is then factored into workload scheduling, and/or a set maximum number of candidates who can be supervised at any given time. Many do have such allowances, but in others the view continues to be taken that, because candidates are working in the member of faculty's own area of research, their supervision is a labour of love to be undertaken in addition to the day job. In such circumstances, supervisors may need to think very carefully before accepting an additional doctoral candidate.

Interrogating practice

What topics in your field do you feel fully competent to supervise?

How might you go about supporting a candidate who is researching in an area peripheral to your own?

Does your institution limit the number of candidates who can be supervised at any one time?

Does your school or department incorporate time spent supervising doctoral students into workload scheduling?

Resourcing matters

Finally, even where the applicant is competent to do the research project and the prospective supervisor is competent to supervise it, there is still the issue of whether the resources will be available to support the candidate and the research project to a successful conclusion. Again, this is less likely to be an issue where the supervisor has designed the project and secured funding which will normally cover the cost of resources. But it still can be an issue in this case depending upon the individual needs of candidates, and almost certainly will be an issue where the project is designed by the candidate. Prospective supervisors then need to consider several areas of concern.

To consider the likely resource needs of the applicant

In identifying resource needs, prospective supervisors need to consider those of the candidate. So, for example, if applicants intend to study part-time and/or at a distance, they may need remote access to the library and other resources. Similarly, if applicants have disabilities, they may need specialist support. It is worth noting that, in many countries, there is a legal requirement that institutions take all reasonably practical steps to anticipate such support needs and make provision for meeting them.

To consider the likely resource needs of the project

Depending upon the nature of the project, resources of one kind or another will be needed to support it, and prospective supervisors need to have a clear idea of what these are likely to be, particularly in terms of equipment, library, and computing resources.

To consider how far these can be met from currently available resources

Once they have determined the resources that are required, the question is then how far these can be supplied from what is currently available. In addition, in so far as current resources can be used, prospective supervisors need to ensure that they will be available at the appropriate time.

Example

The authors are aware of a case in which a science department recruited a doctoral candidate to do work which required the use of equipment in an engineering department. The former had used the latter's equipment extensively in the past, and experienced no difficulty with access, and the supervisor assumed that the candidate would enjoy the same facility. When, however, the candidate needed to work on the equipment, he found that it was being used for another project in the engineering department, and he was unable to gain access. In the event, he was forced to kick his heels for five months before the equipment became available, which added significantly to the time it took him to complete his doctorate. This delay could have been avoided if, at the start of the candidacy, the supervisor had bothered to check with the other department when the equipment would be available.

To identify any additional resources which would be needed to support the candidate and/or the project

By comparing the needs with currently-available resources, prospective supervisors should then be able to determine whether the research project will require additional resources, for example, equipment, books and journals, or computer software or hardware.

To determine if any additional resources can be made available

Once the additional resources have been identified, prospective supervisors can then make enquiries of relevant school, departmental, and services personnel to see if they can be made available or perhaps through on-line access and/or at another institution.

Again, any additional resources need to be available at an appropriate time in terms of the progress of the project.

Such an audit of the resources needed by the candidate and the project should enable prospective supervisors to judge whether the candidate and the project can be effectively resourced and avoid what can be the serious consequences of failure in this regard.

Example

A university in the UK took on a part-time doctoral candidate who lived 75 miles away from the campus. In order to support his research, he was promised remote access to the university's library and other databases, but this was not forthcoming. Subsequently, his thesis was turned down for any award, and the lack of access was among the grounds cited in a judicial case against the university (which failed on procedural grounds) and an appeal to the University Visitor (which succeeded and resulted in a rebuke). See Baty 2003.

Interrogating practice

How can you go about determining the resource needs of candidates?

How can you go about determining the resource needs for research projects?

How can you go about obtaining additional resources?

How can you ensure that resources are delivered to candidates and on time?

Conclusions

Recruitment activities are, of course, crucial in maintaining a steady flow of high-quality applicants to doctoral programmes, and it is in the interests of prospective supervisors to play a role in recruitment activities, whether personal or in the context of institutional initiatives.

Similarly, it is also in the interests of prospective supervisors to have the final say in whether or not they will supervise a particular applicant or candidate. In this, it is crucial to recognise that the decision is based not only upon the suitability of the candidate to undertake the research project, but upon the judgement of the prospective supervisor about his or her competence in supervising the topic and the availability of the resources necessary to support the research. So prospective supervisors have to establish that there is a reasonable match between these elements before they agree to become actual supervisors.

The implication of this, of course, is that where there is an imperfect match which cannot be remedied, prospective supervisors should decline to become actual ones. Such a decision may well not be too popular with students who are anxious to study with the prospective supervisor or with heads of schools, graduate schools or departments who are anxious to maximise the numbers of doctoral candidates.

But there is a strong argument that prospective supervisors ought to be prepared to stick to their guns for their own sakes, for those of candidates, for those of schools or departments, and for the sake of their institution. If supervisors agree to supervise candidates who are not qualified to undertake their research projects, who are operating in a field outside their competence to supervise, or who are inadequately resourced, they can end up spending vast amounts of time trying to compensate for one or other of the deficiencies, often to little result. If candidates are accepted to do projects which they are not qualified to complete, are inadequately supervised, or are under-resourced, they will rapidly get into difficulties which, at best will delay the completion of the project, at worst lead to its abandonment or failure at the final hurdle. Further, where candidates feel short-changed by their experiences on doctoral programmes, they are increasingly resorting to complaints and appeals procedures or, if satisfaction is not forthcoming, to litigation. Schools or departments may suffer if candidates fail to complete on time or at all, or if it becomes known that there have been significant numbers of dissatisfied candidates. Finally, complaints, appeals, and litigation are costly in terms of institutional time and resources, and may damage an institution's reputation.

It is, then, important for all of these key stakeholders that prospective supervisors only agree to supervise students when they are confident from the start that there is a good match between the candidate's expertise, the research project, their expertise, and the resources available.

Chapter 5

Working relationships with candidates

Once a supervisor has agreed to take on a candidate, he or she has to plan how they are going to go about establishing a working relationship with them.

In order to begin to build a good working relationship, there is a need right from the start for all parties to have a clear understanding of institutional requirements of supervisors and doctoral candidates and the first task is to discuss these and, where appropriate, how they are going to be met.

But institutions only define the formal framework for doctoral supervision; how that is interpreted and implemented depends upon the individuals involved, that is, upon the supervisor and the candidate. Because each pairing of individuals is, by definition, unique, then each relationship will be different depending, as McPhail and Erwee (2000: 77) have put it '… upon the supervisor's style of guiding doctoral students [and] the characteristics of the doctoral student …'. Where these are congruent, then there is the basis for a successful relationship; where they are not, the relationship can be marred by problems and difficulties, or even break down completely. Supervisors then need to plan, again at the start of the candidacy, to check the match between their styles and the characteristics and needs of candidates and, where there is a disjuncture, see that steps are taken to align them.

If, in these ways, an appropriate relationship can be established at the start of the candidacy, it also has to be recognised that it should change in the course of time. As candidates move through their doctoral studies, their needs should change, and with that the nature of support that they require from their supervisors. The latter then need to periodically check that there is a continuing alignment between what they are offering and what the candidate needs and, if appropriate, take action to maintain the relationship.

This chapter then looks at planning how to supervise in terms of establishing formal requirements and discussing how they are to be met, ensuring an initial alignment between supervisory styles and candidate needs, and maintaining the relationship.

Establishing formal requirements

Candidates will usually start their doctoral careers with some notions about what will be required of them and what support their supervisor will be required to offer (see, for example, Cryer 2000; Phillips and Pugh 2000; Wisker 2001). But there is no guarantee that these will be complete or accurate, perhaps particularly in the case of those whose previous experience has been of studying in another country with a different educational culture (see Chapter 12). So it cannot simply be assumed that they know about these matters, although obviously it is important for them to do so. For this reason a number of commentators, including Delamont *et al.* (1997) and Grant and Graham (1994), have suggested that it is vital for supervisors to spend some time right at the start with the candidate going through the institution's code of practice or handbook, pointing out the formal requirements, and discussing how these might be met. In some institutions, this has taken the form of an institutional checklist for initial discussions with candidates.

Example

The University of South Australia has a check list for discussions between supervisors and candidates as below:

As a principal supervisor you will need to discuss each of the following issues with your student:

❏ Administration of research degrees by Research Office:

- processes and procedures for admission
- upgrade to PhD
- variations to candidature
- key personnel

❏ Role and membership of School Research Degree Committee
❏ Academic regulations for Masters/PhD
❏ Allocation of supervisors
❏ Roles of Principal and Associate Supervisors, Code of Good Conduct for Research Degree supervision
❏ Schedule of meetings
❏ Annual review process
❏ Grievance procedures
❏ Resources provided by School of Medical Radiation
❏ Resources required for proposed project
❏ Publishing and authorship
❏ Requirements for data storage
❏ Referencing packages
❏ Structured programs
❏ Library access
❏ Time commitments for PhD/Masters by research
❏ Research Proposal

❑ Thesis requirements
❑ Ethics guidelines
❑ Scholarships

Source http://www.unisanet.unisa.edu.au/Resources/researchEducation/
research%20education/Online%20resources/Checklists/check2.doc

In some institutions, it has been made a requirement not only that supervisors and candidates discuss these matters, but that they embody the outcomes in formal learning agreements. The latter have for long been used at the undergraduate and master's level, but not at the doctoral one. However, in the 1990s a number of commentators, including Grant and Graham (1994) and Hockey (1997) began to advocate that the use of learning/ research supervision agreements should be extended to supervisors and candidates as a means of ensuring that both were aware and signed up to their roles in the doctoral process. This has been taken up by a number of institutions.

Example

The Charles Darwin University in Australia requires all doctoral candidates and their supervisors to discuss a range of requirements relating to the supervision partnership and embody these in the form of a research degree supervision agreement. It requires that this should be completed within three months (and preferably one) of the start of the candidature and submitted to the University's Research Committee. The agreement should normally cover:

Induction

Who has primary responsibility, the candidate or the supervisor, for ensuring that the candidate attends induction programmes run by the Faculty and the University for research students and meets other administrative requirements;

Meetings and access

• The level of access that the candidate has to the supervisor (e.g. open access, access by appointment, access as required, access during working hours)
• The frequency of meetings (e.g. weekly, fortnightly, as required or arranged)
• Where meetings are to be held (e.g. supervisor's office, laboratory)
• Whether a written record of meetings is to be maintained and, if so, by whom

- The procedures that apply for the cancellation of meetings by the supervisor and/or the candidate
- The structure/purpose of candidate/supervisor meetings (e.g. to discuss previously submitted material; to discuss work in progress; to review formally work in progress);

Project planning and milestone setting

- Who has primary responsibility for ensuring that all ethical issues are addressed and that experimental or investigative work does not commence before ethics approval is gained from the relevant committee
- Who has primary responsibility for defining the research topic and for developing the initial research proposal
- Who has primary responsibility for developing the research timetable and the project milestones
- What measures the supervisor will take if the research timetable is not adhered to, or if project milestones are not met to a satisfactory standard;

Academic contribution

- The degree to which the supervisor will provide source information to the candidate, or direct the candidate to the source information
- The feedback which the supervisor will give on research practice and performance, written drafts, or seminars, including whether it will be written or oral and always provided in private
- The feedback requirements of the candidate;

Reporting arrangements

- The procedures to be put in place to ensure that candidate and supervisor, jointly, meet institutional reporting requirements;

Intellectual property

- The procedures to be put in place to ensure that candidate and supervisor comply with [national] and NTU policies on intellectual property.

Source: www.cdu.edu.au/research/attachments/svision_agree_example.rtf

Learning agreements of this kind can be useful in ensuring that supervisors and candidates explicate, discuss, and agree expectations right at the start of their relationship. In many institutions they are now mandatory, and copies have to be deposited on candidates' files as evidence that they have been inducted into the framework for their studies.

While codes of practice and learning agreements setting out explicit expectations are a welcome development, it is worth noting that many seem to focus upon the needs of the candidate and neglect those of the supervisor. But the relationship must, of course, be a two-way one. Candidates need to understand that their supervisors are busy people usually with hectic lives, and that they themselves need to put in time and effort to make the relationship work. So, as Repak (2004) has pointed out, it can be useful for supervisors to make candidates aware of the many pressures that faculty face, and of the need for candidates to respect this and reflect upon their own roles in making the relationship work.

Example

The Computer Laboratory at the University of Cambridge makes this explicit in its advice to research students:

> The relationship between you and your supervisor is naturally extremely important, and if it works well you will have found a lifelong friend and colleague. However, do not take too much for granted – you may have to put a lot more time and effort into this relationship than you might expect. Do not leave it to chance, and it can be useful to take every opportunity to get to know your supervisor, both professionally and socially.

Source: http://www.cl.cam.ac.uk/ (accessed 18 May 2004)

Interrogating practice

Do you explicitly discuss institutional requirements with new doctoral candidates?

Do you think that your current practice does, or might, benefit from having a learning agreement at the start?

Do you discuss the pressures on you with the candidate?

Do you make it clear that meeting expectations is a two-way process?

Establishing a match between supervisory styles and candidate needs

In addition to discussing the formal framework for the relationship at its start, it is also vital to discuss the relationship in its human context, namely that of the individual supervisor and candidate.

As was noted in the introduction, individual supervisors may have their own, usually implicit, assumptions about what is involved in the process of supervision, that is, a preferred supervisory style. There is a substantial literature on supervisory styles (see, for example, Grant and Graham 1994; Kam 1997; Delamont *et al.* 2000; Smeby 2000; Pearson and Brew 2002). A review of these and other sources by Gatfield and Alpert (2002) extracted two key dimensions upon which supervisor styles have been arrayed, namely 'structure' and 'support'.

'Structure' refers primarily to the way in which supervisors perceive their roles in the organisation and management of the research project. At one extreme, there is the supervisor who conceives of their role as one of organising and managing the research project themselves and who sees very limited room for autonomy on the part of the candidate; at the other is the supervisor who conceives of their role as offering minimal intervention and giving candidates the maximum autonomy in organising and managing the research project.

'Support' refers to the way in which supervisors perceive their roles in supporting the candidate and the resourcing of the research project. At one extreme, there is the supervisor who conceives of their role as offering the statutory minimum required by the institution, that is, who regards it as the candidate's responsibility to arrange any additional support; at the other, there is the supervisor who conceives of their role as offering a full support service to the candidate personally and in terms of gaining any additional resources required for the research project.

Gatfield and Alpert (2002) then dichotomised these two dimensions into 'low' and 'high' structure and support to yield four paradigms of supervisor styles as shown in Figure 5.1.

The '*laisser-faire*' style is characterised by supervisors seeing themselves as playing a minimal role in the organisation and management of the research project and in the provision of support and leaving both of these matters primarily to the candidate.

The 'pastoral' style is characterised by supervisors seeing themselves as having a significant role to play in providing personal support and resources, but leaving the candidate to organise and manage the research project.

The 'directorial' style is characterised by supervisors seeing themselves as playing a significant role in organising and managing the research project, but leaving it up to the candidate to arrange personal support and, where appropriate, resources.

The 'contractual' style is characterised by supervisors perceiving that they had negotiated roles to play both in organising and managing the research project and in providing support to the candidate.

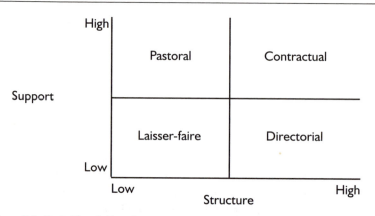

Figure 5.1 Gatfield and Alpert's paradigm of supervisory styles

In absolute terms, there is no right or wrong among these supervisory styles or reason to suggest that one is more valid than another. But there may be in relative terms, reflecting the fact that each of these styles embodies assumptions not just about supervisors and their behaviours, but also about the needs of candidates. So the *laisser-faire* style assumes that candidates are capable of managing both the research project and themselves; the pastoral style that they are capable of managing the former but need support for the latter; the directorial one that they need support in managing the research project but not in managing themselves; and the contractual one that they needed to negotiate the extent of support in both.

As Malfoy and Webb (2000) have suggested, as long as there is a congruence between the supervisory style, the associated assumptions about the needs of candidates, and their actual needs, there should be no difficulties.

Example

Helen Chapman (2002: 1), an Australian student on a professional doctorate, wrote:

> In the beginning, I was not very confident of my scholarly ability. However, I had years of life experience and was an established, mature professional capable of taking control of my actions. I was accustomed to discussing and negotiating agendas and concerns, and to evaluating and prioritising choices. I did not want a supervisor who directed, inspected or controlled my doctoral process. Rather than tell me what to do, I wanted my supervisor to be ... a critical friend – someone who helps others find the limits to the ways they are thinking. I deliberately chose my supervisor for this capacity, and found this type of leadership both an effective and appropriate form of supervision.

So, as in the example, a supervisor with a *laisser-faire* style will be fine for a candidate who is able to organise and manage their project and find their own support or one with a directorial one for a candidate who meets his or her own support needs but requires a strong lead on structuring the research project from their supervisor.

But, by the same token, a *laisser-faire* supervisor will be ill-matched to a candidate who finds it difficult to organise and manage the research project or provide their own support or a supervisor with a directorial style may be ill-matched to a candidate who feels capable of organising and managing their research project.

Example

Wakeford (2001: 3) quotes a doctoral student in the UK who said:

> Being a mature student I pride myself on being able to deal with most situations, but handling my supervisor was not one ... He did not like me discussing my project with others (or) presenting ideas that were contrary to his own ... I began to dread attending meetings in which I would be lambasted and told I was being naive and did not know what I was talking about.

Until comparatively recently, the answer to any mis-match of the type described above would, as Aspland (2002) has argued, be that adjustment would be up to the candidate, and that he or she would swim or sink as a result (and in the case mentioned in the example above the candidate sank). However, one of the consequences of the changes in doctoral studies outlined in Chapter 1, in particular the growth of accountability, has been an increasing expectation that supervisors should be more adaptable. So, as Pearson and Brew (2002) have argued, it is no longer acceptable for supervisors to have one set style and what is now required is to develop a repertoire of supervisory styles which can be adopted as appropriate to meet the needs of candidates.

Clearly, in order to do so, supervisors need to have some idea of their own preferred supervisory style, if any, and of the needs of the candidate. A few years ago Brown and Atkins (1988) and Moses (1992) developed self-administered questionnaires to measure supervisors' preferred styles, which were useful for supervisors but took no account of candidates. Recently, however, these questionnaires have been modified to make them applicable for both supervisors and candidates.

Example

Flinders University in Australia uses a questionnaire. This is based upon original work by Moses (1992) but was developed by M. Kiley and K.Cadman of the Advisory Centre for Education, University of Adelaide, and adapted by Mike Lawson of Flinders. The questionnaire is completed separately by supervisors and candidates, and the results used to inform initial discussions about the supervisory relationship.

The questionnaire is:

A   *Whose responsibility is it?*

Indicate your view of issues in the first table by circling a point on the line in the middle column. Make any comment or clarifications in the right hand column. Who should have responsibility for:

	Supervisor–Student	*Comments*
1 Selection of the student's research topic	1 2 3 4 5	
2 Establishing the theoretical framework for the research	1 2 3 4 5	
3 Identifying a programme of background reading or study for the student	1 2 3 4 5	
4 Developing a schedule for completion of tasks that student will undertake during the degree	1 2 3 4 5	
5 Organising regular meetings between supervisor and student	1 2 3 4 5	
6 Making the student aware of facilities and resources in the department and university	1 2 3 4 5	
7 Preparing the student for public presentations of research ideas or results	1 2 3 4 5	
8 Providing resources that will support the student's research	1 2 3 4 5	

9	Developing a network of fellow students or staff for the student	1	2	3	4	5
10	Ensuring that the student's programme is on track and on schedule	1	2	3	4	5
11	Providing emotional support and encouragement to the student	1	2	3	4	5
12	Maintaining an effective working relationship between supervisor and student	1	2	3	4	5

Who should have responsibility for:

		Supervisor–Student					*Comments*
13	Ensuring that the thesis will be of an acceptable standard when examined	1	2	3	4	5	
14	Ensuring that the current research literature has been identified and read by the student	1	2	3	4	5	
	Other issues	1	2	3	4	5	

B   Do you agree?

Circle the point on the line that represents your views on the following issues:

15	A strong personal relationship between supervisor and student is inadvisable during candidature	1	2	3	4	5
16	The supervisor should assist the student in writing the thesis if necessary	1	2	3	4	5
17	The supervisor should see all drafts of the student's written work	1	2	3	4	5

	Supervisor–Student	Comments
18 The supervisor should provide detailed commentary on all written work submitted by the student	1 2 3 4 5	
19 The supervisor's written comments should normally be returned within two weeks from time of submission	1 2 3 4 5	
Other issues	1 2 3 4 5	

Source: http://www.flinders.edu.au/teach/research/postgrad/Expectations.pdf

By using questionnaires such as the one above, supervisors should be able to assess whether their style is or is not appropriate to the needs of the candidate, and if necessary, consider how they might modify it.

Interrogating practice

What assumptions do you make about what is involved in the process of supervision?

Do they correspond to any of the preferred styles set out above?

If so, what corresponding assumptions are you making about the needs of doctoral candidates?

Does your institution have a questionnaire of the type above to enable you and the candidate to align assumptions about supervision with candidate needs?

Maintaining the relationship

The relationship between the supervisor and the candidate is not a static one, but should change over the course of the candidacy. Usually, at the start the candidate is heavily dependent upon the supervisor and then, as he or she grows and develops towards becoming a researcher in their own right, they become less dependent.

The corollary of this is that, as Gurr (2001: 86–7) has put it:

... the supervisory style needs to be adjusted to a more hands-off approach to allow competent autonomy to be developed ... Unfortunately, in some cases, supervisors adopt a static supervisory approach, or if it is altered, this may not be done in alignment with the growth and emerging needs of the student but on the basis of a teacher-centred ('I know what is best for this student') dogma.

In order to avoid stunting the candidate's growth, supervisors then need to be alert to the need, where appropriate, to ease off the reins and switch from, in terms of the typology used previously, a directorial to a more contractual or *laisser-faire* approach to supervision. This can be a difficult call for supervisors, particularly if their preferred style is directorial, or for candidates who might feel that they are being smothered by their supervisor but feel unable to confront them directly.

In order to assist supervisors and candidates to confront this dilemma, Gurr developed a tool in the form of a graph shown in Figure 5.2.

The idea is that supervisors and candidates can independently plot on the graph where they feel that the relationship is at any given time, and use this as a basis for discussion. On the basis of a small-scale trial, Gurr found that this was effective in allowing supervisors to signal to candidates that the discussion of the supervisory relationship was not taboo and in enabling candidates to raise what could be a delicate subject without offence.

That said, of course, the overall course of the relationship between supervisors and their candidates is unlikely to be a linear move towards the former letting go and the latter become self-directed, for two reasons.

First, doing research is not necessarily a smooth process (see Chapter 7) and candidates may suffer academic setbacks or, for that matter, personal ones as well (see Chapter 10). In such cases, it may, as Gatfield and Alpert (2002) again have pointed out, be necessary for the supervisor to temporarily assume variously a

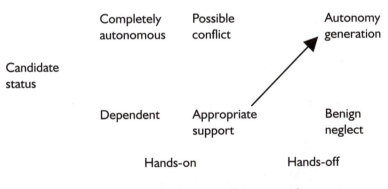

Figure 5.2 Gurr's tool for monitoring the alignment of supervisory styles and candidate needs

more directorial or pastoral role until the crisis has been dealt with and the project and/or the candidate are back on track.

Second, while candidates should become largely autonomous in terms of conducting their research projects, at the end they have to write up the latter in the form of a thesis and get it into a shape where it can be submitted. At this juncture in most cases they become heavily dependent upon their supervisor again for advice and guidance, and supervisors can expect to play a more interventionist role.

Interrogating practice

How can you go about determining whether there is a continuing fit between your supervisory style and that of the candidate over the course of the project?

Conclusions

A good working professional relationship between the supervisor(s) and the candidate is, of course, crucial in enabling them to work together over the months and years of doctoral studies, and is crucial to their outcome. In order to have such a relationship it has been suggested that: supervisors need to make candidates aware of institutional requirements and agree on how they are to be met; that they need to ensure that styles of supervision are aligned with the needs of candidates; and they need to ensure that there is a continuing fit between styles and needs over the course of the candidacy.

Chapter 6

Working relationships with co-supervisors

Historically, doctoral supervision has usually been undertaken by a single supervisor or 'Doktorvater'. But, over the past two decades or so, there has been a move towards co-supervision in the forms of a chief advisor and four or five other members of an advisory committee usual in the United States, or the supervisory team with a main and second supervisor which has become more common elsewhere.

The reasons for this change include the growth of new forms of doctoral study, including multi-disciplinary doctorates, doctorates undertaken in collaboration with industry and commerce, and professional doctorates, all of which mean that one supervisor is unlikely to possess the expertise and ability necessary to fully support the research project and hence that a further supervisor is necessary. In addition, and irrespective of the type of doctorate, there can be benefits both to supervisors and to candidates in terms of having access to a wider range of experience, expertise, and support.

However, as well as having an upside, co-supervision may have a downside as well. The involvement of more supervisors in the process can create a potential for disagreement and divergence within the advisory committee or supervisory team and leave the candidate playing 'piggy in the middle' to the detriment of their research.

The purposes of this chapter are then to look at the benefits of co-supervision, at what can go wrong, and to identify ways in which co-supervision can be managed to make it effective.

The benefits of co-supervision

The potential benefits from co-supervision may include:

- exposing candidates to a diverse range of intellectual perspectives which Smeby (2000: 65) for example has argued '... is no bad thing since variety in perspective should provide intellectual stimulus';
- providing candidates with a broader range of expertise across academic and professional disciplines, which as noted above is particularly vital for those

undertaking research projects that are multi-disciplinary and/or involve research in the workplace;

- enabling a division of labour in supervisor roles, with each fulfilling a particular set of functions in relation to the research project. This can, as Graham and Grant (1997) have suggested, be helpful in enabling main supervisors to cope with larger numbers of candidates by devolving some of their responsibilities, for example, pastoral ones, onto co-supervisors;

- preventing all responsibility for seeing the research project through from falling on the shoulders of one supervisor and making it a shared responsibility of the advisory committee or supervisory team;

- giving candidates access to more than one supervisor in the event that they need to consult or discuss ideas. As the matter was put by respondents to a survey by the Wellcome Trust (cited in Frame and Allen 2002:101), dual supervision was valued '... primarily to ensure accessibility at any time to at least one senior researcher with knowledge and involvement in the research and as a back-up, providing a second person or team, with whom ideas could be discussed'.

- possibly extending the repertoire of supervisory styles and improving the chances of a match to the needs of the candidate. As one of the respondents to the survey by Cullen *et al.* (1994: 67) put the matter:

> Usually in a supervisory panel you get ... somebody who is a particular expert in the field ... but you also try and choose somebody who has perhaps a wider overview of the area and who also perhaps you can turn to if you're feeling in any difficulties and want to talk about more general things. You kind of act as sort of confessors to them when they have bust ups with their boyfriends or get thrown out of home. So you need to have a balance ... so there is somebody you feel comfortable in confiding in for say wider issues.
>
> (Evelyn)

Interrogating practice

Were you supervised by an advisory committee or more than one supervisor?

(If so) what benefits did you feel you gained compared to only having a single supervisor?

(If not) can you see any benefits you might have gained from having multiple supervisors?

What can go wrong?

However, these considerable benefits do not automatically accrue from having co-supervision, and in each case things can go wrong. Differences in practices and perception can occur between supervisors which may handicap rather than enhance the supervision experienced by the student.

Intellectual diversity

Diversity is useful provided that it takes place within a common understanding of the aims and objectives of the research project, but all too often it does not depending upon the intellectual traditions of supervisors and their disciplinary or other backgrounds.

Even within single disciplines, supervisors, particularly in the arts and humanities and social sciences, may come from different intellectual traditions.

Example

Peters (1997: 168) cites a doctoral candidate in economics who said:

I'm in my fifth year and hung up because I can't seem to take control of my committee. They just keep on fighting. The chairman is a neo-classical economist and the second person, influential in the department, is a Marxist. Of course they have totally different interpretations of how my thesis should go. I can't see any end in sight because my advisor keeps asking me to write more and more chapters, saying 'Gee, now you understand this, how about a new intellectual problem'. Meanwhile, the Marxist demands that I re-write everything from his perspective. When I do this, the chairman finds it unacceptable and refuses to sign it off. The worst thing now is that they are both getting angry with me for doing what the other guy says.

If, then, there can be conflict between supervisors within academic disciplines about the research project, the potential is perhaps considerably greater where they come from different academic disciplines. In such cases, supervisors may have no common framework for understanding basic matters such as epistemology, the relative status of theory and practice, ways of locating problems and finding solutions, or the values and ethos of the research. In the absence of a common framework, multi-disciplinary teams may, as Younglove-Webb *et al.* (1999) have shown, be plagued by disciplinary chauvinism and conflicting worldviews.

Example

In their study of multi-disciplinary scientific enquiry, Hagoel and Kalekin-Fishman (2002: 300) quote the case of Lea, a sociologist working in a medical environment:

> Lea discovered that most of her colleagues shared a very narrow interpretation of what a sociologist could or should do. Sociological knowledge was perceived at best as a bunch of skills that enabled the sociologist to generate questionnaires. In team discussions, sociology was derogated as mere common sense that is easily made available to any intelligent person. Medical knowledge was the reference for indications of authoritative solutions to research problems. Whenever there were differences of opinion, there was no question but that a physician was the one to hand down judgement. Clearly, as a sociologist, Lea was confined to the periphery as a perpetual stranger or guest.

Diversity of expertise

Conflict of the kinds described above is, of course, within the academy, but as has been noted earlier, doctoral studies are increasingly involving projects undertaken in collaboration with organisations outside the academy in the public or private sectors.

Expectations of such projects can differ markedly between organisations with different values, norms and interests and hence between supervisors drawn from them.

Example

In their study of collaboration between a university and a public body, which included a PhD studentship, Loan-Clarke and Preston (2002) identified differences of the following kinds:

Academic	Practitioner
Focus on theory	Focus on practice
Generaliseability of knowledge	Specificity of knowledge
Rigour in research method	Relevance of research method
Certainty about the knowledge	Usefulness of the knowledge
Preference for hypothesis testing	Preference for hypothesis generation
Work to long timescales	Work to short time
'Outside' perspective	'Insider' perspective
Detachment/neutrality	Involvement

Similar arguments apply, of course, to professional doctorates, where academic supervisors may be more concerned with the academic rigour of the research project, while practitioner ones may be more concerned with the potential benefits to practice, leaving the student stranded in no man's land between the two perspectives (see, for example, Green 2002).

Supervisor roles

Co-supervision does allow a division of labour between supervisors, but only where there is some measure of agreement between them about their respective roles. But, in the same way that supervisors may have different interpretations of the research project depending upon their academic or professional discipline, they may also view their roles differently.

Perhaps the classic case of this is where one supervisor is from a discipline in which research is conducted within a 'positional' framework where the candidate is effectively an apprentice and the other is from a discipline with a 'personal' framework where the candidate is treated as a potential intellectual equal. The former will expect to play a strong directive role in the research project, while the latter will regard this as spoon-feeding and look for the student to play a much greater role in devising and undertaking the research project.

Similarly, there is considerable potential for similar conflict where there is one academic supervisor and one at the workplace, as in collaborative projects and often in professional doctorates. So, as the authors of a study by the UK Council for Graduate Education (2002) have pointed out, academic supervisors, particularly those accustomed to supervising traditional PhDs, may find it frustrating not to have the project under their sole control. They may be concerned that practitioner supervisors, particularly if they are the candidate's line manager, will be over-directive and not prepared to give candidates their head to explore new avenues and/ or to let them do things which they know could result in failure.

By the same token, practitioner supervisors may be unhappy to play a secondary role, particularly as their organisation is paying the candidate's salary (and possibly the course fees). They may also be concerned about academic supervisors being *laisser-faire* and allowing candidates to spend too much time on the academic side of their doctorates and not enough on the work-related ones (or indeed for that matter on their day jobs). Bearing in mind the investment that the organisation has put into supporting the candidate, the professional supervisor may find it difficult to let the candidate go down a road that could lead to the non-award of the doctorate.

Supervisor responsibilities

While shared responsibility for supervision is fine in theory, it does depend upon all members of team accepting that responsibility and discharging it. However, where supervisors disagree for any of the reasons set out above, it is not unknown for one or other of the supervisors to abdicate their responsibility, leaving the student no better off than if they had a single supervisor.

Further, there is the nightmare scenario where supervisors disagree and candidates are unable to satisfy them and, as Cryer (2000) has suggested, supervisors can pass the buck to each other, leaving the candidate with little or no effective supervision at all.

In such circumstances candidates may, in an effort to make progress and restore responsibility for supervision, align themselves with one supervisor at the expense of the other. While this may well be a rational strategy from the candidate's standpoint, it can have disastrous consequences for the relationships involved in the supervision and possibly the research project (see, for example, Phillips and Pugh 2000).

Finally, it may be noted that the abdication of one or more supervisors may leave the candidate without the necessary overview or rounded view of their research project necessary for them to develop it and, ultimately, submit their thesis or dissertation.

Accessibility

Two or more supervisors should, in principle, mean that candidates have access to one or the other on tap, but that depends as again Smeby (2000: 65) notes, all supervisors being '… really committed to students' research topics and their progress'. If, however, one supervisor does not pull their weight and leaves it to the other, the candidate is potentially no better off than with a single supervisor; if both leave it to the other, the student can be worse off.

Supervisor styles

The argument that the student will benefit from a mix of supervisor styles works well if supervisors do have complementary styles, for example, if one is 'directorial' and one is 'pastoral'. But problems can arise if, for example, both supervisors have a 'directorial' style and end up fighting for control of the research project, or if both are '*laisser-faire*' and leave the student to get on with it. Alternatively, conflict can occur when one supervisor's style is '*laisser-faire*', while the other is 'directorial' with the former regarding the latter as mollycoddling the student and the latter regarding the former as abrogating their responsibilities.

Interrogating practice

Have you experienced difficulties with co-supervisors in terms of expectations of the research project?

Have you experienced difficulties in the fulfilment of supervisor roles and responsibilities?

Have you come across incompatibility of supervisor styles?

Managing co-supervision

If, then, the use of a supervisory team is a necessary condition for achieving the benefits described above, it is by no means a sufficient one, as indicated by the list of things that can go wrong. These can, as Phillips and Pugh (2000) have suggested, have serious consequences in delaying the completion of research projects or even leading to their abandonment. Co-supervision therefore needs to be actively managed with co-supervisors approaching it in the right frame of mind, starting off on common ground, agreeing expectations of the research project and of their own roles and responsibilities and those of students, and keeping their relationships with each other and with the candidate under regular review as the project proceeds.

Approaching co-supervision

It is important that co-supervisors approach collaboration with a mind-set that includes:

- an explicit acknowledgement that diversity exists as opposed to sweeping it under the carpet and hoping to 'muddle through';
- a pluralist approach which accepts that alternative perspectives may be as valid as that of their own;
- a willingness to learn about alternative approaches from within or outside the discipline;
- a willingness to enter into a discourse with co-supervisors to develop a common understanding of how to proceed;
- a recognition that, at the end of the day, it will be the doctoral candidate who suffers if things go wrong.

Starting off on common ground

Supervisors may come from different traditions within the same academic discipline or from different academic disciplines or from professional ones as well. But, they should still have common ground in terms of, first, the institutional requirements for whatever doctorate they will be involved in supervising and, second, formal institutional requirements for supervisors. These matters were covered in Chapter 2, but it is worth noting that, at least in some institutions, co-supervision may be recognised by separate requirements for the 'main' and the 'secondary' supervisor.

Example

The University of South Australia defines the expectations of 'principal' supervisors much as the list on pp. 21–3 and defines those of second supervisors as:

- supporting the principal supervisor in the execution of their duties;
- where appropriate, providing special expertise in support of the student's research project;
- participating in the initial discussions of the project;
- maintaining regular communication with the research student;
- participating in the annual progress review;
- acting as supervisor if the principal supervisor is absent for more than six weeks.

Source: http://www.unisa.edu.au/adminfo/codes/responsibilities.htm

In similar vein, in cases where students have an academic supervisor and one outside the university (for example in professional or project-based doctorates), institutions may delineate a formal division of labour between internal and external supervisors.

Example

The City University of London accords primary responsibility and accountability to internal supervisors but specifies that external supervisors:

- act as coach and counsellor to help the researcher to meet the goals agreed between them and the internal supervisor;
- provide accurate advice and guidance on the project;
- prompt regular reviews of the research plan and the setting of agreed targets;
- maintain contact through regular tutorial and seminar meetings in accordance with departmental policy and in the light of discussion of arrangements with the student;
- are accessible to the student at other appropriate and reasonable times when he/she may need advice;
- request written work, as appropriate, and return such work with constructive criticism and within a reasonable specified time;
- take an active role in introducing the student to other workers in the field, and the appropriate academic bodies and societies;
- maintain records of formal supervision meetings;

> • monitor the student's attendance as appropriate and inform the relevant bodies through the internal supervisor of absence or withdrawal;
> • in conjunction with the internal supervisor, provide guidance, encouragement and counsel regarding the future career plans of the research student.
>
> Source: http://www.city.ac.uk/researchstudies/roles.htm#externally-registered

Institutional requirements for the doctoral award and the roles and responsibilities of supervisors afford at least some common ground no matter how diverse the background of co-supervisors.

Agreeing expectations of the research project and of co-supervisors and the candidate

Armed with the formal institutional requirements, co-supervisors can then meet right at the start of the project and preferably without the student present to try to reach agreement between them on how to proceed. This may be done through formal co-supervisor preparatory training sessions at which they are invited to discuss these matters, or alternatively arranged privately.

The agenda for such a meeting might include:

- Expectations of the research project

    * the formal requirements for the award of the doctorate in question;
    * how each co-supervisor interprets those requirements in the context of their own views and/or disciplinary background;
    * a discussion of examples, for example, of abstracts of successful theses, so that co-supervisors can see what others are looking for in their fields;
    * the identification of key points of agreement or disagreement;
    * in the light of the above, negotiation of joint expectations about the proposed research project.

- Expectations of student roles and responsibilities

    * the formal requirements of students;
    * how each co-supervisor interprets those requirements;
    * identification of key areas of agreement or disagreement;
    * negotiation of joint expectations of roles and responsibilities of students.

- Expectations of co-supervisor roles and responsibilities

    * the formal requirements for supervisors, including those for 'main' and 'secondary' and 'internal' and 'external' supervisors;
    * how each co-supervisor interprets those requirements in relation to their roles and responsibilities;

* a discussion of how each co-supervisor might contribute to the supervision of the research project;
* identification of key areas of agreement or disagreement;
* negotiation of agreed roles and responsibilities, including arrangements for access.

- Co-supervisor styles

  * identification by co-supervisors of preferred styles of supervision using, for example, the instrument developed by Gatfield and Alpert (2002);
  * discussion of compatibility of preferred styles;
  * where appropriate, agreement on adjustment of styles to ensure that the candidate has an appropriate balance of direction and support.

It can be advantageous if the conclusions of discussions of the agenda above are embodied in the form of an agreement between co-supervisors, setting out their joint expectations of the research project, of the student, and of themselves. This may then be discussed at an initial meeting with the candidate and, subject to further negotiation on the latter's role, form the basis of an agreement for all of those involved in the research project.

Regular reviews of co-supervision

As well as starting off on the right footing, there is a need for regular reviews of the relationships of co-supervisors with each other and with the student. Such reviews, perhaps once or twice per year, might be undertaken with the candidate present and include:

- whether co-supervisors feel that project expectations are being met;
- whether they feel that the division of roles and responsibilities is still appropriate and effective;
- whether the candidate feels that he or she is being offered a clear steer by co-supervisors or experiencing difficulties in meeting multiple and diverse demands;
- whether the candidate remains clear about where roles and responsibilities lie for their supervision;
- whether the candidate feels that co-supervisors are accessible;
- whether the candidate feels that they have an appropriate balance between direction and support.

Such discussions, particularly if undertaken in the context of a review of a written agreement, can identify problems stemming from co-supervision at a relatively early stage and before they delay, fatally or otherwise, the progress of the research.

Interrogating practice

Does your institution have a specification of the roles of co-supervisors?

Does it offer training for co-supervisors to discuss in advance the project and how they are going to work together?

Do you think that it would be useful to have agreements between co-supervisors and the student?

Conclusions

Co-supervision is becoming widespread in doctoral studies. In principle, it offers considerable benefits both to candidates and to their supervisors, but these do not automatically flow from simply having more than one supervisor. In fact the latter can lead to the fragmentation of supervision and impose considerable burdens on candidates which undermine their ability to complete on time or, in extremis, complete at all. But these negative consequences can potentially be avoided if co-supervisors approach the project with an open mind, develop shared expectations of the research project and of their roles and responsibilities and those of students, and review these regularly over the course of the candidacy.

Part III

Supporting the research project

Chapter 7

Academic guidance and support

The provision of academic guidance and support is of course one of the key functions of supervisors and supervisory teams, and the central one for those working in the US or US-based systems of doctoral education, as reflected in the use of the titles of 'advisor' and 'advisory committee'.

Depending upon the discipline, academic guidance and support may start with advising candidates about their choice of topic and then assisting them to produce a research proposal. Irrespective of the discipline, it will include making sure as far as possible that they have, or can acquire, the subject-specific knowledge and skills necessary for them to undertake their research topics.

If, in these ways, candidates can be started off on their research projects, sooner or later they are almost bound to encounter academic problems of one kind or another. Original research is, by definition, a journey into the unknown, and it is rarely, if ever, unproblematic. Overcoming these unexpected problems is, of course, part and parcel of becoming an independent researcher, but candidates need support if they are to do so and develop into the finished article.

Traditionally, of course, academic support of these kinds has been provided to candidates on an individual basis. But one of the consequences of the growth in the numbers of doctoral candidates as well as the growth of other demands on academic time has been that supervisors have not always been able to devote as much time as they would wish to individual candidates. For this reason, they may have to consider providing academic guidance and support at least in part on a collective basis to groups of candidates.

This chapter, then, looks at the ways in which supervisors can support candidates in, where appropriate, choosing a research topic, producing a research proposal, acquiring the skills necessary to undertake the project, in overcoming academic problems and, where appropriate, in doing these things on a group basis.

Advising on a topic

As was noted in Chapter 3, it is common in the sciences and engineering for supervisors to identify a topic, produce a research proposal, obtain funding, and then select a candidate. The latter can, then, step into a pre-determined topic, and the need is for the supervisor to explain it to the candidate.

But it is not unknown in these disciplines, and common in the arts, humanities, and social sciences, for candidates to be selected on the basis of a self-defined outline of a possible field of research with the expectation that they will then narrow it down to a specific topic.

This can be a difficult thing for candidates to do on their own. They may, as Delamont *et al.* (1997) have noted, feel that they have little idea about what they are supposed to be looking for or, by the time that they have hit a few dead ends, begun to doubt whether they will ever find an appropriate subject for their research.

While, ultimately, the candidate will have to come up with his or her own topic, supervisors can help in several ways.

Framing the process

Candidates left to create on their own often feel hopelessly adrift and may grab at any angle which seems even vaguely plausible, often to their cost later. Supervisors can assist to prevent this by framing the process. Following Moses (1992) this can be described in terms of:

- deciding within the field upon a topic of potential interest;
- critically reviewing the literature;
- identifying potential 'triggers' for research projects;
- evaluating their suitability.

Discussing potential topics with candidates

Candidates will usually have their own ideas about potential topics, and, of course, supervisors usually have pet projects of their own that they do not have the time or opportunity to follow up themselves but which can be handed on. Here, supervisors need to take care that they listen to the ideas of candidates and take them seriously, and avoid either swamping them with a range of their own projects or funnelling them into a pet project of which they feel little ownership.

Encouraging them to investigate them further

Once a range of potential topics has been identified, candidates should be encouraged to investigate them further by undertaking mini-projects including:

- reading the literature in the field;
- identifying possible triggers for their research;
- producing an outline of how they might go about undertaking the research;
- considering what the possible outcomes might be;

Assisting them to self-evaluate their suitability

Once candidates have undertaken one or more mini-projects, they need to be able to self-evaluate their suitability. Here supervisors can suggest that candidates might consider a list of key questions such as:

- is it worth doing? (is the topic important enough to justify the time spent doing it?);
- can I do it? (am I capable of researching this topic with my present knowledge and skills or, if not, with specified additions?);
- can I do it within the time available? (can it be done within three years?);
- will I do it? (is there enough to sustain my interest for that length of time?);
- will it get me a PhD? (does it have the potential to make an original contribution to knowledge and understanding in the subject?).

Asking them to produce written reports

Once candidates have identified a topic or topics which they consider passes these tests, they can be asked to embody these in written reports.

Giving feedback

Supervisions should be based around the written reports and supervisors should give constructive feedback on whether the project is worthwhile, do-able, viable within the time available, sustainable and, at the end of the day, likely to produce the goods in terms of a doctorate.

This is an interactive process which, hopefully sooner rather than later, should lead to the selection of an appropriate topic.

Interrogating practice

If you select candidates to undertake a research project which you have defined, do you explain the background to them?

If candidates have a choice about their topic, how do you go about assisting them to make an appropriate one?

Assisting candidates to produce a formal research proposal

Once candidates have determined upon a topic which, in principle, is suitable, then it is good practice that they produce a formal research proposal, and in many cases an institutional requirement that they do so within a specified period, for example, three or six months from starting the research.

It may be that institutions or schools or departments have standard templates for the candidate's research proposal, or alternatively this may be left to individual supervisors or the supervisory team.

If the latter is the case, it may be helpful initially to ask candidates to write to a series of headings, for example:

> What is the topic of the proposed research?
> Why is it important?
> What have others written on this topic?
> What are the main and secondary questions which would be addressed?
> What conceptual/theoretical frameworks might be useful in addressing those questions?
> What methods could be used to undertake the research?
> How could the research actually be done in the time that is available?
> Are there ethical considerations?
> What might be the outcomes?
> How would the outcomes have the potential to make a contribution to knowledge and understanding in the topic and meet the criteria for a doctorate?

If candidates draft responses to these questions, then supervisors can give feedback on the answers.

One area where this is particularly important is in relation to the timescale envisaged for the research. This, in principle, is simple enough; the candidate simply plots the activities to be undertaken as set out in the research proposal and plots them against time. But, of course, candidates may have little or no idea of what is involved in terms of the time taken by the various stages of the research, and may need guidance.

Example

Delamont et al. (1997) have developed a useful technique for guiding doctoral candidates in the development of realistic research plans. This involves presenting them with Gantt charts plotting time against task for the research project which deliberately under- or over-estimate the time required to complete key stages of the work schedule. Candidates are asked to review these and see whether they think that they are realistic, and then discuss their conclusions with supervisors and/or peers. The authors have used this technique, and found it to be highly effective in encouraging candidates to self-identify the pitfalls and adopt realistic time horizons.

Usually after several iterations, often involving adjustments in the scope of the project to accommodate the time frame available, candidates should be able to write a formal research proposal.

Example

Wisker (2001) has suggested that a formal research proposal should normally include:

- indicative title
- aim and focus of the study
- questions
- sub-questions
- context for the research
- research methodology
- research methods
- research design
- ethical considerations
- outline plan of study
- draft chapters and areas
- justification for the level of award
- primary texts

This can then, where relevant, be submitted by the candidate for formal approval by the supervisor or supervisory team, institutional panels, or sponsors.

Interrogating practice

Does your institution require candidates to produce formal research proposals?

If so, is there a restriction of time?

How can you go about assisting candidates to develop a research proposal?

How can you try and ensure that these are realistic, particularly in terms of time?

Do you emphasise the importance of the research proposal and plan as tools to help monitor the progress of the project?

It should be noted that, while formal research proposals are normally produced at the start of the project, it can be worth pointing out to candidates that they are not set in stone, that is, that there will almost certainly be changes both to the topic and to the timetable over the course of the project. For this reason, the proposal and plan should not be seen as records which can be put in a drawer to gather dust for the remainder of the candidacy, but as live documents which need to be regularly re-visited and updated. If used in this way, they can be important tools enabling both the candidate and the supervisor to monitor the development and progression of the research and keep it on track.

Supporting candidates in the development of skills relating to the research project

Whether candidates choose or are co-opted into a supervisor-defined research project, there is then a need to ensure that they have the subject-specific knowledge and skills necessary to undertake it.

In the US or US-style systems of doctoral education, of course, there is a specific mechanism to determine this in the form of the qualifying examination, in which candidates have to demonstrate that they are equipped to undertake research in their proposed area before being allowed to proceed to their projects.

Elsewhere, subject-specific knowledge and skills are taken into account in the selection process, but candidates may need to acquire additional ones, particularly in cases where they have only a general expertise in a field but then chosen a particular topic.

Supervisors then need to explore with candidates the knowledge and skills that they will need to undertake the project and ascertain how far they already have them, what additions are needed, and how they are going to acquire new ones.

These skills will, of course, depend upon the specific candidate and the specific project, but there are a number which are, or should be, common across the range of research projects.

Example

The Joint Research Councils and Arts and Humanities Research Board (2001) in the UK have defined these common project-related research skills and techniques as below:

- the ability to recognise and validate problems;
- original, independent and critical thinking, and the ability to develop theoretical concepts;
- a knowledge of recent advances within the field and in related areas;

- an understanding of relevant research methodologies and techniques and their appropriate application within one's research field;
- the ability to critically analyse and evaluate one's findings and those of others;
- an ability to summarise, document, report and reflect on progress.

Many of these skills, including problem recognition and validation, original thinking, and the ability to summarise, document and reflect and report on progress, will be developed as a by-product of the interaction between the supervisors and the candidate throughout the candidacy. But, particularly in the early stages, candidates may need support from their supervisors in acquiring other skills.

A knowledge of recent advances within the field and related areas

While new candidates will probably be trained in how to find the literature using search engines or databases, they may need guidance from supervisors on where to search to find books, papers, theses, and abstracts in their field.

They may also need strong encouragement not to confine their studies to the field but to consider related areas as well. Candidates can be notoriously reluctant to look outside the narrow boundaries of their own topic, either in reading or attending seminars and conferences. Yet, it can be a development in a related field which helps to solve the research problem and, of course, candidates will not ultimately be tested just on their topic, but on its relationship to the wider subject. It can, then, be useful at this stage for supervisors to point out that candidates need to keep a weather eye on developments in related fields, and discuss the means by which they might do so, for example, departmental seminars, conferences, etc.

Understanding research methodologies and their applications within the field

Candidates, particularly those coming from undergraduate backgrounds and/or who have been out of higher education for a while, frequently find research methodologies difficult because they can involve grappling with an array of philosophical, theoretical and empirical matters with which they may be unfamiliar and which they may find difficult to grasp. Supervisors may need to support them by, for example, devoting supervisions to discussing methodologies with them, by arranging relevant training, internally or possibly externally, and by pointing them towards good accounts of methods in books, theses and papers in their field.

Developing skills of critical evaluation

Again, new candidates may have read previously primarily for information, and not necessarily from a critical perspective. This is often evident from the first drafts of literature reviews, which remain at the descriptive level of A said B and C said D with little or no hint of criticism.

Candidates may have to be encouraged to adopt such an approach, perhaps by showing them an academic book review as an example of what they should be doing and/or asking them to write a critical review of a key piece of work in their field and then giving them feedback.

Developing personal research information management skills

In addition to these skills, there is a further project-related skill which supervisors may need to play a role in developing, namely personal research information management. Usually, candidates learn generic information management skills as part of the taught element of doctoral awards, but of course there may also be subject-specific ones in managing information in relation to their research project in terms of storing and retrieving data.

Example

Genoni and Partridge (2000) undertook a study of the personal research information management skills of a small sample of candidates studying at Curtin University of Technology in Australia. They found that:

- many candidates were poorly prepared by previous experience for the personal research management information tasks that awaited them;
- that both supervisors and candidates themselves often assumed that they had the skills to deal with information gathered during the research project;
- that many supervisors and candidates did not see guidance in this regard as an appropriate role for the supervisor;
- that, in consequence, even after they had been doing research for a while, many candidates had not acquired the skills to manage project-related data effectively.

It can then be helpful for supervisors to discuss with candidates how they should go about managing the information generated by their research projects, perhaps by reference to examples of how supervisors go about this themselves.

Interrogating practice

Do you audit the project-related skills of new doctoral candidates?

What skills do you think that you as the supervisor need to support candidates in developing?

How might you go about developing these skills?

Dealing with academic problems

In an ideal world, once candidates are sorted with a topic and the skills to undertake it, all they need to do is to carry on doing the research project until it is completed, that is, that they should have a smooth and trouble free ride. Indeed, when candidates read the literature, they could easily be forgiven for imagining that this is how research is actually done. Published work often, as Martin (1992: 2–3) has put it in the science context:

> ... present[s] a mythical reconstruction of what actually happened. All of what are in retrospect mistaken ideas, badly designed experiments, and incorrect calculations are omitted. The paper presents the research as if it is carefully thought out, planned and executed according to a neat rigorous process.

So what is finally published is usually only the tip of the iceberg; the nine-tenths of barren blood, sweat, toil and tears is hidden. Except in very rare cases, research is inherently a messy business, and many things can and do go wrong.

Particularly if they have come to research from undergraduate backgrounds, candidates may be ill-equipped to cope with the inevitable occasional setbacks of life as a researcher. As Delamont *et al.* (2000: 2) have pointed out:

> Most of the knowledge that undergraduate students are exposed to is pedagogically processed, packaged, and controlled in various ways. Knowledge is carefully doled out in the form of courses or modules, module outlines, course outlines and reading lists, lecture topics and assessment tasks. Students' practical work in the laboratory or 'in the field' is carefully managed and controlled. Laboratory experiments and individual projects are carefully-managed, low-risk activities, conducted within tightly defined parameters.
>
> Students' experience of transition to independent doctoral research is marked by a radical break with such knowledge-reproduction ... students now have to learn craft skills and cultural competencies which are not part of the undergraduate experience. They have to learn how to cope with experiments that do not work. They have to cope on their own 'in the field',

away from the relative safety of the classroom or the seminar. They have to rely upon their personal resources.

Similarly, as Wisker *et al.* (2003b) have pointed out, candidates from professional backgrounds can also experience difficulties in adapting to the uncertainties of academic research.

For these reasons, early encounters with academic problems with the research can be very unsettling and frustrating experiences for candidates. Perhaps the most obvious thing for them to do is to ask for support. But candidates may be reluctant to do this because they are suffering from what Atkins (1996: 2) has described as 'Top Gun' syndrome whereby:

> ... students are seen, largely by themselves, as the best and the brightest. Significant academic achievement has led them to their current place. They are thus unable to admit faults or shortcomings for fear of 'showing themselves up' in the ... academic community. It becomes better to struggle on with barely a clue about what is going on than to admit ... that one does not know what is happening.

So they may not want to tell anybody that they are experiencing problems, perhaps least of all their supervisor(s). In consequence, they can find themselves in the position of the doctoral candidates interviewed by Becher *et al.* (1994: 149) who were '... at sea to the point of having to give up, without anyone being aware of their plight'.

Given this, it is clearly important for supervisors to recognise that, particularly where candidates have limited experience of research, they will need personal support in adjusting from what may have been the certainties of their previous existence to the uncertain and psychologically disturbing uncertainties of life as a researcher.

Such support may, for example, include:

- at the start of the candidacy, modelling the highs and lows of the process by disclosing their own experiences as a 'rookie' researcher;
- keeping all the records relating to one research project, warts and all, allowing candidates to read through the file, and discussing the process with them;
- making it clear to the student that disasters and triumphs are both learning experiences;
- indicating that, in the event of difficulties, the candidate should try to find their own way out, but if they are unable to do so within a reasonable period of time that they should discuss the matter with their peers, where appropriate with members of their research group and, of course, their supervisors;
- reassuring them that they will be met with a sympathetic response and assisted to try and identify ways forward;

- perhaps most importantly, not assuming that, because the candidate hasn't been around for a while, they are making steady progress, but enquiring about the latter.

Example

Where candidates are working in close proximity to the supervisor, for example, the same or an adjacent laboratory, it can be reasonably easy to keep tabs on their progress. Where they are working away from the supervisor, and particularly if they are part-time anyway, it can be much more difficult. However, Morgan and Ryan (2003), a supervisor and a candidate, have suggested a novel solution in the form of a web-based open-state archive of the candidate's work-in-progress, developed by the candidate but accessible to the supervisor. Their original reason for developing it was to encourage more open conversations between them on the various aspects of the research project, but they became aware that it could have uses in enabling supervisors to check remotely that candidates were making progress and, if not, intervene.

While they recognised and explored the tension between their developmental intentions for the archive and its use of the archive for purposes of accountability, provided that the latter is sensitively handled it does have the advantage of giving the supervisor early warning that all is not well and the opportunity to intervene.

With supervisor support and awareness, candidates should, again in the words of Delamont *et al.* (2000: 2) develop 'a ... faith that experiments will work "in the end", that recalcitrant equipment will finally run, that the messy realities of field research will ultimately yield understanding, or that computer models will finally yield solutions'.

Interrogating practice

What perceptions do your doctoral candidates have of the research process at the start of their candidacies?

Do they correspond to reality?

How can you go about aligning candidates' perceptions with the reality of their meeting academic problems during the course of their research?

How can you support them if they do encounter problems?

Giving academic advice and guidance to candidates in groups

In the past, supervisors have been able to give academic guidance and support to candidates on an individual basis. But this has become increasingly difficult to sustain as the numbers of candidates have risen and as academic workloads have increased. One response to this has been the suggestion that, where possible and appropriate, supervisors might consider providing academic support and guidance at least in part on a group rather than solely on an individual basis.

Example

Graham and Grant (1997: 12–13) present a case study of a supervisor in sociology with a large number of doctoral candidates who supervised them in part on a group basis. Candidates were initially screened on the basis of a meeting and an outline proposal for their research, and accepted subject to comparability of the theoretical basis of their studies and a willingness to attend the supervisions and meet writing requirements.

The group met monthly throughout the year. Agendas for meeting were structured by the supervisor in accordance with the stages of the research, and each candidate given time to report upon his or her progress to the group as a whole and to receive feedback. The effectiveness of the sessions was evaluated after each meeting and also at regular intervals with individual candidates.

The group meetings were linked to requirements for the submission of work by the candidate to the supervisor, who provided extensive written feedback prior to each meeting. After six months, group meeting were supplemented by short regular meetings between the supervisor and individual candidates for the duration of the programme.

The claimed advantages of this approach are: that the supervisor saves time by giving general information to the group rather than to each candidate individually; that candidates can support each other, for example, by sharing research materials, working their way together through 'blocks' in their research projects, collectively problem-solving, and meeting socially to encourage each other to keep going; and that some of the supervisory roles can be shared with the peer group.

That said, the use of group supervision is heavily dependent upon candidates undertaking research projects in closely related areas (so that they can understand and comment upon each others' work) and probably most appropriate in the early stages (before their work becomes too specialised for collective comment). Further, it does require organisation on the part of the supervisor in terms of booking rooms for meetings and finding a time when candidates can make it, which is not always easy particularly where they are part-time.

Nonetheless, it may offer a way for supervisors to at least spread some of the burden of offering academic guidance and support to larger numbers of doctoral candidates while encouraging them to support each other both academically and socially.

Interrogating practice

Would it be possible for you to supervise your candidates as a group?

What might be the advantages for you and for the candidates?

What might be the disadvantages?

Conclusions

Particularly in the early stages of the candidacy, it is vital that supervisors provide candidates with adequate academic support and guidance. This includes: inducting them into the research project; where appropriate assisting them in developing a research proposal and plan; auditing their skills in relation to doing research in general and undertaking their own research project in particular; and preparing them for and supporting them through what can be a bumpy ride through problems with the research. By offering such support and guidance, individually or perhaps through group supervisions, candidates can be encouraged to develop both the self-confidence and the faith that things will turn out right in the end which is one of the hallmarks of the independent doctoral researcher.

Chapter 8

Encouraging early writing and giving feedback

Candidates need to start writing early and continue doing it throughout their research projects. The production of written work is essential to enable them to reflect upon where they have been and where they are going, for them to receive feedback from others, and in many institutions it is a requirement for purposes of progression. So candidates need to write early and often. But candidates may, for a variety of reasons, prove reluctant to write in the early stages, and supervisors may need to provide encouragement and support for them to do so.

But it is not just a case of persuading candidates to put pen to paper or, more accurately, fingers to keyboards. They also have to acquire the skills necessary to produce academic writing. These skills may not have been inculcated at earlier stages in their education, but have to be developed over the course of the research project if candidates are ultimately to write a thesis which will be successful and/or have conference papers or articles accepted. Again, supervisors have a role to play in promoting the development of academic writing skills.

Of course the end product of writing is a piece of work that candidates submit to their supervisors for feedback. It is important that supervisors think carefully about feedback, in particular its purposes, its timeliness, the form in which it is to be given, and how it is to be conducted.

The present chapter, then, looks at how supervisors might go about encouraging candidates to write early and often and to acquire the skills of academic writing. The final section looks at ways of giving constructive feedback.

Encouraging candidates to write

It is only at the end of the research project that candidates will have to write up their research project as a thesis, that is, the major writing task lies at the end and not the beginning of the candidacy. But, if writing is left until the final stages, candidates may have to climb a very steep learning curve in terms of acquiring the relevant skills which will, at the minimum, delay the completion of their thesis, at worst lead to them giving up the struggle and abandoning it. For this reason, many institutions require candidates to engage in writing tasks throughout their studies, and expect supervisors to ensure that they do so.

However candidates, particularly those from undergraduate backgrounds, may face barriers to writing. Key barriers identified in the literature (see, for example, Graham and Grant 1997; Torrance and Thomas 1994; Delamont *et al.* 1997; Murray 2002) include:

- Lack of understanding of why they need to write at an early stage. It may not be self-evident to candidates at the start of their studies that they need to bother about writing, that is, they expect to do that only at the end by which time, of course, they should have something to say.
- Lack of experience of writing regularly. Doctoral candidates whose only previous experience is of taught programmes may be accustomed to writing only as and when required by assignment deadlines. So writing is not habitual and it may take some time to develop it into a part of the daily routine.
- Lack of experience of writing longer pieces of work. Again, candidates may, in the past, have written to a fairly short length, perhaps 2–3,000 words. From this perspective, the 8–10,000 required by a chapter of a thesis can seem a mountain to climb and inhibit their willingness to engage in writing. So candidates may be puzzled about why they are being asked to write in the early stages of their doctorates at all, and even if they try find it a difficult task.

In many institutions, these problems have been recognised and the need to write (and the reasons) explained to candidates at their induction. But supervisors may be expected to back this up by encouraging candidates to write as much as possible early on in their studies. Ways of doing this can include:

- Encouraging candidates to keep a reflective diary/research journal. The diary is a daily record of what they have done towards their thesis. It includes a record of time spent on the work, activities, analysis and speculation. By keeping it, students get into the habit of writing every day, recording what they are doing, and reflecting upon it. Further, as Blaxter *et al.* (1996), Murray (2002) and Dunleavy (2003) have argued, it gives candidates a basis upon which to write larger pieces of work.
- Setting candidates mini-projects to complete and write up. Candidates can, at the start of their studies, be asked to undertake mini-projects, for example, reviews of a book or a couple of papers, which both requires them to write and hones their critical skills.
- Make the task of writing larger pieces of work more manageable. This can be done by asking candidates, initially, for a one-page abstract of the chapter detailing the aim (purpose), the objectives (what it would cover) and the possible conclusions (what it would say). With that thought through, the next stage would be to ask for a synopsis fleshing out the abstract and containing the headings and sub-headings to be used. Then candidates can be encouraged to fill in the framework piece by piece until they have a draft chapter.

- Giving permission for candidates to present work that is in its formative stages. Candidates, not unnaturally, want to present written work in its final form which, if they are still developing their skills in writing generally and academic writing in particular, can inhibit them from producing work or at least giving what they have written to their supervisors. But the latter can give candidates permission to submit work that is in its formative stages, that is, make it clear that they do not expect that it is in anything like its final incarnation.

Interrogating practice

Have you experienced difficulties in persuading candidates to produce written work at an early stage in their studies?

What do you consider were the major causes?

Does your institution make it clear that doctoral candidates are expected to write throughout their studies?

How might you personally go about encouraging candidates to write?

Supporting the development of academic writing

If, by these means, candidates can be encouraged to write, they may still need to acquire the facility to produce academic writing. There is no objective definition of academic writing, but it can be said to be characterised by:

- explicitness of intention – at the start of the chapter or section, the intentions should be stated and explicit;
- clarity and coherence of argument and analysis – arguments need to be make and analyses presented in ways which are clear and can be followed easily;
- respect for the conventions of writing in the subject or discipline – each discipline or subject has its own writing conventions which must be respected by researchers;
- substantiation of points – points, arguments, contentions etc. need to be substantiated by appropriate references to the literature or the research findings;
- explicitness of conclusions – conclusions should be drawn out clearly and related to intentions;
- linkages – throughout, there should be clear linkages between what is being written, what has gone before, and what will come after.

Often, again, institutions now provide courses in academic writing to assist candidates in producing it, but it is of course supervisors who read their work, and who need to supply guidance. Such guidance can take the forms of:

- referring candidates to the literature on academic writing (see, for example, Murray (2002) which also contains a comprehensive bibliography of discipline-specific literature);
- referring candidates to a 'model' of academic writing in the discipline and discussing it with them;
- taking a paragraph or two of their own work and discussing how it might be re-written in an appropriate form;
- giving them a checklist to self-evaluate their work, for example,

  * Have I made my intentions clear at the start?
  * Are my arguments/analyses clear?
  * Have I respected the subject/discipline conventions?
  * Have I substantiated the points made?
  * Are my conclusions highlighted and explicit?
  * Have I signposted the links between this section and other parts of the work?

- pairing them with 'mentors' in the form of students further on in their candidacy, who will read drafts and make suggestions for improvements.

If attention is paid to the development of a facility for academic writing at an early point in the doctoral programme, it will not only assist candidates in writing up their research and ultimately their thesis, but also reduce later demands upon their supervisors for support, that is, an investment by both at the start will pay dividends to both at the end.

Interrogating practice

Does your institution provide support for students to acquire a facility for academic writing?

What are the conventions for such writing in your subject or discipline?

How can you support candidates to develop their academic writing?

Giving feedback on work in progress

Once candidates are writing and showing work in progress to their supervisors, then they need to be given feedback. In order to be effective, the latter needs to be purposive, timely, in an appropriate form, conducted in an appropriate way and with due regard for the sensibilities of the candidate.

The purposes of feedback

Brown and Atkins (1988) have suggested that feedback has four main purposes.

1 To enable candidates to appreciate standards

Feedback gives the candidate a feeling for the standards against which their work will be judged. Candidates are unlikely at the start or in the early stages in particular to be fully aware of the standards that they are expected to attain (see Becher *et al.* 1994), and even reading successful theses in cognate areas may have given them little indication of what to aim for at an intermediate stage of the research project. One of the key functions of the supervisor is to enable candidates to appreciate the standards which they are expected to attain. Candidates cannot be expected to gain a PhD (or other doctorate) unless they know the standards, and cannot be expected to have an intuitive grasp of what the standards are. Hence, as Phillips and Pugh (2000) have pointed out, feedback from their supervisors is vital in enabling them to learn what the standards are and enabling them to recognise when they have achieved them.

Hopefully, as candidates learn from feedback, they should begin to internalise the standards and become able to critically assess their own work. This, of course, is part of becoming a successful researcher.

2 To improve their skills

Feedback can also assist in developing candidates' skills, including methodological skills (for example, research design, data collection, data analysis, data interpretation) and writing skills. Candidates may or may not have the expertise to design and implement their research projects, and one of the functions of feedback is to advise on these matters and, in the case of shortfalls, assist the students to acquire relevant skills. Similarly, as noted above, their skills in academic writing are likely to require development, and this is part of the function of feedback.

3 To deepen their understanding

The third purpose is to assist candidates to deepen and develop their understanding of the problem or topic that they are researching through discussion at all of the stages from inception through to completed drafts.

4 To give them a sense of achievement

A further reason for feedback is to give candidates a sense of achievement in what they have accomplished. Too often, supervisors see feedback sessions solely as opportunities to criticise and correct candidates' work, and they forget or ignore the need to give them encouragement or praise where it is due. But positive recognition of their achievements by supervisors that they hold in high esteem can be crucial in motivating candidates, particularly in the early stages of the project before (hopefully) success becomes apparent and becomes an internalised driver in its own right.

In planning feedback, it is important to keep these purposes in mind, particularly the last one.

Timeliness

But, if these purposes are to be achieved, feedback must be timely. One of the most frustrating experiences of doctoral candidates is for them to hand a chapter or chapters of their *magnum opus* to their supervisor(s), and then hear nothing more for weeks or months afterwards (see, for example, Fitzpatrick *et al.* 1998). This, at best, indicates that they lie low down the pecking order in their supervisor's priorities, at worst it can delay the research project.

For this reason, many institutions now have an institutional time limit for giving feedback to candidates, usually between one and three weeks and set out in the initial learning agreement (see p. 60). But even if there is not such an institutional requirement, supervisors should give candidates a clear indication of when they can expect feedback on their work, where appropriate check that this will not hold up the research project (and if necessary adjust it), and stick to the agreed deadline.

The form of feedback

Supervisors also need to consider the form in which feedback will be given. Practice varies considerably, with some supervisors sending candidates written comments in advance, others providing written comments on the day, and others only giving oral feedback. While there is no right or wrong way of doing this, it can be helpful to candidates to have some warning in advance about what will be discussed or at least written comments on the day which will reduce the need for them to spend much of the time taking detailed notes. For these reasons, as well as possibly legal ones in the context of candidates appealing against non-award on the basis that they were not informed of serious deficiencies in their research projects, some institutions require that supervisors give feedback in at least summary written form.

The setting for the feedback

Supervisors often give feedback in their offices, which brings the setting into play. It is important to note that things such as the seating arrangements can have some bearing on the interactions. If supervisors sit behind their desk with the candidate on the other side – particularly if the latter are on a lower level –

then the signal is one of formal interaction between a superior and an inferior. If they are side-by-side, the signal is more one of a discussion between colleagues.

But, whatever the setting, supervisors can make sure that there are no interruptions during the feedback session. It can be extremely disruptive, not to say discourteous if, during the session, academic colleagues or other candidates pop in and out or the phone rings constantly. There is a need to put the 'Do not disturb' sign on the door and divert phone calls for the duration of the session.

Planning the feedback

Once the setting is right, then the feedback can be planned. Again, there is no right or wrong way to do this, but suggestions might be for supervisors:

- To welcome the candidate and thank them for submitting the work – candidates may well be nervous about receiving feedback, and it can help to settle them down if they are made to feel welcome by a smile and perhaps an enquiry about their well-being and a 'thank you' for submitting the work.
- To open by setting out expectations for the session – it can be useful at the start for supervisors to set out expectations for the session. In particular, they should make it clear that the primary objective is to enable further progress in the research project (see Phillips and Pugh 2000). It can be helpful here to make it clear that, where appropriate, they will expect students to challenge their views and opinions, and that this is a normal and essential part of the process.
- To summarise their understanding of the material submitted – one of the most useful things that a supervisor can do is to summarise his or her understanding of the material that the student has submitted. 'So it seems to me that the central thrust of what you are saying is … .'
- To check that understanding with the candidate – once the supervisor has summarised, it can be very useful just to check that their understanding is the same as that of the candidate – 'Have I got that right?' This not only reassures them that their work is being taken seriously, but offers an opportunity to correct any misapprehensions at the start of the session.
- To identify the strengths of the work – supervisors can then identify what they saw as the strengths of the work submitted, which is an opportunity for praise. 'What I thought was really interesting was … what I most enjoyed reading was …'
- To identify the areas for attention – supervisors need, of course, to be honest in their feedback to candidates and, if there is bad news, to give it; failure to do so at best leaves the candidate in ignorance, at worst can invite a formal complaint or even law suit if the thesis is subsequently failed.

Example

A candidate in a UK university whose thesis was turned down for any degree made a formal complaint that, while she had had regular supervisions and feedback from her supervisor, the latter had repeatedly assured her that she was making good progress. The complaint was investigated under the university's internal procedures and substantiated, with the result that the institution had to pay compensation to the candidate – see Baty 2003.

But if supervisors then need to make candidates aware of deficiencies in their work, they should try and do this in ways that are constructive and positive rather than destructive and negative. So, for example, a better way in would be to say, 'Why did you try to solve the problem using method X rather than method Y?' rather than 'Didn't you realise that you could have avoided these difficulties with method Y?'. Another useful device in the bad news context is to say 'If I was your external examiner, then this is what I would say …' which effectively makes the point that it is better to hear it now than in the final examination.

- To invite the candidate to respond – once supervisors have identified the areas, then they can ask the candidate to respond. Here, it is very important that candidates are allowed to engage with the matters that supervisors have raised, and in particular it must be recognised that they will need time to respond to queries about their work. Supervisors must also be prepared to listen carefully and check that the candidate has understood the points being made.
- To summarise the discussion – when the points have been exhausted, then it is important to summarise the discussion. The supervisor may try to draw the threads together and then check it with the candidate or, alternatively, may ask the candidate to summarise. Often, the former is most appropriate when the candidate has done most of the talking, and the latter when the supervisor has contributed most to the session.
- To agree what should be done and by when – on the basis of the summary points, the supervisor and the candidate should agree upon what happens next, and upon a timescale.

In addition, it can do no harm on occasion for supervisors to ask candidates whether they found the feedback session useful, and whether things could have been done in other ways which would be more helpful.

Recording the feedback session and the outcomes

Finally, for the benefit of both the candidate and the supervisor, there should be an agreed written record of the feedback session and the outcomes. This may be written by the supervisor or by the candidate, and it is often an institutional requirement that one is written and possibly that copies are lodged on the candidate's file and/or included in their personal development record.

Interrogating practice

What are the purposes of giving candidates feedback?

Does you institution have a policy on the time within which feedback has to be given?

If not, do you negotiate with the candidate about an appropriate time limit?

Do you make sure that the setting is appropriate and that you are not interrupted?

Do you plan to give feedback in ways that are sensitive to the needs of candidates and which will elicit a positive response?

How do you break bad news to candidates?

How are feedback sessions and their outcomes recorded in your institution?

Conclusions

At least in the past, writing has been generally regarded as something that was done at the end of the doctorate, and the difficulties that this occasioned for candidates unaccustomed to writing long pieces in general, or to producing academic writing in particular, may well have been a factor in explaining the long delays in completing theses. However, writing is now seen as an activity to be undertaken throughout the doctorate and encouraging it and developing academic writing have become parts of the responsibilities of supervisors.

Feedback has always been a key responsibility, but not one necessarily always exercised in ways that have met the needs of candidates or respected their sensibilities. In practice, however, a little thought and planning can go a long way to making feedback sessions effective in the sense of delivering comments and criticisms without destroying the confidence of the candidate in the process.

Chapter 9

Keeping the research on track and monitoring progress

Once the research project is down the slipway and on its journey, it has to be kept on track. While the primary responsibility for this has to lie with the candidate – at the end of the day he or she has to do the research – supervisors have a role to play in supporting them to bring the project in on time.

But, as well as supporting progress, supervisors also have formal institutional responsibilities in monitoring it. In the past, monitoring was often a formality and not always taken very seriously. But, following the revelations in the mid- and late 1980s about long completion times and low completion rates, as noted on pp. 13–14 in many countries sponsors have adopted a much tougher stance. Consequently, institutions have been forced to tighten up considerably on monitoring procedures. Supervisors may then be expected to actively monitor the progress of candidates and engage with formal institutional procedures for assessing it.

The present chapter then considers how supervisors might go about supporting candidates to keep the research project on track, and their role in monitoring and assessing progress.

Supporting candidates to keep the research on track

Research projects can be knocked off track for many reasons not of the candidate's making, including academic problems of the kind identified in Chapter 7. But they can also go astray for reasons relating to the candidate, in particular their skills in managing their project, managing their time, and managing themselves.

Project management skills

In the days when, because it involved an original contribution to knowledge and understanding, a doctorate took as long as it took, there was little need for candidates to have project management skills. But those days are long gone, and candidates are now under considerable pressures from institutions, and often from their bank managers as well, to complete within a few years. In order to do this, they need to have good project management skills.

In many cases, this has been recognised by institutions, and provision has been made in the taught components of research training programmes to include the development of project management skills. In addition to this, some institutions have developed their own self-help tools to enable candidates to reflect upon their progress and, where appropriate, take action to improve it.

Example

The Faculty of Science at the University of Central Lancashire in the UK requires all candidates to maintain a progress file containing, among other things, a reflective journal. Candidates are asked at key points in the progress of their research to reflect upon their achievements to date, how far they have achieved their objectives, what are the strengths and weaknesses of their work so far, what they have learned, what opportunities and problems might lie ahead, what their next set of targets should be, and how they are going to achieve them. See http://www.uclan.ac.uk/other/registry/research/index.htm

Many institutions in the UK also use similar tools based upon templates supplied by professional bodies.

Example

The Royal Society of Chemistry in the UK has developed a Postgraduate Skills Development Record in which doctoral candidates are invited to reflect at each stage of their studies upon a series of statements, see how far they meet them, and where appropriate plan to improve their skills. The statements include:

- I have a clear understanding of the scientific nature of my project, its objectives, and a strategy for meeting targets
- I have an understanding of the relevant literature
- I have my own system for reviewing the literature on a regular basis
- I have become familiar with, and use, literature search techniques
- I have acquired experimental techniques necessary for my research
- I have adapted proven practical procedures to meet my requirements
- I have developed an understanding of health, safety and environmental issues relevant to my research
- I have identified relevant specialist skills to support my research, for example, statistics, molecular modelling

- I have produced precise and informative summaries of my research
- I have planned my research independently and on a daily and weekly basis
- I have kept precise laboratory records and retained a copy outside my laboratory
- I have discussed the need for any changes in direction of my research with my supervisor
- I have presented my research, and have incorporated constructive feedback into planning my research
- I have re-assessed experimental techniques
- I have initiated plans for the structure of my thesis
- I have identified experimental work which establishes and confirms my results and ideas
- I have developed the ability to recognise the amount of experimental data needed to evaluate my results

Crown copyright material reproduced with the permission of the Controller of HMSO and the Queen's Printer for Scotland.

Source: http://www.rsc.org/lap/educatio/pgskills.htm

While these tools are aimed at candidates, it can be extremely helpful if they agree to share their responses with supervisors, and that some time is spent identifying areas to be improved so that candidates can be more effective in managing their projects.

Interrogating practice

Does your institution provide training in project management?

Does it have any tools to enable candidates to develop their project management skills?

Do you discuss these skills with candidates?

Time management skills

A further obstacle to completing the project on time can be candidates finding it difficult to manage their personal time. Particularly for many candidates in the arts, humanities or social sciences, their time can be pretty well their own. This is, on the one hand, immensely liberating in so far as they will have more control over their time than at any point until they retire; on the other hand, it can be an awesome responsibility to be given such freedom. As Welsh (1979: 33) noted in her pioneering study of the first year of doctoral study, it is 'all too easy for the postgraduate student to spend his [her] time pottering about' and fall seriously behind.

As Phillips and Pugh (2000) have noted, supervisors often find it difficult to understand why students seem unable to manage their time effectively and do not take the initiative both for that reason and because they believe that organising and administering their working pace is part of the hallmark of the successful doctoral candidate. But while such a view was perhaps tenable in the days when a doctorate took as long as it took, it is less tenable in an age when candidates have three or at most four years to complete.

On this basis, supervisors are doing candidates a favour, particularly in the early stages of the project, by setting realistic deadlines and insisting that they are met. Certainly in the event of deadlines being consistently missed, supervisors should realise that the candidate may have a problem in managing time, and be prepared to intervene. Such intervention may take the form of, for example, pointing candidates in the direction of the literature for doctoral students on time management (see, for example, Cryer 2000; Phillips and Pugh 2000; Leonard 2001; Taylor 2002; Wisker 2001) or, in extremis, of asking them to keep a record of time spent and discuss it with them (see Graham and Grant 1997).

For candidates in applied science subjects, time management may perhaps be less of an issue in so far as they are expected to turn up at the lab on a daily basis and work regular hours. But here the pendulum can go the other way, in the sense that students spend too many hours in the lab. Their work can become subject to the law of diminishing returns and leave them exhausted and, not infrequently, unable to see the wood for the trees, for example, carrying on doing experiments long beyond the point at which they are producing relevant results.

Again, supervisors may affirm that time spent in the lab cannot, by definition, be wasted, but the counter-argument is that candidates need a reasonable balance between work and outside activities to function effectively. Again, where supervisors suspect that candidates are working themselves to exhaustion for little or no return, they may wish to ask the student about their work/life balance and, where appropriate, give their blessing to a reduction in hours, break or holiday.

Interrogating practice

Do you find that candidates have difficulties in managing their time?

How might you assist them to do so effectively?

Self-management skills – overcoming isolation

One of the most consistent themes in the literature on doctoral candidates over the past three decades or more (see, for example, Rudd 1975, 1985; Bowen and Rudenstein 1992; Becher *et al*. 1994; Delamont *et al*. 1997; Cryer 2000; Phillips and Pugh 2000; Leonard 2001) is the extent to which they can suffer from isolation, both intellectually and/or socially.

An element of intellectual isolation is, as Johnson *et al*. (2000) have pointed out, inherent in the doctorate itself. The latter requires candidates to make an independent and original contribution to knowledge and understanding, which implies that the work must be undertaken on their own and that the outcomes are unique. That said, there is a difference between candidates working on their own on their research projects but with support from their supervisors, and possibly other members of the research team and fellow graduate students, and candidates who are working in an intellectual vacuum.

Clearly, the doctoral candidates most vulnerable to unacceptable intellectual isolation of the kind described above are the 'lone scholars' in the arts, humanities and perhaps parts of the social sciences ploughing their own furrows at a remove from the interests of their supervisors or fellow doctoral candidates (see, for example, Rudd 1975; Bowen and Rudenstein 1992). Those least vulnerable would seem to be candidates, mainly in the applied sciences, working as part of a research team where there are others around who are jointly involved in the project. But, as Becher *et al*. (1994) have argued, this is not a guarantee; teams may function in a highly individualistic way and teams themselves can be isolating in so far as they set boundaries which cut off contact with other research teams.

Irrespective of context, then, supervisors need to keep under review whether candidates are being offered adequate opportunities for intellectual stimulation or interaction, and if not provide them. As well as regular meetings, strategies for achieving this can, as Graham and Grant (1997) and Wisker (2001) have shown, include joint supervision sessions with other candidates (who are encouraged to take an interest in each other's researches), the appointment of negotiated advisors to offer additional support, and mentoring by other candidates further on in their doctoral researches.

If, in these ways, the intellectual isolation inherent in doctoral studies can be kept within acceptable (and productive) limits, there is, as Delamont *et al*. (1997) have pointed out, still a potential issue about social isolation. Candidates need to have a social life inside and outside their work to function effectively, and the absence of such contact can lead to loneliness, depression, and ultimately poor performance in the research project. In this regard, candidates working in the applied sciences would again seem to have the advantage over their counterparts in the arts and humanities, for two reasons.

First, the former are more likely to work in the university in a team environment involving day-to-day contact with other members, while the latter are more likely to work at home and in libraries which, as Rudd (1975: 101) has put it, 'are unpromising places in which to form friendships.'

Second, candidates in the applied sciences may find it easier to treat their research as 'work' and have a life outside, while arts and humanities students bind their lives around their studies. As Wright and Cochrane (2000: 192–3) have hypothesised:

> Scientific research requires the study of purportedly objective phenomena which can be seen as outside the individual. This may enable the scientist to separate their work from the internal world, thus avoiding impinging upon or challenging issues of identity or self-esteem … In some fields of study in the arts, however, study can be perceived as being considerably more subjective and requiring exposure to judgement of elements of the student's internal world, such as their values and belief systems and even ability to demonstrate and convey emotion. Such an element of personal risk and investment perhaps makes the work more intrinsically challenging to an individual's psychological equilibrium …

In short, science candidates may find it easier to switch off because they are less bound up emotionally in their work, while arts and humanities ones may have a greater psychological investment and find it more difficult to put their studies aside.

Clearly, these are, if anything, tendencies, and it is quite possible for scientists to be lonely in the crowd or, conversely, for arts candidates to have rich social lives outside their studies. But the key thing is that social isolation can be a problem besetting doctoral candidates, and one of which supervisors need to be aware. In addition to providing personal support, for example, inviting candidates home for dinner, supervisors need to find out what opportunities there are for candidates to socialise both with faculty and with each other. The list might include staff–student and student seminars, research training programmes, social events, and learned society meetings. Supervisors need to actively encourage candidates to take up such opportunities and, in the process, help them to integrate socially and, at the end of the day, cope more effectively with undertaking their research projects.

Interrogating practice

Do you offer adequate intellectual support to doctoral candidates?

Are there ways in which support could be improved?

What opportunities are there for candidates to socialise with faculty and with each other?

Self-management skills – improving motivation

Candidates commence their dissertations all bright-eyed and bushy-tailed at the apparently glamorous prospect of undertaking original research. But, perhaps a year to eighteen months into the research project, as Cryer (2000) has shown, the glamour can begin to wear off as candidates lose their sense of direction, feel overwhelmed by what little they have done and what is left to be done, suffer loss of confidence, or are bored out of their minds by the endless grind. In consequence, as a number of commentators (see, for example, Becher *et al.* 1994; Delamont *et al.* 1997; Phillips and Pugh 2000) have noted, candidates may undergo a mid-thesis crisis and suffer a consequent loss of motivation.

Example

Mid-thesis crisis is well illustrated by one of Rudd's (1985: 44) respondents who said:

> One starts ... to question why you're there, because the bandwaggon effect of undergraduate work disappears about a year after you've got into the PhD, because you are no longer involved in that corporate body, you don't have to attend lectures, you don't have official things you must do, you don't have to attend a specific tutorial. In other words, there are no longer any clear stepping stones. The only stepping stone is to submit your thesis, and you ask 'Why?' I think people are disillusioned after about eighteen months. I think that's a normal phenomenon you know – 'I'm pissed off with the whole thing. I'm not going to do it ...'

Clearly, if candidates are left to get on with it, there is a danger that their work will fall seriously behind or even that they will eventually give up.

Where supervisors suspect that this is happening, they can help to re-motivate candidates by:

- Praising them – by affirming the value of the candidate's research project to science, humanity, or civilisation, supervisors may boost candidate's self-esteem and hopefully their willingness to complete it. Praise may go a long way, particularly if made in front of a departmental or graduate school audience.
- Negotiating stepping stones – if the problem is, as in the example, that only submission is visible and it seems a very long way off on the horizon, by negotiating interim stepping stones with the candidate. The latter should provide the candidate with realistic targets to aim for and a defined end point.

- Re-focusing the research – often, disillusionment can reflect the fact that the candidate has lost the original focus of the research and is foundering not knowing what to do, a phenomenon which has been described by Phillips and Pugh (2000: 79) as 'getting nowhere' syndrome. Cryer (2000) gives a number of examples of how this has been overcome by supervisors working with the candidate to refocus the research project and drawing up a new research plan.
- Administering a motivational jolt – Delamont *et al.* (1997) have suggested that it can be helpful to give candidates what they describe as a 'motivational jolt'. This could be: presenting a paper at a departmental seminar; presenting a paper at another department; attendance at a conference; a conference paper; a book review; a publication; or organising a workshop on their research. The intention, in each of these cases, is to dangle a carrot in front of the candidate designed to restore their flagging attention to their research project.
- Encouraging them to take a break – perhaps very much as a matter of last resort, supervisors may encourage candidates to 'take a break'. This needs to be short and finite; there are many candidates who took a break and procrastinated about returning until it was too late, giving rise to the phenomenon known in the US as 'ABDs' – All But Dissertations.

By these means, then, supervisors may be able to motivate candidates and overcome loss of motivation with doctoral studies although this is not always possible; there may be students who are better advised to register for a lower degree, or even to withdraw.

Interrogating practice

Do you notice any pattern among candidates of 'mid-thesis crisis'?

How can you go about motivating them to keep them on track?

Monitoring progress

As well as supporting candidates in keeping the project on track, supervisors will in many cases also have responsibilities to monitor their progress on behalf of the institution and report on this matter to progress panels, of which supervisors may be a member.

The basic mechanism for monitoring progress is the formal meeting between the supervisors and the candidate, of which there is normally a minimum number per year required by the institution. At these meetings, supervisors and candidates will review progress towards the objectives set out in the previous meeting and also in relation to the milestones set out in the research proposal or plan. Where objectives have not been met, it is important that supervisors ascertain the reasons why and agree with the candidate any necessary actions to be taken to get the project back on track.

At least in the past, the outcomes of these formal supervisions may not have been recorded at all or perhaps only informally by the supervisor and/or the candidate. But, following the tightening up of monitoring procedures mentioned in the introduction, many institutions now insist that they are formally recorded, and in some cases supply a pro-forma for the purpose.

Example

The University of Birmingham in the UK has the following record for formal supervisions.

Supervision record (routine)

SECTION 1 to be completed by the STUDENT prior to supervision meeting

a) Name:

b) Supervisor's name:

c) Date/time of supervision:

d) Date of last supervision:

e) Work submitted to supervisor since last supervision meeting (with date work submitted *and* returned to you)

f) Work undertaken since last supervision meeting:

g) Issues you would like to discuss in the supervision meeting:

SECTION 2 to be completed by the SUPERVISOR at the supervision meeting

a) Topics covered in supervision meeting (please refer to Section 1(g) above):

b) Your comments on student's progress since last supervision meeting:

c) Overall rating of students progress to date (tick one)
Very satisfactory   Satisfactory   Giving cause for concern

d) If 'Giving cause for concern' please state clearly the steps the student should take to reach a level of satisfactory progress:

e) Work student should undertake between now and next supervision:

f) Work to be submitted to you before next supervision (with dates):

SECTION 3 Date/Time of next meeting:

This form contains a good summary of our meeting

Signatures : Student   Date   Supervisor   Date

A copy of this form should be kept by the supervisor and by the student

Source: http://medweb5.bham.ac.uk/graduateschool/progressreview?o=0

Clearly, if in these or similar pro-formas, there is a succession of 'giving cause for concern' judgements, then something is going wrong. In such cases, schools or departments may well have informal 'early warning' systems whereby the head of school or similar should be notified that a candidate may be failing so that he or she can investigate the matter and see what can be done.

The other main function of these pro-formas is as a primary source of evidence for progress reviews. Most institutions have procedures whereby the progress of candidates is formally reviewed at pre-defined points in the candidacy. In institutions where candidates are initially registered for a lower degree or as candidates-elect, there will normally be a review at between 9 and 15 months to determine whether they should be accorded full doctoral candidate status; where the latter is conferred at registration, there will be a review to confirm that it should be continued; in both cases there will be subsequent reviews of continuation towards the end of further years of study.

Supervisors will normally be asked to send written reports to the panels conducting these reviews on the progress of the candidate. Such reports may be on a separate pro-forma, or include a summary backed by the official records of the meetings.

There is a divergence of practice about whether, as well as submitting reports, supervisors should also be members of progress panels. On the one hand, there is the view that they should not because their judgement may be biased and compromise the independence of the review. On the other, there is the view that it is the supervisors who are in the best position to know whether the candidate should be allowed to progress to doctoral status or to continue in it, and they are members of panels, usually with an additional 'outside' member as well to ensure impartiality.

Again, the form of panel review can vary considerably, both between and within institutions. In some cases it takes the form of a review of documentary evidence in the form of the supervisor's report and evidence of progress submitted by the candidate, usually a report and/or a substantial piece of written work. In others these can be supplemented variously by an interview, a presentation by the candidate, or a mini-viva, or some combination of these.

Example

At the European Institute of the University of Sussex, there is a three-part annual review process. During the summer term, supervisors submit a (second) report on the progress of all their research students. At the same time, all research students submit a form which assesses their progress during the academic year and includes a timetable for the next academic year. Prior to submission, this report has to be discussed with, and signed by, the student's supervisor(s). The third aspect of the Annual Review, is an oral 'defence'. This takes place in the last week of the summer term. Each research student has to appear before a panel usually comprising an SEI co-director and the research student Convenor. The panel lasts about 30 minutes and has two components: a 10-minute presentation by the student on a recent piece of academic work (a chapter of the thesis, an article etc.) followed by questions and answers; a discussion of the written report submitted by the student. The panel then makes a recommendation about re-registration to the GRC co-Director, who then gives authorisation to the Postgraduate Office.

Source: http://www.sussex.ac.uk/Units/SEI/postgrad/researchHBKmonitr progrss.html

It may be that, where reviews involve a presentation or a mini-viva, supervisors are expected to assist candidates to prepare by listening to a rehearsal of the presentation or taking them through a mock viva.

In view of these variations in practice, it is important for new supervisors in particular to know what the precise arrangements are in their institution so that they can play an appropriate part in institutional monitoring procedures.

Interrogating practice

Does your institution require you to record the outcomes of formal progress meetings?

Does it have a pro-forma for the purpose?

Does your school or department have an 'early warning' system for potentially failing candidates?

When does your institution require you to report formally on the candidate's progress?

Are supervisors in your institution involved in progress panels?

What evidence do progress panels consider in your institution?

Do you have a role in preparing candidates for review panels?

Conclusions

In many countries, institutions are under considerable pressure from sponsors to ensure that a significant proportion of candidates complete within an allotted time and this, in conjunction with financial pressures on candidates themselves, places a huge premium in keeping the research on track. Supervisors have key roles to play in this both in terms of supporting candidates to develop the relevant skills to keep the show on the road and in monitoring and reviewing their progress.

It is perhaps worth noting that these twin requirements have added very considerably to the burdens of supervising doctoral candidates in terms of the time and effort that supervisors are required to put in to the process. There is at least an argument that, as in many universities in the United States, these functions could be hived off to faculty mentors, leaving supervisors freer to concentrate upon their academic role.

Part IV

Supporting the candidate

Chapter 10

Personal, professional, academic and career support

In common with the rest of the population, doctoral candidates are subject to ups and downs in their private lives, and these can of course have an impact upon their abilities to undertake their research. Supervisors need to be at least aware of these matters and, where appropriate, to offer support.

As well as personal support, supervisors are also expected to provide support for professional development. Part and parcel of undertaking doctoral research is engagement with the relevant disciplinary and, where appropriate, professional communities so that the candidate can meet, and learn from, colleagues, and make the latter aware of their research and their achievements. As novice candidates are unlikely to have the contacts or expertise to do this on their own, supervisors have traditionally assisted them in developing contacts or networking, giving presentations, and in publishing the outcomes of their research.

Also, supervisors may also play a role in supporting candidates in undertaking teaching duties. Many candidates undertake such duties, partly for interest and experience and partly as a way of financing their studies. Supervisors may wish to encourage candidates to engage in teaching. In such circumstances, they should ensure that they are adequately prepared and supported so that students taught by them have a high quality learning experience.

Historically, of course, these forms of professional development have been important in enabling doctoral graduates to consider an academic career in so far as they emerge with not just a doctorate, but also with a personal profile within the subject community, publications, and experience in teaching and promoting learning. For such candidates, supervisors may have a role to play in directing them towards suitable opportunities to prepare for an academic career and informing them about faculty work and life.

However, in many countries only a minority of doctoral candidates now seek to enter academic life, and of those who do many are called but few are chosen. The vast majority will, if not immediately then certainly after a year or two, find employment in other fields, for which they will need appropriate generic skills. Such skills are increasingly being incorporated by institutions in doctoral programmes, and supervisors are increasingly expected to assist their development.

This chapter then looks at how supervisors might support candidates personally and in professional, academic and wider career development.

Personal support

Supervisors will, in most cases, have some engagement with the personal lives of candidates over the course of their doctoral studies as events in their private lives impinge upon their professional ones.

In order to be able to take account of personal matters, supervisors have to be aware in the first place that candidates are experiencing personal problems of one kind or another that are affecting their research.

The sources of such awareness will depend, at least in part, on the way in which institutions organise the pastoral role. In many institutions, this is divorced from that of their supervisor, and candidates are given mentors or personal tutors who are expected to deal with personal problems and keep the supervisor informed.

But in others, the supervisor or one of the members of the supervisory team has responsibility for pastoral support, in which case they are reliant upon the candidate informing them at least that there is a problem, if not necessarily the intimate details. In turn, the extent to which candidates will be prepared to do that will depend upon whether they perceive this as an obligation and upon what sort of reception they feel that they might get.

Clearly, the chances of them offering information will be greater where supervisors make it clear that they need to be told and where at least one supervisor is seen by the candidate as potentially sympathetic, that is, who in terms of the typology developed by Gatfield and Alpert (2002) has a 'pastoral style'.

Good practice, then, is for supervisors who do have pastoral responsibilities to ask candidates right at the start of their studies to let them know about personal matters affecting the research, and, if possible, for supervisory teams to include at least one member with a pastoral style. If not, it may be possible to arrange for candidates to be given access to a third party with the requisite empathy.

That said, no matter how far they are encouraged to make contact or how empathetic the supervisor(s), candidates may be unwilling to admit to difficulties for reasons relating to their personalities, a sense of shame or failure about their apparent inability to manage their private lives or, as will be seen in the next two chapters, for social and cultural reasons.

Supervisors cannot, therefore, necessarily rely upon candidates informing them, and there is a need for them to also look for other signs of personal difficulties. These may include obvious signs such as a sudden and unprecedented dip in performance, for example, when a normally model candidate fails to turn up for one or more review sessions without notification or hands in a chapter late, or fails to hand it in at all. But they may also include more subtle ones, such as when candidates do turn up for review sessions but are, from their verbal and non-verbal language, distracted from the matter in hand. In such circumstances, it can be useful for supervisors to have a quiet word with the candidate, perhaps in private over a cup of coffee, and at least give them the opportunity to speak out.

Once supervisors have determined, by one means or another, that there is a personal problem, then the next question is how to deal with it. At the very least, supervisors do need to reassure candidates that they can speak in confidence to them, to be prepared to listen to any problems with a sympathetic ear, and to be non-judgmental, even if the problem is clearly the candidate's own fault.

But once they are aware of the problem, of course, the question arises about if, and how far, supervisors should go in advising the candidate. As Cryer (2000) has noted, there tend to be two views about this among supervisors, one that they should not involve themselves at all in solving candidates' problems, the other that it is only natural and helpful for them to do so.

In practice, there are advantages and disadvantages in both approaches. If supervisors decide not to involve themselves, then this may help to maintain the relationship as a professional one, it averts the possibility that they may do more harm than good, and it saves what can be a considerable expenditure of time and energy. The downside is that the student may feel that the supervisor is being unsympathetic and unhelpful, which may not be good for the relationship in the longer term.

If supervisors do intervene, the advantage may be that they can help the candidate, and that this will preserve the relationship in the longer term. But such well-meant intervention has to be seen in the light of two possible dangers. First, and bearing in mind that the supervisor–candidate relationship is, particularly in its early stages, an authority one, supervisors may well be tempted to the 'If I were you … ' solution, and may be seen as imposing a solution upon the candidate. But the supervisor is not the candidate, and what works for the former may not work for the latter. Second, and particularly in relation to more serious problems, few supervisors are trained in counselling and, in this context, a little knowledge can be a dangerous thing.

If supervisors are wary about extending their professional advisory function to a personal one, this is not to say that they should do nothing. What they can do is: to act as a sounding board to help doctoral candidates to think their problems through; to establish the options including, if appropriate, professional assistance from the institution's welfare services; and to find solutions of their own.

Example

In her moving autobiographical account of being a PhD student Johnson (2001: 59) writes that:

> In the space of three years, in mid-life, I lost my parents suddenly; my belief that those I love would be left untouched by serious illness and dreadful events beyond their and my control; any sense, however limited, of justice in life or a 'balancing out'; interest in my career and in my field; any sense of progress in and control over my PhD studies; my self-confidence; any sense that I had anything meaningful to contribute; my capacity and desire to write; my sense of self; and my own voice.

She describes how her supervisors took account of her difficulties by advising her to withdraw temporarily from her studies until her distress reached manageable levels. Throughout, she remained absolutely determined to complete her doctorate. When she had recovered, her supervisors helped her to re-focus the research project and to re-plan it, and she eventually gained her PhD.

While, in the above example, the candidate did pull through and was successful, this was because it was the right solution for her. It can sometimes be hard for supervisors to accept that, although candidates may be exceptionally able and have a doctorate well within their grasp, continuation may not be the right solution for them.

Example

In her study of the doctoral attrition process in the US, Golde (2000) describes the case of Jane, a doctoral student who had a chequered history including a falling-out with a first advisor, residual pain from a car accident, and being dumped by a boyfriend. She was assisted by campus Psychological Services, and began to re-group. She found a new dissertation topic and a new advisor who thought that it was great, and she began to write a new proposal. Then she decided to leave; in her own words (ibid: 11):

> Before I was finished with the proposal, I just decided I didn't want the whole thing. It was really weird. Its like, I am going to get all the way I want to be. I am going to get my dissertation topic, a good advisor, and then, when its all set, when all the ducks are in a row, I make a decision not to do it ... I quit and I have never regretted it at all.

Interrogating practice

Does your institution expect supervisors to provide pastoral support to doctoral candidates?

How can you go about alerting candidates to the need to inform you of personal problems affecting the research?

Is your supervisory style empathetic to candidates' personal problems?

How can you avoid being over-prescriptive in assisting candidates?

What professional welfare services are available in your institution?

Supervisors and support services, then, can do all they can to assist candidates with personal problems, but at the end of the day, it is the latter who have to own and make and live with the final decision.

Support for professional development

Supervisors may provide support for professional development in the six key areas of networking, giving presentations, publications, teaching and learning, academic careers, and the acquisition of generic skills.

Networking

Academics are, of courses, located in their individual institutions, but operate within disciplines spread across a range of institutions locally, nationally, and internationally. Networking, then, in the sense of making and maintaining contacts with colleagues in the discipline is an integral and important part of academic life.

In the same way that networking is vital for faculty, it is also vital for doctoral candidates. They also need to be able to make and maintain contacts with colleagues working in their field for the purposes of furthering their research, establishing a profile within the discipline, and perhaps ultimately providing an entrée to an academic career.

But, at least at the start of their studies, doctoral candidates are unlikely to have contacts of their own and/or may lack the necessary self-confidence to make them. In this context, supervisors have a key role to play in helping them to establish and maintain networks. So, as Becher *et al.* (1994: 120) have said:

> Among the tests of a good supervisor is the extent to which he or she helps graduate students to set up professional contacts with other academics working in closely related fields.

In particular, and adapting Blaxter *et al.* (1996), supervisors may have roles to play in the following areas.

Encouraging candidates to take networking seriously

Candidates may not, at the start of their studies, be fully aware of the importance of networking to their research and possibly to their future careers. Supervisors can draw their attention to the benefits in terms of opportunities for dialogue, for professional support, for collaboration, for profile in the subject, and for career prospects, perhaps using their own experiences as an illustration.

Helping them to target appropriate networks

Candidates may take networking seriously but, particularly at the start of their studies, have little if any idea of the appropriate networks to target. Supervisors can help by drawing their attention to relevant subject and professional associations and to the key players within them.

Identifying opportunities for networking

Supervisors are more likely to be aware of opportunities for networking in the form of seminars and conferences run by professional societies, which can be brought to the attention of candidates.

Assisting in finding funding to attend conferences, etc.

Attendance at events of course requires funding for travel, subsistence and perhaps accommodation, as well as the cost of producing papers, etc. Often part of any grant provided to a department or school to support the candidate will include an element of financial support for such activities, or alternatively there may be an internal fund for this purpose. Supervisors need to be aware of funding sources, and able to assist candidates to tap them in appropriate cases.

Introducing candidates to leading figures in the field

It is one thing for a candidate to attend a conference, and another for them to engage in cold-calling leading figures in the field. If the supervisor is present at the conference or seminar or meeting of the professional society, a personal introduction can be helpful, or if not a letter in advance can smooth the path.

Encouraging candidates to record their networking

Candidates need to be encouraged to keep a record of whom they have met in terms of names, contact details, and what was discussed to provide a basis for future networking.

Interrogating practice

Do you encourage your candidates to actively engage in networking?

What sources of funding are available in your Department or School to support their attendance at seminars, conferences etc?

Do you encourage candidates to record, reflect upon, and review their networking activities?

Encouraging them to reflect upon and review their networking activities

Finally, candidates need to be reminded of the need to reflect upon the contacts they have made, follow up those which seem likely to be fruitful, review the coverage of their contacts, and identify any outstanding areas where further contacts need to be made.

Giving presentations

Increasingly, doctoral candidates are required by institutions to give presentations on their work in progress, usually at the end of each year of study. These may take the form of departmental or school graduate student research conferences where candidates present to each other and/or formal presentations to a panel which determines whether they should be allowed to proceed to the next stage. Additionally, of course, supervisors may encourage candidates who are some way down the line with their research and have some worthwhile results to give papers or presentations at other institutions or at academic or professional conferences. This can, as Cryer (2000) has noted, be of immense value to candidates in staking out a claim in the discipline and bringing their work to the attention of the subject community and, providing all goes well, establishing their reputation and enhancing that of their supervisor and of the school or institution in which they are studying.

Institutions often provide support for the development of presentation skills as part of the taught components of doctoral training programmes.

Example

The Universities of Newcastle upon Tyne and Northumbria in the UK run a joint training programme in presentation skills for doctoral candidates. This starts with a presentation on how to give presentations and how to give feedback on the presentations of others, followed by an opportunity for candidates to prepare presentations on their research. Candidates are then put into small groups, and each member gives a presentation which is videoed. The presentations are then replayed and feedback given by the group.

But if, in this way, presentation skills can be developed generally, they have of course to be applied within the particular context of the candidate's own research. It is here that supervisors can play a role by encouraging candidates to rehearse their presentations in front of them and by giving them feedback.

Example

A template for feedback could be as simple as the one below.

Introduction
Was the introduction clear?
Were the aims and objectives defined and communicated?
Content
Was there too much material, too little, or was it about right?
Structure
Was the talk logical and easy to follow?
Conclusion
Were the conclusions clear?
Was there a summary?
Was this related to objectives?
Visual aids
Were the aids well prepared?
Were they used effectively?
Delivery
Was the presentation audible?
Did he/she speak clearly?
De he/she vary their tone?
Did he/she address the audience?
Did he/she have any distracting mannerisms or irritating phrases?
Did he/she keep to time?
Overall
Did the presentation meet its aims?

Interrogating practice

Does your institution insist that candidates give presentations on their work?

Does it provide training?

Do you identify opportunities for doctoral candidates to give papers and presentations?

Do you help them to prepare for these events?

By these means, supervisors can assist candidates with presentations and hopefully help them to give good ones, which of course also reflect upon the supervisor as well as the candidate.

Publications

As well as assisting with presentations, supervisors have a further role in assisting candidates and doctoral holders to publish the results of their research.

In some countries, for example those in Scandinavia, it is a requirement that all or part of the materials presented for a doctorate have previously been published, and it is an integral part of the role of the supervisor to advise candidates about publication. But in others, the requirement is that work submitted for the doctorate contains material which, in the judgement of examiners, is worthy of publication, not that it has actually been published.

But, clearly it is desirable that the outcomes of doctoral research should be published in paper or electronic form, for three main reasons. First, and most obviously, it is vital that any original contribution to knowledge and understanding should be made available to the disciplinary and/or professional community for scrutiny and the advancement of research in the subject. Second, publications can enhance the status of doctoral candidates or holders and are, of course, particularly important if they are seeking an academic career. Third, publications reflect well upon the supervisor and/or research team (who may be co-authors), upon the department, upon the institution, and upon the research sponsor.

If, for these reasons, publications are desirable, it is by no means axiomatic that, left to their own devices, candidates or doctoral holders will necessarily be able to achieve them. As Dinham and Scott (2001: 46) have put the matter:

> For the novice researcher ... the task of gaining publication may be daunting ... The arcana of seeking out appropriate conferences and journals, preparing and sending off suitable proposals and manuscripts are not things which can be easily appreciated or accomplished by the uninitiated.

The implication of this, of course, is that candidates or doctoral holders need to be assisted in gaining publications by the initiated, in practice by their supervisor or supervisory team. Dinham and Scott (2001) go on to present evidence that the availability or otherwise of supervisor assistance was strongly correlated to chances of the outcomes of doctoral research being published rather than being left to gather dust on a library shelf.

If, then, supervisors or supervisory teams have a vital role to play in assisting candidates and holders to publish, the question then is how they should go about undertaking it. This may include the following suggestions.

Setting expectations at the start of the candidacy

Clearly, in doctoral systems where publication is a requirement for work to be presented for a doctorate, candidates should be aware at the start of the need to publish. But in systems where publication is not a pre-requisite, it can be useful at the start of the candidacy to make it clear that doctoral research should lead to publication, and where appropriate this could even be made part of the learning agreement.

Encouraging candidates to attend training programmes

Many institutions, schools or departments now run training sessions on 'getting yourself published', including drawing up shortlists of potential outlets, ranking them in terms of impact, targeting specific conferences, journals or publishers, and finding out requirements for submission in terms of style and substance. In other cases, editorial teams may run events on how to prepare a submission for their journal, often at academic conferences. Such sessions may be mandatory parts of research training programmes, but if not supervisors can encourage candidates to attend.

Modelling the process of gaining a publication

Supervisors can show doctoral candidates or holders how they themselves went about publishing a key paper, including targeting an outlet, responding to requirements, and where appropriate taking on board the comments of referees prior to final publication.

Writing a paper with the candidate

Perhaps the most effective way of assisting candidates to publish is to write a joint paper with them for publication and take them through all of the stages from initial conception through to the appearance of the paper in print or electronic form.

Encouraging candidates to 'publish as they go'

Once candidates are some way in to their doctorate and have some results or something worthwhile to say, they can be encouraged to seek immediate publication. This can be a difficult call for supervisors.

On the one hand, it can be seen as a diversion from the main purpose of producing the thesis, and hence as an unnecessary distraction. On the other, it is a feather in the cap to be published as a doctoral candidate; it may help to stake the candidate's claim in the subject area; given that, as Mullins and Kiley (2002) have noted, examiners are likely to regard already published material from the thesis as an indication that it is clearly passable; and, if the candidate is considering an academic career after the doctorate, publications strengthen their hand in what is a competitive job market.

Any decision will depend upon how much of a distraction is involved in writing a piece for publication (which in turn depends upon its closeness to the central topic of the thesis) and upon disciplinary norms (for example, in some of the sciences the norm is for new research findings, including those by doctoral candidates, to be published as and when they are confirmed whereas in some arts subject the norm is for the doctorate to be completed and then published as a book).

Maintaining contact with doctoral graduates and assisting them to publish

Finally, and particularly if no publications have resulted during the period of doctoral study, supervisors may need to stay in touch with candidates, encourage them to prepare their work for publication, and assist them with the selection of an appropriate outlet.

Interrogating practice

What proportion of doctoral work in your department or school is published?

Does your institution, department or school offer training in 'getting published'?

Do you encourage and support candidates to 'publish as they go'?

Do you support doctoral graduates in the publication of their work?

Teaching and learning

For generations, doctoral candidates have undertaken teaching duties, for example, conducting seminars or demonstrating in the laboratory, often on courses for which their supervisor is responsible. This can, of course, be highly beneficial in so far as the supervisor is relieved of some of his or her teaching while the candidate gains valuable experience of teaching and promoting learning while earning an income to help them to finance their studies.

But, in contemplating the employment of a doctoral candidate to undertake teaching duties, supervisors have to be aware of two responsibilities, one to the candidate and one to those whom the latter is engaged in teaching.

With regard to the candidate, supervisors and others with teaching within their gift have, at least in the recent past, been in a powerful position. They have held all of the cards in terms of whom they employ, for what, and for how long, while candidates have been desperate for any opportunity to earn enough money to continue their studies. In such circumstances, there may be favouritism in allocating teaching duties to particular candidates and a temptation to dump as much bread-and-butter teaching upon them as possible in the knowledge that, for financial reasons, they find it difficult to say 'no'. Allied to that, candidates have often only been paid for classroom contact hours, and not for the – often many more – hours spent in preparation or marking assignments, to the detriment of their ability to complete their doctoral programmes.

In consequence, many teaching assistants have felt that they have been discriminated against and/or exploited as cheap labour. Particularly in the United States, where teaching assistantships are, of course, a common way of financing doctoral studies, there has been a considerable backlash against such perceived exploitation as reflected in recent years by the formation of graduate employee unions on a large number of campuses (see, for example, Junius and Gumport 2002; Rhoades and Rhoads 2002) to push for equal opportunities and better pay and conditions.

As well as candidates, supervisors also have a responsibility to the students who are taught by teaching assistants. If the latter are thrown into it without adequate preparation, it can end up being a very poor learning experience for those whom they teach. For this reason, national quality assurance bodies have begun to take a keen interest in how higher education institutions are assuring and enhancing the learning experiences of students taught by graduate teaching assistants (see, for example, Quality Assurance Agency for Higher Education 1999).

In order to, on the one hand, prevent favouritism and the exploitation of graduate teaching assistants and, on the other, to try and ensure that students taught by them have a good learning experience, many institutions have adopted policies and procedures or codes of practice.

Example

The University of Leicester in the UK has a 'Code of Practice for the Employment of Part-Time Teaching Assistants'. The code covers:

Qualification

Teaching assistants are required to normally have a good undergraduate degree and be registered for a higher degree, and preferably to have postgraduate experience.

Recruitment

It is required that teaching opportunities are openly advertised and accompanied by a job description.

Selection

There is a requirement that departments should have written and transparent selection procedures which are in accordance with institutional equal opportunities policies. Candidates are required to complete an application form and be interviewed by the head of department and the member of staff whose course they would be teaching on to determine their suitability.

Training

Applicants without a teaching qualification or appropriate experience are required to attend a training programme, for which appropriate payment is made.

Teaching and learning practices

All teaching assistants must be given a written statement of teaching and learning practice in the course(s) they will be involved in teaching. This should cover issues such as teaching and learning modes, student backgrounds, expectations concerning student workloads, assessment practice, marking of essays and other assigned work, and departmental practice concerning student neglect and student weakness.

Workload

In the case of doctoral and other candidates for research degrees, the normal maximum should be six hours of teaching per week, subject to consultation with the supervisor.

Mentors

Each teaching assistant has to be assigned a mentor who should have regular contact and provide guidance on matters such as selection of tutorial and essay topics, how to deal with 'difficult' students and/or groups, assessment procedures and standards, and time management in relation to preparation and assessment.

Departmental facilities

Arrangements must be made for teaching assistants to be contacted and seen by students outside normal class times, where possible in a private space. Where appropriate, teaching assistants should also be given access to secretarial, photocopying and other teaching-related resources of the department.

Pay

The full range of duties must be made clear in advance to the teaching assistant, and accompanied by an assessment of the total hours involved, including preparation, delivery, and marking. Payment should be related to the total hours involved, not just contact hours in the classroom.

Monitoring

Teaching undertaken should be monitored, particularly in the early stages, to identify and deal with problems to ensure the delivery of a sound learning experience to students. Classes and tutorials should be monitored by appropriate evaluation procedures, including student questionnaires, and the outcomes made available to the teaching assistant, the mentor, and the head of department.

Source: http://www.le.ac.uk/personnel/docs/codeofpracticeteaching assistants.htm

It is clearly important that, in seeking to employ doctoral candidates for teaching duties, supervisors take their responsibilities to both candidates and the students they teach seriously, and that they abide by institutional policies and procedures or codes of practice.

Interrogating practice

What policies and procedures are in place for the recruitment, selection and appointment of doctoral candidates for teaching duties in your institution?

What support is offered to help them to prepare for undertaking these duties?

Are there limitations upon the number of hours candidates are allowed to perform these duties?

Do hours and arrangements for payment cover the full range of duties, including preparation and assessment?

Support for academic careers

While the days when gaining a doctorate was a guarantee of an academic career are long gone, there are still many candidates who undertake it primarily with a view to becoming faculty or who decide to pursue such a career during the course of their studies. In order to recruit the faculty of the future, it is clearly important that such candidates are identified and given at least the basic information about academic work to enable them to make up their minds.

One, perhaps the, most obvious source for such information is their supervisor. However, a recent in-depth longitudinal study of a sample of doctoral candidates in the US who aspired to academic posts by Austin (2002) found that their supervisors tended to assume that doctoral candidates either arrived with an understanding of academic work or acquired one by a process of osmosis during their studies. For this reason, they rarely discussed possible academic career routes with candidates, or volunteered information about what was involved in academic work. In consequence, many candidates were poorly informed about a possible academic career option, with the potential result that some candidates who were unsuited would go forward while others who were suited would be put off.

For these reasons, Austin suggested that supervisors should make the effort early in the candidacy to discuss career intentions. Where these leant towards an academic career (or where promising candidates could be persuaded to consider pursuing one), she suggested that they should at least be prepared to discuss what is involved in an academic career, including research, teaching and promoting learning, academic administration, public service outreach activity, and possibly entrepreneurial activity.

In addition, she suggests that supervisors may also have a role to play in preparing candidates for academic careers by, for example, pointing them in the direction of institutional or national programmes designed to improve their awareness, knowledge, and skills.

Example

The Council of Graduate Schools and the Association of American Colleges and Universities have established Preparing Future Faculty (PFF) programmes for graduate students intent upon an academic career. The PFF has been defined by Pruitt-Logan *et al.* (2002: 3) as:

> ... a configuration of ideas designed to promote expanded professional development of doctoral students who aspire to an academic career. It embraces the doctorate's traditional emphasis on research, but it also brings knowledge about the diverse colleges and universities that constitute the higher education landscape – particularly those primarily serving under-graduate students into doctoral preparation. For those interested in a faculty career, PFF introduces the students to the academic profession and to the diversity of institutions with their different missions, student bodies, and expectations for faculty. PFF gives graduate students an opportunity to experience faculty life in a protected educational context at a variety of

colleges and universities, allowing them to decide if they do really want an academic career and, if so, to determine what kind of institution is right for them.

The PFF includes: a planned apprenticeship in teaching, research, and services; exposure to the range of professional responsibilities in a range of institutions; mentoring by staff in their own and other institutions; integrated professional development; and structured contact with 'consumers' of doctoral graduates to find out what institutions ask of new faculty. The programme has been extensively evaluated with, Pruitt-Logan *et al.* (2002: 49) report, 'universally positive' results from candidates, faculty and institutions.

While programmes such as the PFF may not be available to many candidates interested in an academic career, their supervisors can still, as Austin (2002) again has suggested, assist variously by:

- encouraging candidates to take up opportunities within the institution for professional development, for example, taking a teaching certificate;
- encouraging candidates to self-reflect upon their interests and areas of strength and weakness in relation to an academic career, how their values and commitment articulate with the profession, and upon their place and competence within it;
- providing regular ongoing advice, feedback, and assessment of their progress of scholars and future faculty;
- arranging mentors, perhaps in other institutions, with whom candidates can discuss their development as potential faculty.

By these means, supervisors can play their part in the crucial processes of academic regeneration and renewal.

Interrogating practice

Do you discuss potential career paths with doctoral candidates?

What institutional or other support is available for candidates to develop themselves as potential faculty?

What steps can you take to assist them to develop in this way?

Supporting the development of generic skills

As well as supporting candidates to develop the skills necessary if they are to follow an academic career, supervisors may be accorded a role in assisting them to develop the generic skills necessary to follow other careers.

As outlined in Chapter 1 the global drivers for the acquisition of such skills are, on the one hand, the fact that the vast majority of doctoral graduates will end up working in business, industry, or commerce, and, on the other, the perceived need for researchers trained in Mode 2 knowledge-production to run the knowledge economies of the future, and so contribute to economic growth and national prosperity. These drivers have led to demands by research sponsors, including governments, that candidates should, during the course of their studies, acquire the skills that will make them 'employment-ready' by the time that they graduate.

Such attempts to graft generic skills relating to employability onto the doctorate, particularly the traditional PhD, have met with scepticism from some sections of the academic community on the following grounds.

Inappropriateness

Many have questioned whether promoting employability is an appropriate purpose for the doctorate. So, as one respondent to Nyquist and Woodford's survey (2000: 8) of the attitudes of faculty in the US put the matter:

> I think fundamentally the PhD is a research degree, and the idea is to give people the foundations of the discipline and an opportunity to become engaged when they're still students under the supervision of a mentor. I don't care what industry people or government people would like to say about PhDs; research is the essential heart of the PhD. And anything that undercuts that is, I think, doing damage to it.

On this view, training for future employment is considered inappropriate in a doctoral programme (and best carried out by employers themselves).

Being misconceived

The employment skills argument is underpinned by the belief that there is a clearly defined set of core skills which can be acquired during the course of doctoral studies and then transferred directly into practice in employment. But, as Rowland (2003) has written:

> ... there is little agreement about what such skills are and even less evidence that they can be readily transferred from one context to another. It is not obvious that the creative philosopher can use the skill of creativity in financial management. Even the preparation of a CV is radically different in, say academic and creative arts contexts.

Being an additional burden on candidates

With candidates already under severe pressures to complete their doctorates within shorter and shorter spaces of time, it can be argued that the imposition of additional requirements to gain generic skills is an additional burden upon them which they could well do without.

Being an additional burden on supervisors

Similarly, the need to impart generic skills imposes an additional burden on supervisors, and one which many are ill-equipped or motivated to meet. As Rowland (2003) again has pointed out:

> The implication is that academic staff should be required not only to fulfil the daunting task of supporting their students, but also to give them an ill-defined set of supposedly transferable skills. This presupposes not only a belief in the existence of such skills, but also the ability to train students in them. Few academics are able to do this or are interested in doing this.

But these objections have not carried weight with policy-makers who have continued to demand that the doctorate be broadened to incorporate employment-related skills.

Example

The Joint Funding Councils of the UK (2003) have required that all doctoral students should acquire a prescribed set of skills. These include both skills relating to the research project and its management that are part of normal doctoral research, but also a range of generic skills relating to personal effectiveness, communication skills, networking, team-working, and career management. Students are expected to be able to spend ten days each year acquiring these skills and institutions which failed to provide appropriate opportunities have been warned that there could be consequences in terms of funding.

As a result, many institutions have introduced generic skills components into their doctoral programmes. Supervisors may, then, be asked to assist candidates to acquire such skills by, for example:

Helping candidates to analyse their training needs

Where generic skills do form part of doctoral programmes, institutions may ask supervisors or supervisory teams to go through checklists of generic skills with candidates at the start of their studies to establish those they have already met and those which they will need to cover over the course of their doctoral studies.

Helping candidates to identify opportunities to fill gaps in skills

Where there are gaps in candidates' skills, supervisors or supervisory teams may be asked to help them to identify suitable opportunities to fill them, for example, from internal or external training programmes.

Encouraging candidates to attend appropriate workshops

Supervisors or supervisory teams may be asked by institutions to encourage candidates to take the time out from their research to attend appropriate events to acquire or improve skills.

Encouraging candidates to record the acquisition of skills

For purposes of providing evidence to sponsors and/or employers, institutions may require that candidates record the acquisition of skills, for example, in a log book or portfolio, and supervisors may be asked to make sure that this is undertaken.

Monitoring and reporting on candidates' acquisition of generic skills

Finally, supervisors or supervisory teams may be asked to periodically monitor the extent to which identified training needs have been met and report upon this, for example, as part of the annual progress review.

Interrogating practice

What provision, if any, does your institution make for candidates to acquire generic skills?

Do supervisors have a role in supporting candidates to develop generic skills?

Do they have a role in monitoring and reporting the acquisition of such skills?

Conclusions

While supervisors clearly need to be aware of any personal circumstances of candidates that are affecting their research and to be supportive, the extent to which they should be supportive is a grey area. On the one hand there is the argument, accepted by many institutions, that the relationship should be professional and that personal factors should not be allowed to intrude; on the other, there is the practical point that they do intrude and that supervisors may be willing and able to assist. This clearly poses an ethical dilemma, to which the answer depends in part on the particular supervisor and their own 'take' on their personal and pastoral responsibilities.

There has not, at least traditionally, been any such dilemma about professional support in an academic context. Supervisors have always had key roles to play in supporting candidates to acquire a range of skills relating to their development as members of the subject community. Similarly, they have always had a role in, where appropriate, supporting the development of candidates who are interested in a faculty career (giving information about academic life, encouraging reflection, giving feedback on scholarly development).

But there is a further dilemma about the roles of supervisors in supporting candidates in the acquisition of generic skills relating to employability. There are, as has been seen, some serious question marks about both the wisdom and the practicality of this development. But it seems to be becoming an increasingly important component of doctoral studies, and hence of supervision, as the doctorate become more aligned to producing key workers for the knowledge economies.

Chapter 11

Responding to diversity – domestic candidates

Reflecting historical patterns of access to higher education, traditionally doctoral candidates have been disproportionately male, from high-status social-economic backgrounds, members of majority ethnic and/or racial groups, and without a disability (see, for example, Bowen and Rudenstein 1992; Conrad 1994; Humphrey and McCarthy 1999). In the main, they have been young, entering doctoral programmes directly after completing bachelor's or master's degrees, and funded for three or four years of full-time study. Finally, and except for fieldwork, the vast majority have undertaken and completed their studies on campus.

However, as noted on p. 17, over the past two decades or so access to higher education has been extended in many countries to include historically under-represented groups, and this has significantly diversified the pool of potential doctoral candidates. In particular, more candidates have been and are being recruited who are: from lower-status backgrounds; who are female; who are from minority ethnic and/or racial groups; or who have a disability. In addition, and reflecting not just numbers but a changing social climate, there have been more candidates who are openly gay, lesbian, bi-sexual or trans-gendered (GLBT).

Moreover, candidates have, mainly for financial reasons, been deferring entry to doctoral studies until a later age, often in their 30s. Because they are older and have family and career responsibilities, many are studying part-time for their doctorates. While this trend has been less apparent in the science and engineering disciplines, where research may be heavily dependent upon access to equipment, it has been marked in the arts, humanities, and social sciences, where in many institutions a majority of candidates are part-time.

As such, of course, they are less likely to be able to spend time on campus. In part to accommodate their needs, many institutions have developed programmes of study designed to support candidates in learning off-campus, that is, distance learning. This has, of course, been greatly facilitated by advances in technology, particularly of course email and the Web, which have enabled communication and the delivery of education to candidates' workplaces and/or homes.

So, from candidates being full-time and being on campus for the duration of their studies, the norm in many disciplines has become for candidates to be part-time and on campus for a greater or lesser proportion of the time. This may vary from perhaps a day or a couple of evenings a week in programmes with no or limited off-campus learning support through, in the case of those delivered mainly through distance learning, to a weekend or two a year.

Overall, then, the population of domestic doctoral candidates has become more diverse socially and in modes and methods of study. Such candidates may, compared to their predecessors, face what Dedrick and Watson (2002) have described as a series of 'barriers' to undertaking and succeeding in doctoral studies. These barriers variously include lack of confidence, lack of role models, isolation, discrimination, multiple competing priorities, and lack of access to resources and facilities. Clearly, to offer effective supervision, supervisors need to appreciate what these barriers are and to consider how they might go about assisting candidates to overcome them. This chapter describes the nature of such barriers and suggests ways in which supervisors might assist candidates to overcome them.

Lack of confidence

Historically, as Johnson *et al.* (2000) have argued, doctoral supervision has been based upon the assumption that, by virtue of having made it onto a doctoral programme, candidates would necessarily have the confidence to cope with its academic and social demands. This assumption was, arguably, always dubious, as demonstrated by high non-completion rates and long completion times two decades ago, when the candidate population was highly elitist. But it is even more so in the context of a diverse population where, as Yeatman (cited in Johnson *et al.* 2000: 137) has put it:

> … many supervisees are barely socialised into the demands and rigours of an academic scholarly and research culture. It is especially inadequate to the needs of many PhD aspirants who, by historic cultural positioning, have not been invited to imagine themselves as subjects of genius. These include all those who have been marginalised by the academic scholarly culture; women, and men and women from the non-dominant class, ethnic or race positions.

Such lack of confidence may, for example, take the form of self-doubt about whether candidates have the right to be on a doctoral programme at all.

Example

When Appel and Dahlgren (2003: 100) asked a sample of women doctoral students in a Swedish university to write narratives on their experiences, they found that:

> In many of the narratives … the idea of postgraduate studies was considered a 'really tremendous undertaking', almost unattainable, and something for

the exceptionally gifted. The informants did not feel that they belonged to this group ... female students in particular need encouragement.

Alternatively, it can take a more subtle form whereby the candidate begins to perceive that they do not 'belong' in the social milieu in which they find themselves.

Example

One of the doctoral candidates who responded to the survey by Delamont *et al.* (2000: 51) reported that:

I've come to recognise more and more things like class. I come from a working-class background. I was first person from my very extended family to get to university and I never thought of class being at all important. But since I started doing the research I realised just how much submerged knowledge there is that presumes some kind of middle class background ... I've gained a sense of where I come from. In fact, there's a lot of things I didn't know, which I ought to have, and that is something that isn't spelt out at all for the sake of maintaining the right image ... its a different social world, it really isn't for me.

Candidates with disabilities may also be lacking in confidence. This may derive from negative educational experiences earlier in their lives which scars them and leaves them with a poor self-image. So, and despite the increasingly widespread availability of assistive technology, they retain doubts about their ability to succeed at the highest levels.

Supervisors then need to recognise that candidates from non-traditional groups may be lacking in confidence compared to their traditional counterparts and, where appropriate, to offer additional reassurance and support. In particular, in the early stages of doctoral studies, supervisors need to show candidates that they have a genuine interest and concern for them and that they want them to do well. Obviously where justified, praise, particularly public praise, can do wonders for their morale and self-belief.

Interrogating practice

Have you found that candidates from non-traditional groups are less confident in approaching doctoral research?

How might you encourage them to develop confidence?

Lack of role models

A further barrier for doctoral students from non-traditional groups may be a lack of role models, particularly among the faculty. Role models, in the sense of someone similar who has not only achieved a doctorate but gone on to an academic post and become a distinguished researcher can, as a number of commentators (see Conrad 1994; Dedrick and Watson 2002; Leonard 2001; Phillips and Pugh 2000) have suggested, help to inspire candidates to emulate their achievements.

However, most faculty are male, white and without a disability, which yields a plethora of role models for candidates with similar characteristics, but obviously not for candidates who are from minority ethnic and racial groups and/or female and/or who have a disability. Clearly, such candidates may be less likely to imagine themselves as, in Yeatman's phrase quoted above, 'subjects of genius' than if they had a role model to follow.

Supervisors then need to see whether there may be advantages in identifying suitable role models for candidates from non-traditional groups in the department or research group and, if not, consider identifying one – not necessarily in the same institution – and putting the candidate in touch. Clearly this needs to be done unobtrusively and with a high degree of sensitivity, but, as Dedrick and Watson (2002) have suggested, it can pay off in terms of establishing and maintaining confidence.

As well as lack of role models from a similar background, of course students who are studying for their doctorates at a distance may not have access to role models at all, reflecting the fact that they are rarely present on campus to engage face-to-face with faculty. For this reason, in its guidelines for distance graduate education, the US Council of Graduate Schools (1998) has recommended that attention should be paid to providing such candidates with mentors who, among other things, will be role models, and in establishing means of visual as well as aural or written communication, for example, through video links during office hours and 'C U See-me' technology.

Interrogating practice

Are there role models for candidates from non-traditional groups in your research group or department?

If not, can you identify appropriate role models?

What arrangements does your institution make to enable candidates studying at a distance to interact with mentor/role models?

Isolation

Isolation can, as noted in Chapter 7, be part of the lot of doctoral candidates generally, but it can be more severe for those from non-traditional groups and/or who are studying part-time (see, for example, Deem and Brehonm 2000; Leonard 2001; Phillips and Pugh 2000). For obvious reasons, it can be most apparent among candidates who are studying at a distance and who may rarely appear on campus at all (see, for example, Macauley 2000). Such candidates may have little or no face-to-face interaction with supervisors and peers, but rely instead upon the telephone, fax, or email. It is, of course, much more difficult for candidates and supervisors who do not, or seldom, meet face-to-face to build professional and personal relationships, and candidates can be left feeling out on a limb. This can be compounded by similar difficulties in building relationships with fellow candidates, making the isolation more complete.

Example

It was concern about these matters that prompted the US Council of Graduate Schools to set out guidelines for institutions putting on graduate-level distance learning programmes, including doctorates. With regard to the latter, the Council advised:

- that all distance-learning programmes should include an initial residency or attendance requirement so that candidates could meet academic staff and fellow candidates face-to-face;
- that during this period they should be attached to mentors who would get to know them personally and could support them when they were studying off-campus;
- that staff involved in supervising candidates at a distance should be offered training:

  * in the needs of distance learners and how to respond to them;
  * in electronic communications strategies;
  * in the use of the technology;
  * in ways of dealing with academic honesty and security concerns.

- that institutions offering distance learning doctorates should make appropriate arrangements to replicate the campus social and intellectual experience electronically by means including open discussion forums, peer counselling, and doctoral student organisations run through electronic bulletin boards.

Source: http://www.cgsnet.org/pdf/DistanceGraduateEducation.pdf

So through these means, it may be possible to counter isolation among candidates studying for most of their time off-campus.

While such candidates have more potential for isolation than those studying part-time on campus, the latter can also suffer from limited contact with the institution and its staff and students, leading to feelings that they do not 'belong'. Here, Kember et al. (2001) have suggested that, where possible, part-time students should be treated as a cohort, and given collective opportunities for intellectual and social interaction, for example through induction, the training programme, peer mentoring, and social events.

But isolation may not only be a barrier simply because candidates are studying at a remove from the institution and/or part-time, in so far as it may be social in origin. As such, the extent of social isolation will depend in part on how many others in the milieu share a similar background. It is least likely where, as Leonard (2001) has suggested, there is a 'critical mass' of staff and candidates from non-traditional groups. But where there are few or no compatriots it can be a solitary existence, for example, the lone female working away in the laboratory, the lone black among a sea of whites in the lecture theatre for the research training programme, or the lone openly GLBT candidate among the heterosexuals.

But isolation can also stem from social assumptions by supervisors and/or other colleagues. So, for example, the social life of the research group may centre around the pub or the football or baseball game. On the assumption that 'they wouldn't want to go', older and women and GLBT candidates may be left out or disabled candidates excluded.

Example

One of the authors is involved in a project in the UK looking at barriers to doctoral candidates with disabilities, and involving interviews with the latter. In one case, a respondent who was hearing-impaired reported that he was unable to join in the coffee-time conversations with his research group because the chairs were arranged inappropriately so that he was unable to hear the discussion. In another case, a candidate who was blind had been unable to attend the inaugural social event at the start of his studies because the venue was inaccessible, and had remained socially isolated for some time thereafter.

Of course, even if they are invited and venues are accessible, some candidates, because of other commitments, may not be able to attend.

> ### Example
>
> One mature student quoted by Golde (2000: 209) said:
>
> > Most people were younger than I was … I was married. Most of the people weren't. So I had someone I need to go home to at night … I couldn't go after work and have a beer somewhere … In that sense, I wasn't part of the student group as many people were.

For these reasons then, candidates who are from non-traditional groups may be more vulnerable to social isolation.

It is then important that supervisors and, where appropriate, other members of research groups, are aware of this possibility, and that they extend the same social opportunities to these candidates as to others.

Interrogating practice

What arrangements are made in your institution to counter isolation among candidates studying at a distance?

What arrangements are made to counter isolation among part-time candidates?

What is the dominant pattern of social interaction in your research group or department?

Does it include candidates from non-traditional groups?

If not, how can you and your colleagues include them on the same basis as other candidates?

How can you seek to ensure that appropriate opportunities are available to disabled candidates?

Discrimination

Candidates from non-traditional groups may experience direct or indirect discrimination on account of their gender, their membership of an ethnic and/or racial group, their disability, or their sexuality.

In the case of gender, women may be directly discriminated against by male supervisors. The latter may, as Dedrick and Watson (2002) have pointed out, regard women as inherently unfit to undertake doctoral studies and be actively hostile towards them and towards their research projects, particularly if the latter have any whiff of feminism about them. So Phillips and Pugh (2000) cite the example of a female candidate whose confidence was destroyed by an anti-feminist male supervisor who rubbished her written work. Similarly, Becher *et al.* (1994) quote the cases of a group of women scientists who were allocated research problems which were marginal to the group and of female researchers being bundled together in a physical outpost of the main building.

Worse, women may be treated by male colleagues as sex objects, that is, be subjected to sexual harassment and exploitation. This may show itself in forms varying from leering and joking through to the abuse of power by supervisors in demanding sexual favours from women candidates. The frequency of such behaviours is not known but, as, for example, Appel and Dahlgren (2003) have shown, it does happen and is very distressing for candidates.

Similarly, candidates may be discriminated against on the grounds of their ethnic or racial groups. This may be overt, in so far as such candidates are subject to racial hostility and abuse (see, for example, Dedrick and Watson 2002; Phillips and Pugh 2000), or it may be more subtle. So, for example, Carter (cited in Leonard (2001: 203) found that ethnic minority candidates in supposedly liberal UK universities 'felt that they were constantly battling against being typecast by ethnicity and sex and resented having to jump over extra hurdles'.

Disabled candidates may, as Dedrick and Watson (2002) again have suggested, suffer from hostility and abuse, as well as from assumptions that they are inherently less capable of undertaking demanding academic work. The latter is particularly the case where candidates have disabilities affecting their speech and/or writing and where this is misinterpreted as reflecting upon their abilities.

Candidates who are openly GLBT (or who are suspected of being so or unintentionally 'outed') may, as Goody and de Vries (2002) have shown, be subjected to hostility and abuse because of their sexuality both by fellow-students and by supervisors.

Discrimination of these kinds is outlawed in most countries and in most institutions of higher education, which have strict codes of conduct designed to ensure that candidates have equal opportunities. Supervisors need to know and understand both their legal and institutional obligations and, if they feel unable to fully comply with them, acknowledge that their prejudices may harm the chances of candidates and disqualify themselves from supervising them.

As well as direct discrimination, candidates from non-traditional groups can also suffer from indirect discrimination. So, for example, Phillips and Pugh (2000) suggest a classic case of this whereby male supervisors consider that it is inappropriate to criticise the work of women candidates because it might upset them. While there is some evidence that women are perhaps less likely than males to react to criticism in a combative way (see, for example, Leonard 2001), this does not of course mean that criticisms should not be made at all; the consequence is that it leaves candidates believing that all is well with their research when this is not the case, which is hardly helpful to them. Perhaps a reluctance to criticise is a reason why it has been found (see Conrad 1994) that, without being conscious of doing so, male supervisors are likely to give less time to supervising female than to male candidates, which again is a form of indirect discrimination.

Fortunately, few supervisors are overtly misogynists, racists, or prejudiced against the disabled or against GLBT students, and the main concern needs to be the avoidance of indirect discrimination. Supervisors then need to consider carefully whether, even with the best of intentions, they are discriminating against non-traditional candidates, and what they can do to ensure that opportunities are equal. So, it is worth reflecting on whether they are treating students in the same way and, for example, timing a few supervisions to see if they roughly balance out in length for non-traditional and traditional candidates.

Interrogating practice

Does your institution have a code of conduct for supervising students?

Can you abide fully by it?

Are there ways in which you might unintentionally discriminate against candidates from non-traditional groups?

Multiple competing priorities

A barrier for some candidates from non-traditional groups may be balancing multiple competing priorities. So, for example, women candidates are, as Appel and Dahlgren (2003) and Leonard (2001) have shown, still expected to do more in the way of domestic chores even when there are no children and, if there are children, they are often still expected to do the lion's share of the work of bringing them up.

Similarly, mature candidates generally may have responsibilities towards partners and towards children and perhaps aged parents. Some disabled candidates may have responsibilities in terms of maintaining their health, which may necessitate frequent medical treatment and absences from campus.

These barriers may be difficult enough to surmount for candidates who are studying full-time, but of course many of these and other candidates are studying part-time and combining their doctorate with a family and/or a career. They may, then, be forever juggling with competing priorities, of which doctoral studies are only one. As Evans (2002: 160) has put the matter:

> ... part-time students' doctoral study is likely to be their second or third priority which means that when significant demands or changes occur to their higher priorities there may be implications for their doctoral research. In some instances this may lead to their withdrawal or non-completion.

Given these potential consequences, it is obviously important that supervisors take an interest in the circumstances of candidates. In this context, it can be helpful to spend some time at the start of the relationship discussing the wider commitments of candidates and how they are to be managed. Here students can be referred to the literature (see, for example, Wisker 2001) for both reassurance and assistance. Further, supervisors need to be aware of any institutional facilities which may be helpful in supporting the candidate, for example, a creche. Finally, supervisors have to be willing to make allowances for the impact of these additional demands, for example by being more flexible over the submission of written work.

Interrogating practice

Are you aware of the pressures upon candidates juggling multiple commitments?

Does your institution have facilities to assist them?

Are you flexible in allowing for the impact of multiple pressures?

Access to training, facilities, and resources

Access can, of course, be a major hurdle for candidates with disabilities, particularly where their mobility is impaired. It is obviously important that disabled candidates have the same access as others to training, facilities, and resources for their research, and supervisors need to be aware of their needs and, where appropriate, of any assistance which may be available to meet them, for example, through the institution's disability office. It is worth noting that, particularly in Australia and the UK, there is legislation which places a responsibility upon higher education institutions to anticipate the needs of students with disabilities, and which gives a right to sue in law if all reasonably practical steps are not taken to do so.

For a different reason, access may also be a problem for candidates who are studying part-time. Despite the rapid growth in the numbers of such candidates, many institutions are still geared around catering for the traditional full-time candidate. This can be reflected to the restriction within the normal working week of induction programmes, research training programmes, seminars for doctoral students to give presentations on their work, lab opening hours, library opening hours, access to computing facilities, and the availability of student services. Candidates who can only attend the institution during the evenings or at weekends may, then, be severely disadvantaged.

Clearly this is unacceptable, and it should be the responsibility of the institution to ensure that part-time candidates have equal access with others to the training, facilities and resources to support doctoral programmes. However, this is not always the case, and all too often the supervisor is placed between the rock of the institution's restrictive policies and the hard place of the ire of candidates who are unable to take time off work or from childcare to attend events and activities.

Here, supervisors need at least to know what are the restrictions on access and, where appropriate, to bring them to the attention of the relevant authorities. They may also need to be flexible themselves, for example in scheduling the timing of meetings with the candidate for the evenings or weekends. Of course, access to training, resources and facilities is even more crucial for candidates who are studying at a distance.

Example

In its guidelines for distance graduate education, the US Council of Graduate Schools (1998: 41–3) recommends that institutions should ensure that all students should have 'appropriate access to instructional materials, facilities and services needed to complete programme requirements'. The latter include:

- access to physical or online bookstores to acquire course materials;
- access to libraries' online catalogues, data bases, and search facilities;
- training in identifying materials, using databases, and requesting materials;
- on-line support for specific requests;
- where appropriate, to on-line lab simulations and/or lab facilities at the institution, at another institution or at the candidate's work place;
- induction to the institution and the programme;
- telephone and/or on-line access to an academic advisor;
- telephone and/or on-line access to counselling services;
- telephone and/or on-line access to financial advice.

Interrogating practice

Do candidates studying part-time on campus have appropriate access to training, facilities, and resources?

If not, how can you bring this to the attention of the institution?

How can you, as a supervisor, accommodate the needs of such candidates?

What arrangements are made in your institution to provide access to training, resources and facilities for doctoral candidates studying at a distance?

Conclusions

The expansion of doctoral programmes over the past two decades or so has been accompanied by a growing diversity among the domestic candidate population, with many more coming forward from non-traditional groups, and a growing diversity of modes and methods of study. Such diversity has meant that supervisors have to be aware of, and respond effectively to, a wider range of needs. Hopefully, the present chapter has indicated both the range of needs and how supervisors might respond.

Chapter 12

Responding to diversity – international candidates

Historically, there have always been candidates who have studied for their doctorates in countries other than their own, particularly, of course, in the United States. But, over the past decade or so there has been a sharp increase in demand particularly in the developing countries for trained researchers, which has led to more funding being made available to send students abroad to undertake doctoral training.

Because such students pay fees that are often substantially higher than those paid by 'home' students, a lucrative market has developed which has been eagerly tapped by cash-strapped higher education institutions in the major providers of doctoral education. While, at least before 9/11, the United States remained the most rapidly-growing share of this market, other major players have emerged, in particular Australia and the UK, while other West European countries have also begun recruiting actively overseas.

As a result of these trends in demand and supply, there has been a large increase in the numbers of international candidates on doctoral programmes. Such candidates too face barriers to doctoral success. Some of these are common to those faced by non-traditional domestic candidates, but with an added dimension for international candidates, while others are more specific to the latter. All, however, need awareness from supervisors and, where appropriate, assistance with surmounting them.

This chapter then looks at the barriers faced by international students in common with many domestic ones, and those which are more specific to them.

Common barriers

International candidates, in common with domestic ones from non-traditional backgrounds, may be vulnerable to isolation, deficient in role models, and subject to discrimination.

Isolation

In the case of isolation, this can be more complete for many international candidates because, of course, they are living and working in another country, often far from home, often with a different language and culture (see, for example, Knight 1999). Moreover, if they have brought their families, the latter can also feel as if they have landed on another planet, and this can lead to intense domestic unhappiness.

With international candidates, then, supervisors need to be aware of the potential for isolation and particularly vigilant in terms of monitoring the extent of this among candidates and, where appropriate, their families. They need to be personally and professionally supportive, for example, by inviting them and their families for dinner, ensuring that they are included in departmental social events, and by making them aware of relevant organisations and societies on campus for candidates and where appropriate their partners and children.

Role models

Similarly, international candidates may have few or no role models from their own cultures within their supervisory team or research group. In the same way as for non-traditional domestic candidates, it can be helpful for supervisors to point candidates towards appropriate role models. In some institutions these may be provided in the form of faculty from the candidate's country or region of origin, whereas in others it may be necessary to contact a colleague, if necessary in another institution, perhaps even with a view to a mentoring relationship.

Discrimination

Again, and in common with their non-traditional counterparts, international candidates who are female and/or members of ethnic and/or racial groups may face discrimination outside or inside the academy. Particularly if, as is often the case, they are from majority and high-status groups in their countries of origin, they can find themselves treated as inferior and low status in their so-called 'host' countries and be the object of insults, taunts, and violence. This can contribute to 'culture shock' (see below).

Additionally, international candidates can face direct discrimination within the institution in which they are studying. So, as Phillips and Pugh (2000) have noted, supervisors, particularly in ex-colonial countries, may take a patronising and paternalistic stance towards international students which is both offensive and, particularly in an authority figure, upsetting.

Finally, international candidates can also be the subject of indirect discrimination stemming from insensitivity towards their religion and/or culture, both outside or inside the academy. The latter may include, for example, institutions insisting that Muslim women share shower facilities with men (see Leonard 2001) or even the timing of research training events or supervisions at the regular time for prayers for Islamic candidates.

While supervisors may be unable to do very much about discrimination, direct or indirect, outside the academy, they need to be aware that it happens and that it is hugely distressing for international candidates. So there is a need for empathy, and, where appropriate, a knowledge of services to which students can be referred for assistance.

Supervisors can do something about discrimination inside the academy. Those who regard international students as part of the 'white man's burden' should recognise the contribution made by them socially, culturally, and not least, financially and treat them equally to their domestic counterparts and in accordance with institutional codes of conduct. Similarly, supervisors need to be aware of the possibility of indirect discrimination and make sure that candidates are not discriminated against through, for example, arrangements for accommodation or the scheduling of essential activities and events.

Interrogating practice

Do you monitor the extent of social isolation among international candidates?

Do you make efforts to support them personally and professionally?

Can you think of role models who would be appropriate for specific international candidates?

Do you value the presence of international candidates in your research group or department?

Are you aware of any indirect discrimination against international candidates in your institution's arrangements for accommodation, research training, or supervision?

Barriers to international candidates

As well as the above, international candidates can also meet barriers in terms of culture shock, different expectations of academic roles, different learning styles, lack of experience of research, and difficulties in communicating verbally, non-verbally, and in writing.

Culture shock

Culture shock is the well-recognised process (see, for example, Cryer and Okorocha 1999; Kiley 2000; Phillips and Pugh 2000) whereby people transferring from one country to another and hence from one culture to another go through an initial honeymoon period followed by the shock of new and unexpected experiences which are unfamiliar and painful, often leading to confusion, disorientation, and loss of identity.

The extent of culture shock of this kind is, of course, largely dependent upon the cultural distance travelled; so, for example, a UK student undertaking doctoral studies in Australia (or vice versa) may experience a very limited cultural shock, while a woman from a traditional Middle Eastern country moving to a Western one (or again vice versa) may experience a much greater shock.

Many receiving institutions make arrangements to try and minimise culture shock, including in some cases an initial induction programme in the country of origin, and in most a fuller orientation programme immediately after candidates arrive. But, while induction programmes can tell candidates what to expect, they still have to cope with the experience personally, and they may well evince a burning desire to 'go home' to what is familiar, normal, and certain. Some do drop out at this early stage but others persist and, in the fullness of time, are able to move on by re-affirming their identity, rejecting unwanted differences, becoming self-assured and so achieving bicultural competence.

Clearly it is necessary for supervisors to be aware of the possibility that international candidates may suffer from culture shock and, particularly in the early stages, to empathise with the fact that they are in the process of adjusting to a new culture with all that that implies. Supervisors may, if they have studied abroad, care to reflect upon their own culture shock, or even if they have experienced it on holiday.

In order to play their part in assisting candidates to overcome culture shock, it can be helpful that, if supervisors know little of their country of origin, they take the trouble to find out, which is not difficult given the existence of the Web. This will not only help them to understand what cultural distance the candidate is seeking to travel, but also, of course, indicate that the supervisor is interested in the candidate's country of origin and interested in learning about it.

It also provides a topic of conversation, which supervisors may bring up from time to time in order to monitor how candidates are coping. If, perhaps in the course of such a conversation, supervisors suspect that the candidate is experiencing serious difficulties in adjusting, it can be helpful to direct them towards either a designated advisor or to a colleague who has specialist knowledge, for example, one from the candidate's country of origin.

Additionally, supervisors need to be conscious that, while candidates are coping with culture shock, this is an additional pressure upon them and this may need to be taken into account in terms of meeting their academic workload.

Interrogating practice

Have you ever experienced culture shock?

Can you imagine what it is like for an international candidate?

How much do you know about the candidate's country of origin?

What support is available to international candidates in your institution?

How might you adjust your expectations of candidates to allow for cultural adjustment?

Different expectations of academic roles

Many international students come from cultures where teachers are venerated as all-knowing, and where the teacher is the fount of all wisdom (see, for example, Okorocha 2000). This can lead to an expectation among doctoral candidates that their supervisor will play a similar role. As Ryan (2000: 69) has put it:

> ... international students ... are likely to expect a hierarchical relationship with their supervisor where the supervisor exercises tight control over the research. Many international students will expect their supervisor to take the initiative and adapt a role close to being a guide and/or parent. They may expect the supervisor to make major contributions towards the research and the thesis.

Again stemming from cultural norms in their country or origin, international students can view their own roles as, essentially, being an empty vessel into which accumulated wisdom is poured. The idea that they should have their own opinions and values may not only be novel in itself, but perceived as disrespectful. As Okorocha (2000: 9) has put the matter:

> Consequently, when removed to a Western system, the student finds it inconceivable even to consider entering into a debate with supervisors. It would be impossibly rude to imply that supervisors' judgement could be anything but perfect, and it would be arrogant to assert their own ideas and opinions. Their role, as they see it, is to follow whatever instructions their academic superiors choose to give them.

While, as suggested in Chapter 5, supervisors need to discuss formal roles with all candidates at the start of the research project, it is especially important that this is done with international students. Supervisors need to find out what such candidates expect and, where appropriate, discuss with them what they (the supervisor) will do and what the candidate will do, particularly with regard to undertaking the research itself and writing it up.

As well as discussing formal roles, again it is important for the supervisor to discuss how these will pan out in practice. The key point here is, as Cryer and Okorocha (1999) have suggested, to make it clear to the student that, for the relationship to work, they must put forward their own ideas and concepts etc. and that the supervisor will take them seriously.

Finally, it can also be useful to point out to international candidates that, at the end of the day, it is the student's own independent work which is examined, and that they will receive no credit for the work of others, including their supervisor.

> **Interrogating practice**
>
> What assumptions do international students bring with them about the roles of supervisors and students?
>
> Where these are inappropriate, how can you work with them to understand what your respective roles will be?

Different thinking and learning styles

If international candidates have, in their previous experience, been expected to be largely passive learners, then they may have acquired thinking and learning styles that may be inimical to successfully completing their research projects.

In this respect, there is an extensive literature (see the summary in Cadman 2000) about the differences, real or apparent, between so-called 'Confucian heritage cultures' which stress the reproduction and regurgitation of knowledge as opposed to 'Western' ones which stress critical thinking and problem-solving. The latter are, of course, crucial in doctoral studies, and hence the argument runs that international candidates from these cultures may need to adjust their learning styles to undertake them successfully.

In some cases, this may be done at institutional level.

> **Example**
>
> Anglia Polytechnic University in the UK has, for a number of years, recruited PhD students from Israel. Review of the progress of an early cohort suggested that they were experiencing difficulties in completing which it was thought might be a product of their culturally-determined learning styles. As part of an action research project, a learning styles questionnaire was administered. It was found that these students had an 'accumulative' style of learning which, as Wu et al. (2001: 293) have said:
>
> > ... proved to be a trap for many of them, because it could lead to the accumulation of more and more facts, with less and less chance of establishing meaningful links between them, or even of establishing which facts were relevant or logically useful towards a solution of the research problem ... students could waste years of research time vainly gathering more and more information, until they sank beneath it, while still believing that one day they would gather enough for everything to fit together 'if only the last piece of the jigsaw could be found'.
>
> In view of this, a development programme was put in place to assist students

to develop a wider repertoire of learning styles, which was successful in enabling students to complete their theses (see Wisker, *et al.* 2000 and 2003a).

If it is not, then supervisors have a role to play in assisting candidates to adjust. But this is one which needs to be undertaken with a considerable degree of cultural sensitivity; as Wu *et al.* (2001: 293) have noted:

> … it [is] important for supervisors to avoid cultural imperialism and not simply foist onto the student a 'Western' style of learning … with which the supervisor [is] familiar. At the same time, it would be an abdication of the supervisor's role not to intervene when they saw students carrying on with an unsuitable and futile method … just because they had always used it.

In order for supervisors to be sensitive, it is clearly helpful to know something about the candidate's learning style in the first place, which gives a point of departure, and to indicate to the candidate that there is nothing 'wrong' or 'stupid' in their style but only that, for the purposes of doctoral study, it has to be developed.

Example

Both sensibility to the student and respect for her original style on the part of the supervisor are illustrated by a doctoral student cited by Aspland (1999: 36) who wrote:

> [My supervisor] would ask me what I was thinking about … I would just know the main ideas, and he would help me find the hidden meanings in the books I am reading. One paragraph at a time he would explain things and show me the argument that he would make. I soon learned that making this argument was not easy but as I changed my ways, I could do it too. He showed me how to do this. He knew that I was not stupid because he understood the Chinese ways. I have never thought this way before and I am learning it is a good way to think. At the moment I'm not perfect but I'm getting better.

Interrogating practice

Do you find that international candidates have different learning styles?

How can you go about helping them to acquire a learning style appropriate for their doctoral studies?

Lack of experience of research

Again it follows that, if international candidates have hitherto been expected to be passive learners, they may have little or no experience of undertaking research. So, as Ryan (2000: 69) has pointed out: '[International students] may have no experience of literature searching, critical reading, or specialised research skills. They may be lacking in library, computer, and laboratory skills …'.

Hopefully, deficiencies in these areas will have been remedied as part of the general research training and this is of course one reason why the US-style PhD with its longer and more extensive initial training has been so attractive to international candidates (and been recently copied outside the US in the form of 'New Route' PhDs in the UK and elsewhere).

But supervisors should not simply assume that international candidates are research capable, and this should be discussed with them at the start of their projects. Where the candidate's experience turns out to be limited, supervisors may be able to assist in a number of ways.

Directing students to the literature on how to do doctoral research

There is now an extensive literature on how to do research (see, for example, Cryer 2000; Greenfield 2002; Phillips and Pugh 2000; Wisker 2001). It can be helpful for supervisors to go through the many exercises in one or other of these books together with candidates, which should considerably enhance their knowledge and understanding of the research process.

Modelling the process of research

Supervisors can spend some time discussing their own research with candidates, and taking them through a successful project from the initial idea right through to the results and publication. This can illuminate the process of research, and provide a model for candidates to follow themselves.

Setting mini-research projects

If the candidate's experience is very limited, it can be useful at the start of the research project to set them mini-projects involving key elements such as literature searches, literature critiques, reviews of methods, setting up experiments, etc. to give them experience of doing research.

Interrogating practice

How research-capable are your international candidates?

How can you help them to develop research capabilities?

Verbal and non-verbal communication

International candidates can include those whose first language is the same as that in which they are doing their doctoral studies; those whose first language is not the same but whose education has been conducted in that language; and those whose first language is not the same and who have not been educated in that language. The first group are native speakers, and are usually competent in the language. It is usually the second and third groups who are required by institutions to meet language standards on entry or shortly afterwards, but meeting these may not necessarily guarantee that candidates are fully competent, and many experience difficulties.

Difficulties can, in extreme cases, mean that candidates cannot communicate their ideas and thoughts to supervisors or to fellow-students and some may have difficulty in communicating even basic information (see, for example, Cryer and Okorocha 1999). Moreover, international candidates not only have difficulty with the language *per se*, but may be unaware of the appropriate use of language due to a lack of awareness of social conventions in the 'host' country.

As well as experiencing difficulties with verbal communication, international students may also have difficulties with non-verbal communication. So, for example, eye contact is a sign of attention in most Western cultures; in others, at least in the teaching or supervision context, it can signal disrespect. So an international student who is looking away is not necessarily inattentive, but may be following his or her own cultural conventions (see, for example, Okorocha 2000).

Another instance of cultural difference is in terms of 'social space'. In some cultures, attentiveness is signified by sitting close by the teacher or supervisor, closer than is usual in many Western countries, and this can be disconcerting for supervisors. Alternatively, of course, in many Islamic cultures women may not be expected to be alone or near to a male other than their husband and immediate family, and hence candidates may feel uncomfortable in a one-to-one supervisory situation.

Of course, most institutions offer language programmes for candidates who need to improve their skills, and many will also give an introduction to non-verbal conventions in the 'host' country as part of their induction programme. But, while it is not their primary responsibility to ensure that candidates are competent in the language and aware of conventions, supervisors still need to take communication, verbal and non verbal, into account.

Supervisors need to reflect upon their own communication from the standpoint of non-native speakers who are listening

Here, it can be helpful for supervisors to reflect upon a time when they themselves were trying to follow perhaps a conference presentation in a language other than their own. Experience might suggest that, while factual information can probably be imparted at a normal pace, arguments and concepts may need to be stated at a slower pace and, if at all possible, with means of reinforcement – a picture or a diagram can be worth far more than a thousand words in a foreign language.

Supervisors need to allow time for non-native speakers to respond

Again, it can be helpful here for supervisors to reflect upon, for example, a paper they have given in a language other than their own. Unless they were linguists, they may not have been able to 'think' in the foreign language, but would have needed to translate questions and queries into their own language, work out an answer, and translate it back, all of which takes time. In the context of doctoral candidates, it is important that supervisors give candidates permission to take that time until such a point as they begin to think in the language.

Supervisors need to be aware of non-verbal differences between cultures

If candidates indulge in what seems inappropriate non-verbal communication, they should be given the benefit of the doubt while discreet enquiries are made about the prevalence of such behaviours in their own cultures. If behaviours are culturally-specific and supervisors find them uncomfortable, then as Cryer (2000) has suggested, they need to gently point this out to the candidate.

Interrogating practice

Have you ever listened to a presentation in a language other than your own?

If so, what where the main problems that you found in understanding?

Have you ever given a presentation in a language other than your own?

What were the main problems you found in trying to respond to questions?

How can you assist international candidates operating in a second (or sometimes third or fourth) language?

Have you found differences in the non-verbal communication of international candidates?

Do you find out about non-verbal communication in candidates' countries of origin?

Written communication

Again, as with verbal and non-verbal communication, international students who are non-native writers may face problems in written communication, in three main ways.

The first and most obvious is that they may be writing in a foreign language, which is difficult enough in itself.

But, second, they may have had little or no experience of writing extended pieces of work at all, and may only have been required to take lecture notes and regurgitate them in examinations. So, not only are they writing in a foreign language, but at the same time they are learning how to write much more extensive pieces of work than ever before.

If this is not enough, third, candidates are expected to produce what can be a new type of writing, that is, the Western model of academic writing. As noted on p. 100, this can be said to be characterised by a clear formal structure, explicitness of intention for the work as a whole and its component parts, clarity and coherence of argument and analysis, respect for writing conventions in the subject, the substantiation of all points made, and the explicitness of conclusions.

Such a model of academic writing may be very different from that prevalent in other cultures. So, for example, as Ryan (2000: 74) points out:

> The use of proverbs, stories and literary illusions ... are commonly used in Asian and African writing to demonstrate one's educational level and accomplishment, to win the reader over to the author's point of view, and to establish credibility. Classical sayings or poetic phrases will be used to make the writing look 'well-educated' and to establish empathy. The writing process takes a more circuitous approach, where the reader is gradually taken along a journey where the argument, or the main thesis, is only found at the very end. The thesis will begin by saying what the topic isn't before writing about what it is.

Students accustomed to writing in this way may find it difficult to adjust to the Western model.

Clearly, there is an issue here about why they should have to adjust, that is, modify or abandon their own style of academic writing for another. *Prima facie*, styles of writing may be different, but there are no objective reasons to necessarily infer that one is better than another. Here the brutal fact is that most doctoral providers are in the West, that such providers operate within the rational–scientific paradigm of research, and hence at the end of the day the expectation is that doctoral dissertations will conform to the associated model of academic writing. Candidates, then, would seem to have little choice in the matter.

There is a further issue here about who, if candidates have not previously acquired either good general writing skills in the language or the specific ones required for academic writing, should be responsible for training them. Here, as

Strauss and Walton (2002) have shown, there is a conflict between the views of many supervisors, who consider that it is the institution's responsibility to recruit students who are capable of writing, and those of candidates who consider that, if the institution has accepted them, it has an obligation to teach them writing skills, particularly in relation to academic writing.

Institutions do, of course, screen international candidates for general writing skills, and many in addition run courses on academic writing for them. But candidates often still experience difficulties and, however unfairly, the burden falls upon the good natures of their supervisors. In such cases, supervisors can assist in the following ways.

Finding out the style of writing used by international students

In order to provide a starting point, it is very useful for a supervisor to be aware of the style in which the student has been accustomed to write. An example of good practice in this respect is cited by Aspland (1999: 35–6) of a supervisor who had a new student who was from China. Having seen her written work – and it is, of course important to check – he told the student that:

> ... my writing was the most important thing to change. He said in China we were good at writing shopping lists, 1,2,3. You see we just learn and write these long shopping lists but he told me ... it has no argument. You can't pass if you write shopping lists ...

Encouraging candidates to write critically and analytically

Students then need to be encouraged to write critically and analytically. Strategies can include:

- pointing students towards the literature, for example, the excellent book by Bonnet (2001) on 'How to Argue';
- recommending model articles, for example, review articles in the subject literature;
- providing checklists of the characteristics of analytical and critical writing for use when writing (see, for example, Bruce and Braneld 1999);
- working with students to improve their academic writing skills, for example, by going through drafts and indicating how they might be re-written in terms of academic writing.

Encouraging candidates to write regularly and giving feedback

One of the key things for all candidates is, as argued in Chapter 8, to encourage them to write regularly from the start of the programme onwards. But this is particularly critical for international candidates writing in what may be a second or third language where, understandably, the acquisition of the high-level writing skills demanded for a successful doctorate will take longer. So writing, even short amounts, regularly is helpful to enable them to become accustomed to writing, particularly if it is accompanied by regular feedback not just on the substance of their work, but the writing style as well.

Of course, supervisors can go further than this, and it is not unknown for them, under the guise of proof-reading, to re-write substantial parts of doctoral theses. Clearly, there are ethical issues involved here in relation to the independence of the work, issues which can sometimes be highlighted in thesis defences where examiners find a mismatch between the quality of the writing before them and the oral competence of the candidate. In an ideal world, of course, this would not happen because institutions would only recruit international candidates who were competent in writing or provide full support for the development of the latter. But, while institutions are dazzled by the pounds or dollars brought in fees by international students, supervisors within them may face what can be a very difficult dilemma.

Conclusions

International candidates have always been a major segment of the doctoral population in the US, but have now become so in a number of other countries as well. Such candidates are faced with a range of potential barriers which make doctoral studies potentially much more complex and difficult than for domestic candidates. But, as has been seen, there are numerous ways in which supervisors can support international candidates to overcome the barriers. Inevitably, this means that supervisors must often make a significant investment in time and effort to work with international candidates, particularly in the early stages and when they are writing up, a fact that is not always appreciated by institutions in workload planning.

But this, of course, presumes that international candidates are studying within the institution, and increasingly this is not the case. Technological developments mean that international candidates are increasingly able to spend all or part of their period of study at home, thus avoiding both the cost and inconvenience of living and working in another part of the world. From the supervisor point of view, this can compound the issues of working effectively with international candidates with those of working with distance learning candidates which, as Wisker *et al.* (2003c) have shown, requires a special range of skills to be developed to enable supervision to be effective. This, clearly is one area which requires research into practice to develop appropriate supervisory and support strategies for the future.

Part V

Completion and examination

Chapter 13

Completion and submission

Once candidates have substantially completed their research projects, they then have to think about writing up their theses. The latter will almost certainly be the largest scale and most complex writing task they have ever undertaken, or indeed in many cases will ever undertake. Even if they have been writing regularly since the start of their candidacy, producing the thesis may still be seen as a huge mountain to scale. So while, during the latter stages of the research project, they should have been operating virtually autonomously, the chances are that they will need considerable support from their supervisors in producing their theses.

Once, and usually after several iterations, they have produced what they regard as the final version, then the issue is whether it should be submitted for examination. In some systems of doctoral education, this is ultimately the decision of the candidate. While they would be foolish not to seek the advice of their supervisor (or if negative to ignore it) they are at liberty to do so, that is, the supervisor has no power of veto.

But in other systems of doctoral education, the supervisor is required to sign-off the thesis as worthy in principle of defence, and it cannot go forward without his or her agreement. This, of course, requires supervisors to make a judgement about whether, in principle, the thesis is likely to meet the standards for the award. For old hands who have supervised a number of doctorates and acted as examiners, it is perhaps easy to reach a preliminary conclusion, but it can be a difficult call for those new to supervision and examination, particularly if they only have their own experience as a doctoral candidate to rely upon.

This chapter, then, is about the ways in which supervisors can support candidates in writing up their theses, and can determine whether the latter are likely to meet the standards for the award.

Supporting the writing of the thesis

In supporting the writing of the thesis, supervisors need to discuss with candidates what they are writing (a thesis), what should be in their thesis (content), how it should be organised (structure), how the parts should be balanced (planning), how it should be presented (presentation) for whom they are writing (the audience), and finally how long it will take (the timetable).

The thesis

It can be helpful at the point at which candidates are starting writing up just to remind them of what the end product should be. This does vary somewhat and, for example, in a number of countries (and some disciplines) the end product can be a compilation of published articles. However, in the vast majority of cases, the requirement is that they produce a thesis. The key point here is that a thesis involves much more than simply writing up the research that has been done but entails making an argument or case and substantiating it with reason and evidence.

The fact that a thesis involves an argument or case and substantiating it by reason and evidence means, of course, that producing one is not a case of candidates retailing everything they have done over the past few years, topping and tailing it with an introduction and conclusion, and hoping for the best. As Torrance and Thomas (1994: 108) have put the matter:

> [Thesis] writing is not simply a description of the researcher's activities, but a constructive process that uses research findings as raw materials to build upon one of several possible accounts of a programme of research.

So it can be helpful to remind candidates that what they are about to engage in is a process of knowledge creation whereby, to use the analogy of a sculptor, the work that they have done is the block of marble from which the final statue – the thesis – will eventually emerge.

Content

To continue the analogy, it follows that, as the statue begins to take shape, inevitably some of the marble will have to be discarded, that is, that the creation of the thesis will require the candidate to discriminate among the mass of research findings that they have accumulated and emphasise the ones that are relevant and marginalise or omit those which are not.

Candidates can find this difficult. As one of Rudd's (1985: 73) sample put it:

> I was ... unable to differentiate between what was absolutely essential and what could be dispensed with. So my problem was really a sort of *embarras de richesse*. I mean, there was so much material, and it all seemed fantastic. And I couldn't put it all in, but I tried to. And of course this made the whole thing of mammoth size, totally unwieldy.

This candidate was so unable to see the wood for the trees that he never finished his doctorate.

It can, then, be helpful for supervisors to point out that, as the thesis develops, there will be choices to be made about what should and should not be included, and that the ability to determine what is relevant and what is not is one of the hallmarks of a successful doctoral candidate. It can be comforting to candidates naturally anxious to include all that they have done to remind them that, if they do marginalise or discard findings, there is always the prospect of including them in later publications.

Structure

A further part of writing up which candidates often find difficult is structuring their account, that is, deciding what goes where in the thesis. In this context, one possible strategy which has been identified (see Cryer 2000; Taylor 2002) is to ask candidates to think of themselves as explorers who have undertaken a journey and who are writing a guidebook to where they have been, and what they discovered in the process. As authors of the guidebook, they need to explain:

- where they started from
- what guidebooks they read
- why they decided to undertake the journey
- how they decided to approach the journey
- the route they decided to follow
- the discoveries they made on the way
- where they arrived at the end of the journey
- how it differed from the starting point
- where they would go from here in future.

So it can be suggested that candidates start by literally drawing a map of their intellectual journey, containing the main topic headings and the linkages between them. Once they are satisfied with that, they can then begin to unpack each of the topics into sub-headings. By the end of the exercise, there should be a complete map of the thesis, probably with 200–300 key words upon it. The advantages of this type of approach are that:

- it helps candidates define an overall framework for their thesis;
- it divides the writing into manageable tasks;
- it clearly highlights the key things candidates need to bring out in terms of discoveries (originality), added knowledge and understanding (the differences between the start and end point), and future research in the area (where the subject goes now);
- it translates readily into a common structure for a thesis in a number of subjects, that is:

Starting point	Introduction
Guidebooks	Literature review
Reasons	Trigger
Approach	Methodology
Route and discoveries	Substantive research chapters

Arrival	Analysis and results
Differences	Added knowledge
Future	Directions of research

Supervisors can encourage candidates to undertake this or a similar exercise prior to getting down to writing, and discuss the route map with them at each stage, which should help both to understand the way that the thesis is heading.

Planning

As well as getting the overall structure reasonably clear, candidates also need to plan how much they are going to write to make sure that they are operating within any word limits and that, within this, there is an appropriate balance between what they write under the headings of each of the parts of the thesis.

With regard to the total, many institutions have word limits on theses, and it can be helpful for supervisors to point these out to candidates, along with other factors such as whether the limits include the bibliography or whether appendices are allowed and so on.

But, within the total permissible length, candidates need to allocate at least rough targets for each part of the thesis. Given that theses are going to be examined primarily on the original contribution that they make to knowledge and understanding in the subject, candidates would be foolish to aim for half of their thesis to be taken up by the literature review, a further quarter by the methodology, and only a quarter for the original scholarship.

In this context, some institutions produce guidelines.

Example

The guidelines of the University of Warwick (cited in Blaxter *et al.* 1996: 217) are set out below:

	% of thesis
Introduction	10
Literature review	20
Methodology	15
Research findings	20
Discussion	20
Conclusions	5
Bibliography	10

Again it can be helpful for supervisors to direct candidates towards any institutional guidelines or, if there are none, to discuss with them what would be appropriate.

Presentation

A further area where candidates may need advice is in relation to presentation. Here, candidates may need to be advised about meeting any disciplinary style conventions or particular institutional requirements. Candidates then need to be directed towards appropriate sources of information about these matters, for example, exemplar theses in the discipline or the institution's requirements for the form in which theses are submitted.

But, while advice on these matters is a legitimate part of the role of the supervisor, presentation also includes matters such as errors in spelling or grammar. While many supervisors cannot help themselves but correct these errors as they read through drafts, technically it is normally the responsibility of the candidate to make sure that the thesis is error-free. Supervisors may wish to make this clear to candidates and advise them to use grammar and spell-checkers and/or to have a friend or colleague check their work for errors and typos.

The audience

In order to drive home all of these points, it can be helpful to remind candidates that they are writing their thesis for a particular audience, namely the examiners. Here, supervisors can point them towards the excellent advice of Cryer (2000), namely that examiners face multiple calls upon their time and energies and are likely to respond better to theses that are well-structured and well-presented and which highlight the contribution made towards knowledge and understanding in the subject.

Further reinforcement can be added by pointing candidates to examples of the advice of examiners to doctoral candidates.

Example

In his 1996 address to the University of Canberra Postgraduate Students Association, Professor Arthur Georges advised candidates to self-address the following questions (Georges 1996):

- Does the thesis contain a succinct critical review of what is currently known so that the examiner is not left pondering as to how the work fits into the broader scheme of things?
- Is there sufficient background provided so that the examiner can appreciate the research problems that you are to tackle, and the objectives of the thesis?
- Have the deficiencies in our current knowledge been clearly identified and the significance of addressing them been established?

- Has the scope of the current work been clearly articulated so as to avoid a mismatch in the examiner's expectations and what is actually delivered?
- Have the research objectives been stated with sufficient precision to enable the examiner to assess whether they have been achieved or not? Is it possible *not* to achieve the objectives, and if it isn't, then the objectives are not of substance.
- Do the objectives fit comfortably with (a) the critical review, do they arise from (b) the significant deficiencies in our current knowledge or understanding, and do they lie within (c) the scope of the study?
- Have the principal results and conclusions been stated early, usually in the abstract, so that the examiner knows where the thesis is heading from the very beginning? Do not leave the examiner in the dark.
- Are the materials and methods detailed enough to ensure that the work is reproducible?
- Is the use of novel or non-standard methods or approaches fully justified in a way that convinces the examiner that the candidate is fully conversant with the subject?
- Is the experimental design clearly articulated and appropriate to the objectives, and are the methods of statistical analysis appropriate?
- Are the results unequivocal and of substance? Does the thesis make an original contribution to knowledge?
- Is the significance of the results fully explored in relation to the current literature, especially where the results are at odds with current understanding?
- Are the substantive discussion points brought home with finality?
- Has clear ownership of your contribution been established? 'This is the first time this has been demonstrated for any vertebrate group', if in fact that is the case.
- Are all the linkages between discrete elements of the results brought together where they are relevant to substantive conclusions?
- Are all the conclusions and is all of the discussion clearly linked to the results or to the established results of others?

Source: http://aerg.canberra.edu.au/pub/aerg/eduthes4.htm

Example

In a recent research study conducted in Australia by Mullins and Kiley (2002: 378–9) examiners were asked what were the negatives that caused a thesis to fail, what the positives were that were associated with a pass, and what make a thesis outstanding. What they came up with was:

- Negatives

  * lack of coherence
  * lack of understanding of theory
  * lack of confidence
  * researching the wrong problem
  * mixed or confused theoretical or methodological perspectives
  * lack of originality
  * lack of connection between the conclusions and the remainder
  * of the thesis
- Positives
  * originality
  * coherence
  * confidence
  * student autonomy
  * well-structured argument
  * well-presented
  * sensible research question
  * sufficient quality (2–4 journal papers)
  * reflection
- For an outstanding thesis:
  * artistry
  * creativity
  * design (all parts fit)
  * elegance
  * well-sculpted

So, all of the previous messages are not just good practice in themselves, but will help to meet the needs of the eventual audience, the examiners who will have the final say in recommending whether they are awarded a doctorate.

The timetable

Finally, supervisors need to agree with candidates a timetable for writing up. This should start by agreeing a target date for the production of the thesis in its final form.

It is then possible to work backwards and include the time to be allowed for re-drafting, a hand-in date for the first complete draft, and hand-in dates for individual chapters.

It may be comparatively rare for candidates to be able to stick rigidly to such timetables given that, as noted above, thesis writing is a process of knowledge creation and as such difficult to complete to order. But a timetable at least serves as a marker for candidates to aim at and for supervisors to check on their progress and, if they are slipping, try to find out why and help them to get back on track.

One common cause of slippage is because candidates are suffering from that curse of writing up, namely 'writer's block'. Candidates try to write parts of their thesis, read through what they have written, consider it rubbish, delete it and start again, whereby the process repeats itself. Particularly at a time when they are under pressure to stick to deadlines, this can be an unnerving experience leading to dejection and despair.

In fact, 'writer's block' is a recognised phenomenon and there are a number of techniques for dealing with it. These (see, for example, Murray 2002) include:

- encouraging students to 'freewrite' – to just put down whatever is in their minds on the topic without regard for style, punctuation, etc. – and then leaving writing for a day or two. Often, when they return, they are surprised at the ideas they have expressed and carry on further;
- advising them to change the writing task to another and easier part of the thesis to restart the process;
- advising them to take a short break and go off and do something completely different before returning refreshed and, hopefully, unblocked.

Interrogating practice

Do you remind candidates of the fact that they are writing a thesis?

Do you discuss with them the need to be discriminating about the content?

Do you help them to produce a structure?

Do you advise them about word limits and the balance of the parts of the thesis?

Do you advise them about disciplinary styles and institutional requirements?

Do you make them aware of the audience for their thesis?

Do you negotiate a timetable?

If they are experiencing difficulties in writing, how can you assist them?

In these ways, then, supervisors can assist candidates to keep the writing flowing and the chapters coming until, eventually, they have a first complete draft. Supervisors can then give feedback on it and subsequent drafts until a final one is produced.

Submission

Once the candidate has produced what he or she sees as the definitive draft of their thesis, the issue then arises about whether it should go forward for final examination.

Here, as was noted in the introduction, supervisors may have only an advisory role, or they may be required to sign off the thesis as worthy in principle of defence. Either way, it can be a difficult call for supervisors at least if they have little experience of supervising or of examining. In such cases, what supervisors can do is to explicate the criteria, evaluate the thesis in the light of them, and, depending upon their role, decide how to advise the candidate or whether to let him or her go forward to final examination.

Explicating the criteria

Before reviewing the thesis, it is important for supervisors to explicate the independent criteria that they are going to apply to evaluate the work. Such criteria may fall into three categories, those relating to the research project, those relating to the thesis, and those relating to the award.

Criteria for the research project

Clearly, supervisors have to satisfy themselves that the research project upon which the thesis is based is adequate and appropriate, that is, define appropriate criteria.

Example

Partington et al. (1993: 76–8) have developed useful checklists of criteria, both generic and discipline-specific, for application by examiners. These can also be used or adapted by supervisors. So, for example, generic criteria include:
- The context:
  * that the research questions have been placed in their academic and, where appropriate, industrial, commercial or professional contexts;
  * that, in the case of a thesis undertaken as part of a team project, the relationship of the research to the overall project is set out along with the contribution of the candidate relative to other team members.

- The literature
  * that the relevant literature or an appropriately justified section of it has been covered;
  * that the literature is reviewed in ways which are critical and analytical and not just descriptive;
  * that the review demonstrates clear mastery of the literature;
  * that explicit links are made between the literature and the topic of the thesis;
  * that there is a summary of the literature in so far as it relates to the thesis topic.
- Methodology/methods
  * that there is an awareness of the range of methodologies/methods which might be used to tackle the topic;
  * that there is adequate justification of the methodologies/methods adopted for the research;
  * that the methodologies/methods are related to the design of the research;
  * that practical problems and issues are identified and discussed;
  * where applicable, that ethical considerations are outlined and discussed;
  * where applicable, that matters of reliability and validity are identified and discussed.
- Design of the study
  * that the design of the study is appropriate to the topic;
  * that there is an awareness of the limitations of the design adopted.
- Substantive research
  * that the research design has been properly implemented;
  * that the relevant sources of evidence have been explored.
- Analysis
  * that appropriate theoretical and, where applicable, empirical techniques are used to analyse evidence;
  * that the level and form of the analysis is appropriate to the evidence.
- Outcomes/results
  * that the outcomes/results identified relate to the topic;
  * that the outcomes/results are justified on the basis of the analysis of the evidence;
  * that the outcomes/results are presented clearly;
  * where appropriate, that patterns and trends in the outcomes and results are accurately identified and summarised.

- Discussion
  * that the main points emerging from the outcomes/results have been picked up for discussion;
  * that there is an awareness of the limitations of the outcomes/results.
- Conclusions
  * that the conclusions relate to the initial focus of the study;
  * that the conclusions are justified by the study;
  * that the implications for the field of knowledge have been identified.

Supervisors can, then, develop criteria similar to those above upon which to base their evaluation of the research project.

Criteria for the thesis

The research project is, of course, written up as a thesis or dissertation, for which there are additional criteria. These are more likely to be standard across disciplines, and key ones would normally include:

- Authenticity – the thesis should be the candidate's own work and not plagiarised from the work of others, published and unpublished. All sources used should be appropriately acknowledged using a recognised form of referencing.
- Scholarship – the thesis should conform to the normal canons of scholarship in the discipline, displaying critical discrimination and a sense of proportion in evaluating evidence and the opinion of others. Sources should be cited accurately, consistently and correctly in the text and bibliography.
- Professionalism – the thesis should demonstrate that the candidate has acquired or extended a repertoire of research skills appropriate to a professional researcher and his or her field and has a clear understanding of the role of such a researcher.
- Structure, writing and presentation – the thesis should be clearly structured and orderly in arrangement, and well-written and presented. Similarly, any composition, exhibition, artefacts or other products of practice arising from the research should be arranged and presented in an orderly and coherent way.

Criteria relating to the award

The final criteria are those relating to the award, which are normally defined by institutions, and may include that the research has been undertaken independently by the candidate, that it makes an original contribution to knowledge and understanding and/practice in the academic and/or professional discipline, and that it contains material which is, in principle, worthy of publication.

Evaluating the thesis

Once supervisors are clear about the criteria to be applied, the next step is to evaluate the thesis. Supervisors will, of course, have their own methods for doing this, but the important thing is that they are systematic and cover all of the criteria. Again, Partington *et al.* (1993) suggest that one way to proceed is as follows.

Start by reflecting upon the application of the criteria relating to the research project to the topic and consider what they would expect

It is then useful for supervisors to reflect and consider how the criteria relating to the research project might be applied to the topic in question, for example, the literature they might expect the candidate to have read, the range of methods that might have been used, how the study might have been designed. By the end of this, the criteria should be effectively translated into a set of clearly-defined questions to be asked about the thesis. In addition, the reflection may well lead to new questions about the research.

Read and note

Supervisors can then carefully read each section of the thesis with the relevant questions in mind. They can note those where they are satisfied with the answers, those where clarification is needed, and those where answers are not convincing. As, in the course of the reading, additional questions occur, these may be noted and views recorded on how well the candidate has answered them in the present chapter or in others.

Consider how far the work meets the criteria for the research project

By now, supervisors should have a clear idea how far the research project meets the relevant criteria. They should reflect on this, and summarise what they see as the strengths of the project, the weaknesses, and the areas where clarification is needed.

Consider how far the work meets the criteria for the thesis

In the process of reading the thesis section by section, supervisors should have begun to form a preliminary view about how far it meets the general criteria relating for the thesis relating to authenticity, scholarship, professionalism, and structure, presentation and style. They should now consider how far the work meets these criteria, and note where it does, where there are doubts, and where it does not.

Consider how far the work meets the criteria for award

The last area for consideration is whether the thesis meets the requirements for award. In particular if and how far it makes an original contribution to knowledge and understanding and, where relevant, practice, and whether it contains material which, if not already published, would be accepted for publication in a peer-reviewed journal or as a book.

Reaching a conclusion

On the basis of their review, supervisors can then reach a conclusion about the suitability of the thesis to go forward for examination. This may be, for example:

1   that it fully meets all of the relevant criteria;
2   that it fully meets the criteria relating to the award and the thesis but there are minor weaknesses in the research project;
3   that it is genuinely marginal in meeting a number of the criteria, including those relating to the award;
4   that it does not fully meet the criteria for the award, the thesis, or the research project.

In the first case, the supervisor can sign-off the thesis as worthy of examination; in the second case the supervisor may, bearing in mind Mullins and Kiley's (2002) dictum that 'It's a PhD not a Nobel Prize', be inclined to do the same; and in the final case, the supervisor would obviously be unable to advise or certify that, in its present form, the thesis should proceed to examination.

This, of course, leaves the third, difficult case where there is genuine doubt about whether the thesis meets the criteria and hence about whether it will pass or fail. In an ideal world, supervisors presented with such a thesis should be able to explain their doubts to the candidate, discuss the problem areas, indicate how the thesis should be strengthened, and devise a plan for re-writing and/or undertaking additional research prior to the production of a revised thesis.

However, this is not always possible because of time constraints on the candidate's ability to continue with his or her studies or because non-submission would jeopardise meeting departmental targets set by research sponsors and possibly incur penalties. In such cases supervisors are left on the horns of a dilemma – should they advise the candidate to submit or certify the thesis as worthy of examination knowing that there is a risk of it being referred for further work or should they advise against submission or refuse to certify it pending revision knowing that there is a risk that the candidate might be unable to complete it or that submission targets would be missed?

Clearly, there is no easy answer to this dilemma. On the one hand, it can be tempting for supervisors to take a gamble and advise or authorise the candidate to proceed to examination in the hope that a generous view of the shortcomings will be taken by the examiners; on the other hand, they have to recognise that, if the gamble fails, there will be serious consequences for the candidate and, of course, possibly for their own reputations as supervisors. The latter, then, have to assess the risks, and act in accordance with their judgement.

Interrogating practice

Does your institution require you to certify that theses are worthy of defence?

Are you aware of the criteria for evaluating the research project?

Are you aware of the criteria for evaluating the thesis?

Are you aware of the criteria for evaluating the award?

Have you ever been in a dilemma in advising candidates to submit or certifying that their thesis is worthy of defence when you had serious doubts?

Conclusions

When candidates have completed their research projects, they then enter another tunnel called 'writing their thesis'. This is not simply a matter of putting all they have done before into the pot and hoping for the best. Supervisors can help them to realise this by spending time at the outset discussing the key issues, in particular what they are trying to produce and whom they are producing it for, and subsequently giving feedback on successive drafts.

Once a final draft has been produced, then supervisors have the onerous responsibility of advising candidates whether to submit, or determining whether they should be allowed to do so at all. This can be a difficult task, but one which can be systematised by determining the criteria, applying them, and reaching an academic judgement. In most cases this will hopefully be clear but, particularly with theses that are marginal, there is a grey area within which supervisors may have to balance risks. This can be distressing for supervisors and, in the event of getting them wrong, candidates, but appear to be part and parcel of the tightening of time limits on the modern doctorate.

Chapter 14

Preparation for examination

Once the thesis has been formally submitted, this will trigger the procedures for examination, starting with the appointment of examiners. The latter may include the advisory committee plus one or more other examiners internal to the institution (as in many institutions in the United States) or a mixture of internal and external examiners (which is the norm elsewhere), and they may, or may not, include the supervisor. But, irrespective of whether the latter are examiners or not, as the subject specialists they can expect to be consulted about whom it would be most appropriate to approach to act as examiners.

After the examiners have been appointed, what happens next varies in different countries. In Australia and South Africa, it is normally only the thesis which is examined, and not the candidate, and oral examinations are only used in rare cases where the thesis is marginal and clarification is required. It can also vary within countries, for example, in Germany some institutions only examine the thesis while others also examine the candidate (see, for example, Eurodoc 2003).

Elsewhere, it is normally mandatory for the examiners to examine not only the thesis, but the candidate as well, that is, this is a requirement for the award of a doctorate. The reasons for this include the needs: to check that the work has been undertaken by the candidate and that he or she understands it; to ascertain that they have developed appropriate research skills; to see whether they have a wider knowledge of the field to which the research relates; and to establish whether they are capable of defending their thesis to experienced researchers drawn from the subject community. So, no matter how good their thesis, candidates have to undergo an oral examination or viva.

As candidates may have limited experience of this form of examination, supervisors normally have a responsibility to assist them to prepare for it.

The present chapter, then, looks at the role of supervisors in advising about examiners and, where appropriate, in advising the candidate about the oral examination.

Advising on examiners

In seeking to advise on possible nominees, supervisors need to be aware, first, of the relevant criteria to be qualified to examine a doctorate. Many institutions now have explicit criteria (see, for example, Powell and McCauley 2002; Tinkler and Jackson 2000), as do some professional subject bodies (see, for example, British Psychological Society and Universities and Colleges Staff Development Association 1996). These may include the following criteria.

Rank and qualifications

In some institutions, particularly in continental Western Europe, examiners must be full professors, while a normal requirement in many others is that examiners should have a doctorate themselves or equivalent research experience.

Subject expertise

A universal requirement is that examiners should have recent and relevant expertise in the candidate's area of research as demonstrated by, for example, recent publications.

Standing within the discipline

A further requirement may be that the examiner has a high standing in the discipline, that is, that he or she commands the respect of the disciplinary community.

Previous experience of examination and/or successful supervision

Examiners who have little or no previous experience of examining or of supervising may, as Mullins and Kiley (2002) have suggested, have little experience of the standards which should be applied and be too tough because they have not experienced the scrutiny of their own students. In order to avoid over-critical inexperienced examiners, institutions may insist either that examiners have previously examined or, if not, that they have undertaken usually two or more successful supervisions.

Independence of the research project

Institutions may require that examiners have not previously been involved in the research project in any substantive capacity.

Independence of the institution

Institutions may require that external examiners should not have worked at the institution for a specified period before the examination, for example, five years, or that they should not have examined at that institution on more than a specified number of occasions within (say) the last three years.

Willingness to examine within the specified period

A final requirement may be that examiners are willing to examine the thesis and that they will do so within the period specified by the institution, for example, three months from receiving the thesis. This is not a negligible requirement; examining a doctoral thesis properly is time-consuming and done as an act of professional service rather than for money.

It may be noted that these requirements are, of course, designed mainly with the PhD in mind, and meeting them can create difficulties in finding examiners for other doctorates. In particular, in practice-based or professional doctorates, it can be desirable that one of the examiners is a professional practitioner, but it can be problematic to find examiners who both fit this bill and meet the institution's criteria. In such cases, institutions may have procedures for exemptions, or they may have other criteria for examiners of such doctorates.

Once supervisors are clear about the institution's criteria, they are then in a position to draw up a longlist of potential examiners. If the candidate's subject is sufficiently esoteric, the longlist may be comparatively short, that is, the examiners will be self-selecting. But in other cases the longlist may be larger than the number needed for the examination, and there will be a need to make up a shortlist.

The question, then, is who to put on the shortlist, and at this stage supervisors may be required to, or they may consider, consulting the candidate about possible names. In this context it is worth enquiring whom the candidate considered would be most appropriate to examine their doctorate and, perhaps more importantly, the names of any to whom they would have strong objections. This might at least assist in identifying examiners who, because they are opposed to the approach adopted in the research or whose life's work has been attacked, might be less objective about the thesis and the candidate. Also, supervisors have to think very carefully before proposing examiners whom candidates feel will not give them a fair crack of the whip.

As well as consulting students supervisors may, in drawing up the shortlist, begin to think, consciously or unconsciously, of 'horses for courses', that is, which examiners might be most appropriate given the thesis and the candidate. This may be illustrated by three hypothetical cases.

The first is where supervisors consider that the thesis is outstanding and that, where there is an oral examination, they are confident that the candidate will shine under stringent questioning from examiners. In such cases, supervisors can confidently recommend virtually any name on their list, confident that the candidate will sail through with flying colours. Under such circumstances, the temptation can be to advise the institution to go for the most prestigious examiners. While they may be hyper-critical and give the candidate a hard time, at the end of the day the fact that they have recommended award will lend status to the doctorate in the eyes of the subject community and may even help candidates in their careers.

The second, and more usual, case is where supervisors consider that there are some minor weaknesses in the research project but that otherwise the thesis is sound, and that the candidate will be reasonably able to cope in the oral examination. Supervisors may consider that it could be tempting fate to invite the top leaders in the field, and instead advise the institution to ask others who are highly rated within the field, and are known for giving theses and candidates thorough but objective scrutiny. They will be reasonably likely to recommend a pass, and a doctorate awarded on their recommendation will be well regarded within the subject community.

The third, and most difficult case, is where supervisors considered that the thesis is marginal, and that the candidate may wilt under questioning in the viva. In such a scenario, the temptation can be to recommend that the institution go for examiners who may not be very highly regarded in the field, but whom the supervisor knows will be more likely to be understanding about the thesis, more likely to give the candidate an easy passage in the viva, and at the end of the day will probably recommend award of the degree. The upside is that the candidate will get the degree; the downside is that the thesis will carry less weight among the subject community.

In an ideal world, dilemmas of these kinds would not occur, but they do (see, for example, Phillips 1994). Clearly, there is no inherently 'right' or 'wrong' decision for a supervisor in such cases; he or she has to balance the interests of the candidate who has done three or four or more years work to gain the award against the risk that the doctorate may be regarded as suspect and, as McWilliam *et al.* (2002) have argued, damage their own reputation and that of the institution or even the doctorate itself.

Interrogating practice

What are the criteria in your institution to be appointed to examine doctorates?

Do they distinguish between criteria for examiners of the PhD and other doctorates?

Does your institution require you to consult the student before proposing examiners?

(If not) do you think that this would be an appropriate practice?

Are you aware of attempts to match examiners and candidates?

Do you think that this practice is defensible?

Advising the candidate

Candidates may have had experience of oral examinations as undergraduates and/ or on master's programmes, as well as during their doctoral programmes when first presenting their research proposal for approval or in annual progress reviews. But, while these are valuable experiences, they may not prepare candidates sufficiently for what can be the formality and rigour of the oral examination for the doctorate.

In some cases, advice is provided to candidates by institutions, but this practice is far from universal. Supervisors may, then, need to advise candidates about what to expect in and how to go about planning for the oral examination, preparing for it, and how to make sure that they turn up on the day in the best possible shape to do themselves justice.

What to expect

In many institutions, particularly in continental Western Europe and the US, oral examinations are public events, and candidates can go along to one or more and experience the context and the proceedings. However, for example in the UK, it is often not possible for candidates to do this because oral examinations are *de facto* or *de jure* private events with only the candidate and the examiners present. So, as Burnham (1997: 30) has written 'To all but the initiated, what occurs in the lengthy "judgely huddle" from which postgraduates emerge either victorious or distraught is a mystery.' This can leave candidates in the position of simply not knowing what to expect which, as Phillips (1994) and Delamont *et al.* (1997) point out, is a fertile breeding ground for misconceptions and misapprehensions which can undermine their confidence and performance.

Clearly, one thing that supervisors can do is to de-mystify the process by pointing candidates in the direction of an explanation of what goes on in an oral examination. Such an explanation may be found in the institution's handbook for the examiners of doctorates, or it may be that the institution can provide or give access to resources.

Example

Two UK universities, Leeds Metropolitan University and the University of Strathclyde, have produced training videos on oral examinations for candidates (and examiners). Both are based on actual oral examinations and show all of the stages from the examiners' pre-meeting through the examination itself and the outcome, followed by an interview about the experience with the candidate. The authors have found that, in training candidates for their oral examinations, these videos have been highly effective in priming them about what to expect.

Advising on planning

While, because no two doctoral theses are alike, no two oral examinations are alike, it is still possible for candidates to undertake some planning in advance. The following are useful general things that supervisors may wish to advise candidates to do.

Re-read their thesis

Once candidates have written their theses, there is an obvious temptation to think that they know it backwards and don't need to re-read it. But within quite a short space of time it is possible for them to forget at least some of the detail of what they have written. If this extends to the oral examination, the impression is created that they don't know their own work, which obviously creates a poor impression upon the examiners. The importance of such re-reading was one of the key factors which emerged from Hartley and Jory's (2000) survey of doctoral candidates and their experiences. When their sample was asked the question 'Based on your experience, how would you advise others to prepare for their vivas?', fully 61 per cent responded 'knowing your thesis inside out', more than twice the percentage giving any other answer.

Find out about examiners

Where appropriate, candidates may be advised that it is worthwhile making a special effort to find out about the interests of examiners and what they have written. This should give them at least some clues about possible lines of enquiry in the examination, and in any case it does no harm for candidates to show examiners that they are familiar with their contributions to the subject.

Keep up to date with the literature in the field and surrounding areas

It can take from a few weeks up to several months from the submission of a thesis to its examination, and in that time it is perfectly possible for new work to come out which has a direct or an indirect bearing upon the topic. In order for candidates to be able to demonstrate to examiners the currency of their knowledge and their command of the subject, they should be advised to check all likely sources for new papers with a bearing on their research topic.

Advising on preparation

The next thing that candidates can be advised to do is to prepare for the oral examination. Of course, the form of the latter does differ between systems; in a number of countries, candidates make a formal presentation to the examiners usually lasting around 20 minutes, which is followed by questions; elsewhere, the format is normally question and answer. So the two main forms of preparation may be putting together a presentation and/or anticipating questions.

Presentations

It is, to say the least, a discipline – albeit a good one – to boil down the results of what can often be a 400-page thesis into a 20-minute presentation, and candidates may not know where to start. Here, supervisors can usefully remind candidates of the advice of Fitzpatrick *et al.* (1998: 32) that:

> It is best only to present something similar to your abstract. Highlight your problems and purpose for the research. Reiterate your research questions and hypotheses, and identify the strategy or focus of your literature review ... You should briefly outline your methodological strategy of choice and bring forth your most important findings, those that either have emerged or were found significant. End your discussion with your general conclusions or findings and your recommendations.

Once candidates have done this, they then need to give some thought to how they are going to undertake their presentations. Here, perhaps the most effective medium is to use PowerPoint slides. The preparation of such slides is not difficult (and amendment is easily possible if need be up to the last minute) and they can be used to list the key points which candidates can then address in their talk.

Once candidates have decided what they want to say and prepared slides, they may be advised to rehearse their presentation and pay particular attention to the timing. Usually, and understandably, in their desire to impress the examiners with the scope and originality of their work, candidates often prepare too much and their presentations end up well over time. If this happens, then candidates need to go back to the drawing board and cut out any extraneous material, and then time the presentation again. At the end of this iterative process, they should have a presentation that will convey the essentials in the time allotted.

Finally, once they have such a presentation, they may need to be advised to consider how it should be delivered, preferably by delivering it with someone else present. If the supervisor is an examiner, it may be inappropriate for them to do this, but it might be possible to ask a colleague or even another graduate student to listen and give constructive feedback. This can help candidates to avoid obvious pitfalls, for example, addressing the screen or data projector rather than the examiners, and improve their performance and hopefully their confidence. It can also give candidates the chance to practise 'thinking on their feet' in response to questions.

Questions

With regard to questions, candidates can be advised to consider the sorts of questions they are likely to be asked. These might include general questions and specific ones relating to the research project.

Trafford (2003) analysed the questions put to candidates in 25 vivas and found a pattern of sequential phasing of questions, divided into three stages which he named 'Opening', 'Consolidating Opinion' and 'Closing'.

In the first phase, 84 per cent of candidates were asked 'Why did you choose this topic for your doctoral research?'. Other questions in the 'Opening' phase covered conceptualisation, doctorateness, professional relevance, content and methodology. In the 'Consolidating Opinion' phase practice differed between hard and soft sciences. In the hard sciences the vivas were longer and questions were asked on a page-by-page basis, whilst in the softer science-based vivas there was more thematic exploration of issues.

Questions in the 'Closing' phase were similar for all topics using questions such as 'What was your contribution to knowledge?' or 'What plans do you have to publish?' In 75 per cent of the vivas the final question invited the candidate to comment on anything they felt had not been covered. In an appendix Trafford gives an example of a complete set of questions for both a successful and unsuccessful doctoral viva.

Candidates can be advised to think in advance of how they would respond to these sorts of general questions.

With regard to specific ones relating to the research project, it can be suggested to candidates that, as they are re-reading their thesis, they should consider the sorts of questions that they would ask about it. While this can be useful in encouraging candidates to reflect upon their work, they are, of course, biased and it may be helpful for supervisors to suggest that candidates enlist the aid of a fellow candidate to read key sections of the thesis and 'question spot' for them.

Of course it is one thing spotting questions and thinking about possible answers, and another actually defending the thesis in front of examiners. Here, it can be very helpful if supervisors can arrange for them to have a 'mock' oral examination. Because the supervisor is close to the work or may be acting later as an examiner, it may be preferable to ask a couple of colleagues, perhaps including at least one who has acted as a doctoral examiner, to examine the candidate for half an hour on key chapters and, at the end, to give them constructive feedback. In this way they can gain some experience and, if appropriate, improve their performance.

Such 'mock' vivas are particularly vital if candidates are being examined in a language other than their native one which, of course, is often the case with international students. The prospect of spending two hours or more under close questioning with so much riding on the outcome can be absolutely terrifying for non-native speakers, and it is important that they are given the opportunity to practise and given feedback on how they presented themselves. Here, it can be important to stress that, if they do not understand the question, they should ask the examiners for clarification until they are satisfied that they know what is being asked, and that they should take all of the time that they need in responding.

Similarly, 'mock' vivas are also vital for candidates with a disability, particularly if this affects their hearing, and/or speech. In cases where, for example, candidates are both hearing- and speech-impaired, it may be necessary to make special arrangements for the examination, for example to sit the candidate in a position where he or she can lip-read the questions of examiners and to provide a signer who can understand the candidate's responses and communicate them to the team. Clearly, this can be a complex operation, and it needs to be rehearsed, possibly a number of times so that arrangements can be perfected for the day.

On the day

Additionally, it may be worth mentioning to candidates about what to do on the day itself.

It can be helpful to remind them about any formal dress conventions, for example, the wearing of a gown, and about the need to wear other clothes in which they are comfortable – they may be sitting for a couple of hours and possibly longer.

Again, they can be advised to take with them into the examination:

* a copy of their thesis in loose-leaf form (in some systems it is a requirement that theses be submitted in bound form but it makes it easier for the candidate to refer to it in the examination if it is in loose-leaf form);
* pen and paper if they need to jot questions down or possibly draw diagrams;
* copies of any original results, print-outs, or raw data which may be helpful in substantiating key points made in the thesis.

Finally, it can be worth making the points that virtually all candidates will feel nervous on the day, but that they should remember that – within limits – this is a physiological sharpening of the senses which can help them to respond more effectively.

Interrogating practice

How can you assist candidates to appreciate what is involved in the oral examination?

How can you help them to plan?

How can you help them to prepare?

What advice do you give about the day?

Conclusions

Once the process of examination has started, supervisors are normally consulted about the choice of examiners for the thesis and, where appropriate, the candidate as well. In most cases, this is straightforward, but in some there can be risky decisions in balancing, on the one hand, the relative strength of the thesis and the candidate, and on the other the reputations and known proclivities of possible examiners.

Thereafter, in most systems, supervisors have a key role in assisting candidates to plan and prepare for the oral examination. While, of course, they can be assisted to do this down to the last detail, perhaps the most important piece of advice that supervisors can give them is, as Murray (1997: 10) has written, ' Do not go to the viva thinking you have prepared for all possible questions … be ready to engage the brain'.

Chapter 15

Examination

In the UK system, and those based upon it, supervisors are normally debarred from acting as examiners and, in many cases, are excluded from even attending the oral examination. However, following disquiet about the possibility of abuse, supervisors are increasingly being invited to sit in as observers to see fair play.

Elsewhere in Europe, supervisors are expected to take part in the oral examination of candidates, usually as part of a team including three to five external examiners. In the United States and systems based upon it, of course, the chief advisor and the advisory committee constitute a majority of the examiners, usually with the addition of one or more other faculty from the institution to give an independent perspective.

So supervisors may, depending upon the system, be expected to observe or participate in oral examinations. If all goes well and the examiners agree to recommend the awards of the doctorate, then that may be the end of the story. Where, however, it does not, supervisors may have to support candidates in revising their theses or, in extremis, advising them about appeals against the decision of the examiners.

This chapter, then, looks at the roles of supervisors in observing oral examinations, conducting them, and where the outcome is unfavourable supporting the candidate to prepare work for re-submission or an appeal.

Acting as an observer

In systems such as that of the UK where supervisors have usually been excluded from oral examinations, their role historically has been to accompany the candidate along to the room where it is held, wish them good luck, and hand them over to the mercies of the examiners.

Provided that those mercies are tender, the examination should be conducted fairly and properly. But, at least historically, there has been little attempt to ensure that this will be the case; as Tinkler and Jackson (2000) have shown, few institutions have provided rules of engagement to either the candidate or the examiners, or offered the latter any training in how to conduct an oral examination.

In consequence, there has been a potential for abuse which Anderson (cited in Morley *et al.* 2002: 264) has rightly described as 'awesome'.

While the vast majority of examiners have been scrupulous in behaving professionally in questioning the candidate, this has not been universal.

Example

Jackson and Tinkler (2001) surveyed a number of candidates who had been orally examined for a doctorate and asked them about what they thought about the experience. A majority of 60 per cent were positive about the experience, but 20 per cent described it in negative terms. Comments about the purposes of the viva (from candidates who had passed) included:

> To subject the candidate to the most unnecessary form of misery and humiliation. Then, to check that they really are responsible for the work presented for examination. Finally to remind the candidate that they have a long way to go before they can achieve the knowledge of senior academics. I never felt more of a failure and a fraud than when I passed this examination.

> Perhaps to make me suffer a bit for induction into the Guild of Doctors.

The infliction of such misery, humiliation and suffering is, as Morley *et al.* (2002: 269) and Powell and McCauley (2002) have noted, less likely in systems where oral examinations are public (as in much of Western Europe) and/or where there is a large number of examiners present (as in the US), that is, it may be more a feature of the UK system.

If it is a feature, it is clearly an undesirable one, and for that reason, as Tinkler and Jackson (2000) have shown, a number of UK institutions now permit, or in a few cases require, the supervisor to be present at the oral examination as a 'silent witness'. Where this is permitted, it is normally subject to the agreement of the candidate, and the expectation, which may be set out in guidelines, is that the supervisor will monitor whether the examination is being conducted in line with the institution's procedures and in a way that is proper and fair to the candidate. This may reassure the latter that he or she is not going to be the victim of examiner egos and, of course, if there is any question of appeal against the outcome because of prejudice on the part of examiners and/or procedural irregularities, it provides an additional source of evidence. This seems good practice and in the UK it has been proposed (Joint Funding Councils 2002) that all students should have the right to be consulted about whether their supervisor should be an observer in their oral examinations.

> **Interrogating practice**
>
> Does your institution allow, or require, the supervisor to be present at the oral examination?
>
> If so, does it have guidelines for supervisors observing oral examinations?

Acting as examiners

While their counterparts in the UK may only have observer status, members of advisory committees in institutions in the US and supervisors in institutions across continental Western Europe are expected to act as examiners in the oral examination.

Supervisors who act as examiners have to plan and prepare for the oral examination, to liaise with other examiners, and to play their part in conducting it.

Planning for the oral examination

While there may be some variation between institutions, the primary reasons for holding oral examinations of candidates normally include enabling examiners:

- to take up any issues arising from the thesis with the candidate;
- to verify that the thesis and the research project on which it is based is the candidate's own work;
- to verify that the candidate is able to defend the thesis to the satisfaction of experts drawn from the relevant subject community;
- to verify that the candidate understands the relationship between their work and the wider field of study to which it relates.

Supervisors will, in most cases, have certified that the thesis is worthy of examination, and, as outlined in the previous chapter, already formed a judgement about whether it fully meets all of the criteria for award, meets the key ones, but with some minor weaknesses in the research project, or is marginal. On this basis, they can determine the main areas to be covered in the examination. So:

- if the thesis fully meets the criteria, the main areas will be determining whether it is the candidate's own work, whether they can defend it, and whether they have a knowledge of the wider field;
- if the thesis meets the criteria but with minor weaknesses in the research project, then the main agenda will include exploration of these weaknesses plus testing for authenticity, ability to defend the thesis, and knowledge of the wider field;
- if the thesis is marginal, then the main agenda will include exploration of the areas of uncertainty, as well as the testing of the candidate.

On this basis, then, supervisors can begin to plan the oral examination in terms of the ground that they need to cover.

Preparing for the oral examination

Once supervisors have planned the oral examination, it is possible to prepare in the sense of sorting out the questions that need to be asked of the candidate. In particular, it can be useful to consider whether these should be asked in 'open' or 'closed' form.

Open questions

Open questions are, essentially, an invitation to the candidate to expand on particular topics. They can be particularly useful to check that candidates have done the work themselves, and thought about the wider implications of their work. Such questions might include:

- 'Why did you choose that particular method?'
- 'What problems did you experience in collecting the data?'
- 'Tell us how you went about analysing the data'
- 'What do you think the implications of your thesis are for the subject?'

Closed questions

Closed questions are essentially an attempt to gain a factual response from the candidate, and their main use is in explicating specific matters relating to the topics of the viva. So, for example, with the research project, they might include:

- 'Your literature review only mentions X's paper in passing, even though it would seem to be central to the argument put forward on p. YY. Can you tell us why?'
- 'X has suggested that the method you adopted may be biased because of Y. Do you think that they might have a point?'
- 'Can you tell us how you made that inference from the data?'

It is a good idea in an oral examination to plan for a mix of 'open' and 'closed' questions; all 'closed' questions will only test the candidate's recall, while all 'open' questions will put the candidate under considerable strain.

Once examiners have a list of questions, they should then check that these do indeed cover all of the points that they need to be satisfied on to cover their agenda.

Liaising with the other examiners

Oral examinations are always undertaken by more than one examiner, and there is obviously a need for the examiners to liaise with each other before the examination takes place. In particular, they need to discuss and calibrate their preliminary judgements about the thesis, if possible agree the purposes of the oral examination, and then determine:

- the key matters to be raised with the candidate;
- the order within which they are to be raised;
- who will 'lead' on each issue.

Trafford (2003) terms this the 'Prelude' phase of the viva which, in addition to the above, determines the academic relationship between examiners.

Conducting the oral examination

Finally, examiners need to actually conduct the oral examination. Each one will, of course, be unique in terms of its subject and the actors involved, that is, the examiners and the candidate, and hence there must be an element of discretion left to examiners in how they are conducted. That said, such discretion should be exercised in ways that avoid bad practice and are consistent with good practice.

Bad practice for examiners

Partington *et al.* (1993) have suggested that bad practice in conducting the examination would be for an examiner to act throughout in the following ways.

Be an inquisitor

This examiner behaves like a TV interviewer quizzing a politician during an election campaign, rapidly shooting out hostile questions, interrupting the answers, and generally trying to score points. Often this is because, as Baldacchino (1995: 71) has put it:

> Examiners may be more intent to impress ... rather than, or in preference to, listening and engaging with the student. Examiners may feel that their reputation is at stake unless they somehow prove to be more knowledgeable or to be capable of prising open an argument.

Such an approach may intimidate the candidate so that he or she is unable to respond or anger them to the extent that the examination becomes an adversarial confrontation.

Be a hobby horse rider

This examiner has strong feelings or prejudices about one area of the subject and keeps returning to questions on this while neglecting others to the detriment of the candidate's ability to show his or her wider knowledge and abilities.

Be a kite-flyer

The kite-flyer has identified a – usually fairly tenuous – link between a topic and another subject and persists in exploring this to the detriment of the breadth of examination of the candidate, that is, effectively examines a thesis which the student did not write.

Be a reminiscer

This examiner continually regales the candidate with stories of their own adventures during their own research careers to the detriment of the examination of the candidate's work.

Be a proof reader

This examiner takes candidates line by line through their theses asking questions about errors of spelling, punctuation and grammar. If these are exceptionally poor, instead of proof reading in the examination, examiners can make it a requirement that the dissertation is re-word processed or hand the candidate a list of corrections after the viva.

Be a committee person

The committee person takes the candidate through the thesis page by page questioning each matter as it arises rather than synthesising points into key issues relating to the trigger for the study, the methodology, the design, etc.

Good practice for examinations

To ensure that the facilities are adequate and appropriate

Where possible, examiners need to make sure that the room is appropriately laid out for the occasion, that the candidate is comfortable, has space to make notes if need be, has a glass of water, etc.

To ensure that other examiners introduce themselves to the candidate

Where candidates do not know their other examiners personally, it is courteous for them to be asked to introduce themselves.

To explain the process of the oral examination to the candidate

It can be helpful to explain the process to be followed to the candidate, for example, that they will give a presentation for 20 minutes and then be questioned upon it for a period, following which they will be asked to leave while the examiners reach a recommendation.

To settle the candidate down

Candidates can be extremely nervous, and it is important to try and settle them down at the start of the examination. This can be done by, for example, saying something commendatory but non-committal, for example, 'We found your dissertation very interesting', 'we particularly enjoyed ...'.

Where appropriate, to listen actively to presentations

Where, as in the US and similar systems, candidates start with their presentation, it is important that examiners are seen to be listening actively to what they have to say, as indicated by appropriate body language.

To start with easy questions

At the beginning or once the candidate has finished his or her presentation, it can be helpful to ease them into responding mode by asking questions which should have been anticipated and which should be easy to answer, for example, why did you study this topic?, why at this university?

To move on to the substance

Further questions should then be asked covering the key issues and in the order previously identified. In questioning the candidate, examiners should:

- Ask questions in a constructive and positive way. Examiners should try to ask questions in ways that are constructive and positive rather than destructive and negative.
- Recognise that candidates may need time to prepare to do something or to answer. Particularly when asked open questions, candidates may need some time to gather their thoughts together and produce a coherent answer. Examiners need to recognise this, for example, by telling them to 'take your time'.
- Praise a good answer. When candidates give a particularly incisive or interesting answer, it can be helpful to their morale to praise them.
- Give candidates a chance to recover from a poor answer. When candidates give a poor answer, this may be through misunderstanding or nerves.

Rephrasing a question and asking it again gives the able candidate the opportunity to recover the position or may confirm the inability to respond of a weaker one.

To conclude the viva

Once examiners are satisfied that they have gathered the relevant evidence, they should indicate this to the candidate, thank them for answering the questions, ask whether there are any concluding comments which they wish to make, explain again that the examiners will now consult about the outcome, and tell them when they will hear about it.

Reaching a judgement

Once the candidate has departed, the examiners need to confer and agree:

* whether the thesis and candidate have satisfied the criteria for the award outright or with minor corrections (usually spelling and grammatical errors);
* if not whether the thesis and/or the candidate have the potential to satisfy the criteria in future, and if so what they need to do (which should be agreed in detail for subsequent communication to the candidate);
* what recommendation should be made to the institution.

Supporting the candidate after the oral examination

In some cases, the recommendation will be the immediate award of the degree with no strings attached. However, few theses are entirely free from textual errors, and it is more common for examiners to recommend that the doctorate be awarded subject to making the necessary textual corrections. Usually, rather than re-convening the full examination panel, the requirement is that these are made to the satisfaction of the supervisor. In such cases, the latter need to be aware of any institutional time limit on the period within which such corrections have to be made, and if necessary to remind the candidate to get them in on time.

In other cases, examiners may require that sections of the thesis are revised, often because candidates are seen to be claiming more in their concluding chapter than can be justified on the basis of their research. On occasion, corrections may be more serious, and candidates are required to re-write large sections of their thesis. In such cases, examiners should provide a detailed list of the revisions or re-writing required, and they should also stipulate a time limit within which they need to be made and, where appropriate, requirements for re-examination. Again, supervisors need to work with candidates to make the required changes within the time allotted so that they can present themselves for re-examination.

Lastly, there is the case where examiners decide that the thesis and the candidate do not have the potential to meet the criteria for award, and recommend that a lesser degree be awarded or that no award at all should be made. This should not happen, and rarely does in systems where supervisors and/or examiners can prevent unsatisfactory theses going forward for examination. But it can and has happened in other systems, as shown by the example below.

Example

Morley *et al.* (2002: 263) cite correspondence from one PhD candidate about:

> ... the sad experience that I went through in the 1980s when I undertook a part-time PhD ... I had little contact with my supervisor, except when I sent him draft chapters and he gave me (limited) feedback on them ... I got fed up with it after about four years, but was encouraged to continue – with the implication that it was OK. I completed and had a viva without any preparation or information about what to expect. The only thing I remember about the viva was the external examiner asked why I had included such a long appendix ... I was awarded an MPhil without any feedback as to why – my supervisor never made any further contact with me (ever) ... I didn't know of any appeal procedure ...

If such behaviour on the part of the supervisor was acceptable even two decades ago, it would certainly not be in the more student-centred climate of today, not to mention the more litigious one. If, then, candidates are awarded a lesser or no degree, it is important that their supervisors offer an explanation and support and make them aware of their right to appeal against the recommendation.

Interrogating practice

Do you plan how you are going to approach an oral examination?

Do you prepare appropriate questions?

Do you liaise effectively with other examiners?

Does your institution have guidelines for conducting oral examinations?

Are you aware of bad and good practice in the conduct of oral examinations?

Are you aware of institutional regulations on time limits for the revision or re-submission of theses?

Are you aware of your institution's policies and procedures for appealing against the recommendations of examiners of doctoral degrees?

Conclusions

With the major exceptions of Australia and South Africa, the oral examination is the final rite of passage for the candidate on the way to being awarded the degree.

In many institutions in the UK, supervisors have been wholly excluded from participating in this rite of passage. However, as has been seen, revelations of potential abuse in the latter have recently led in many institutions to their being granted, usually at the behest of the candidate, observer status. In this capacity, they are there to see fair play within what remains an essentially private occasion.

Elsewhere, the viva is usually held in public, and it is normal for supervisors to act as examiners. In this capacity, supervisors need to prepare in the same way as other examiners and to conduct their part of the oral examination in accordance with good practice.

Where the outcome of the oral examination is that the thesis be revised then supervisors will need to console candidates and advise them how to proceed so that they can re-submit on time. Similarly, where no recommendation to award is made, supervisors will have to offer candidates support and, where appropriate, advise them on an appeal.

But, in the vast majority of cases, the recommendation of the examiners should be positive, and all that the supervisor will have to do is to join them at the customary dinner or drink to celebrate their achievements.

Part VI

Improving practice

Chapter 16

Evaluation and dissemination

For many years, teachers of taught programmes have regularly evaluated the quality of their teaching, using a range of methods including student questionnaires and/or focus groups, peer observation and feedback, and self-evaluation. However, at least historically, supervisors have been reluctant to use similar methods to evaluate the quality of their supervision. But, clearly, if supervisors are to be able to improve their practice, they need to evaluate their performance, determine their strengths and weaknesses, and build upon the former and address the latter.

The corollary of this is that, if supervisors do evaluate their performance and identify what they consider might be good practice, then they should disseminate it for the benefit of other supervisors. This has happened relatively rarely in the past, but, in recent years, opportunities for dissemination have multiplied, and it is at least arguable that supervisors should take advantage of this both to receive recognition for their efforts and to assist others to develop their practice.

This chapter then is concerned with the responsibilities of supervisors to evaluate their practice and, where appropriate, disseminate it.

Evaluation

The historical reluctance of supervisors to ask candidates to evaluate the quality of their doctoral supervision may, as Taylor (2002) has suggested, reflect two main factors. First, many supervisors have believed that formal instruments for evaluation would violate the sanctity of the professional relationship with the candidate, that is, that they are inappropriate. Second, there have been understandable concerns on the part of candidates that criticism of their supervisors could lead to their being penalised to the detriment of their chances of completing their research projects or of their career prospects, particularly in academia.

However, the failure to evaluate has serious consequences for both candidates and their supervisors; the former are effectively disenfranchised in terms of commenting upon the quality of the supervision that they are receiving or have received, while supervisors have no basis upon which to reflect upon, and where appropriate improve, their performance. It would then seem appropriate that, both for their own sakes and those of their candidates, supervisors should make efforts to evaluate the quality of their supervision.

One possible way of doing this was outlined in Chapter 5, namely the independent completion of questionnaires by candidates and their supervisor(s) followed by a private discussion of their respective responses. This method has been widely used in Australian universities, a number of which have developed dedicated questionnaires for the purpose (see, for example, University of Western Australia 2003). Such an approach would seem to, on the one hand, preserve the privacy of the supervisor–candidate relationship while on the other allowing systematic evaluation.

A further method which has been suggested is to administer exit questionnaires to doctoral graduates. This can overcome the fears of candidates that adverse comment might affect their futures, although there is of course a built-in bias in so far as such questionnaires are not administered to those who drop out or are unsuccessful.

Example

The Biotechnology and Biological Sciences Research Council in the UK has developed an exit questionnaire designed for supervisors to gain feedback from graduates who have successfully completed their doctorates. The questionnaire is:

Exit questionnaire regarding my PhD supervision

Dear ....
Now that you have completed your PhD/MSc training, it would be of considerable help to me personally if you could complete the following assessment of the training that you received and in particular my role as supervisor. Please try to be as objective and honest as possible. Your answers will provide me with some feedback to help me improve my own practice as a supervisor and teacher. They may therefore be of some real help to students who follow in your footsteps. Please score each question on the basis of the supervision that you actually received

0 = Abysmal!
1 = No!
2 = Poor! / room for significant improvement
3 = Acceptable / adequate
4 = Yes!
5 = Brilliant!

If there are any questions you feel unable or uncomfortable answering, or which are not relevant please leave them blank.

Student: ....

Supervisor: ....

Question

1 At the start of your project, were you given a clear idea of what you could expect from your supervisor(s) and what they expected of you as a student (the informal contract)?

2 Were these guidelines broadly adhered to throughout the project?

3 Was the paperwork and bureaucracy associated with your PhD adequately organized by your supervisor (was the organization of your registration, examinations, examiners etc handled smoothly)?

4 Was your supervisor readily available to you if you needed them?

5 Did your supervisor ensure that there was sufficient time (on a regular basis) for discussion and analysis of your work? (Did your supervisor keep up to date with the progress of your work?)

6 Was the time you spent with your supervisor well used and valuable?

7 Does your supervisor keep up to date with the literature and have the scientific expertise required to supervise a PhD project? (Did they suggest a reading list?)

8 Are you happy with your supervisor's current level of ability / training as a teacher and supervisor?

9 Were you provided with practical guidance / written methods / instruction for specific laboratory techniques, particularly in the early stages?

10 Were you given clear guidance in effective experimental design and execution?

11 Were you given clear guidance in record keeping / lab notebooks, data, figures etc?

12 Were you given help in preparing with presentations and talks?

13 If your immediate supervisor was unable to guide you in a particular technique, or subject area, did they recruit other supervisory team members, or were other members available to help and advise you?

14 Was feedback on your laboratory work, written reports (e.g. transfer report, thesis chapters etc) and oral presentations (e.g. seminars, journal clubs etc) provided by your supervisor ?

15 Were you encouraged to present your own project at internal seminars and discuss your work with other staff members and students?

16 Were you encouraged to attend scientific meetings, either in the UK or internationally and, if possible, present your own data?

17 Were you encouraged to attend appropriate training courses, lectures and seminars (encouraged to keep a record of attendance)?

18   Were you given clear guidance on health and safety issues (how to use equipment safely (e.g. centrifuges), handling of dangerous chemicals, handling of virus, etc.).

19   Were you given support by your supervisor socially, or on pastoral issues?

20   Was there a commitment by your supervisor to high scientific standards and good practice?

21   Was there a commitment by your supervisor to high ethical standards?

22   Does your supervisor practise equal opportunities?

23   Does your supervisor comply with Institute harassment policy?

24   A PhD has been described as starting as an assistant and ending up as a colleague. Do you think your supervisor provided appropriate levels of advice, support, and academic freedom at each stage?

Source: http://www.iah.bbsrc.ac.uk/TAPPS/Student-Exit-Questionnaire.htm

As well as the evaluation of supervision by candidates, there are two other ways in which supervisors can evaluate their performance, both of which are widely used for taught programmes.

So, in many institutions, staff regularly observe each other's classes and give (usually) confidential feedback on the strengths and weaknesses of what they have seen. In principle, and given the growth in co-supervision, there is no reason why co-supervisors should not do the same for each other, perhaps using an adapted form of one of the questionnaires for candidates.

Further, of course, there are numerous self-evaluation questionnaires covering the main types of teaching which teachers can fill in and maintain a record of what went well, what did not, and what they would plan to do about any issues next time round. Again it would seem possible, and certainly good practice, for doctoral supervisors to also self-evaluate their supervision.

Of course, the use of all of these means would enable 360-degree evaluation of supervisory performance by candidates, co-supervisors, and self.

Interrogating practice

Does your institution have a questionnaire to assist supervisors and candidates to evaluate the quality of supervision?

(If not) Could you use or adapt a questionnaire from another institution?

Do you think that there would be any benefit in administering exit questionnaires to graduates?

Do you think that it would be useful to gain feedback from co-supervisors?

Do you think that it would be useful to self-evaluate your supervision?

Dissemination

If supervision is to be evaluated, then it follows that where good practice is identified it should be disseminated both within and outside institutions. In the past, however, and probably reflecting their view of doctoral supervision as an essentially private activity, few supervisors seem to have considered that others could learn from them, and hid their light under a bushel.

Example

One of the authors facilitated a workshop on 'Reviewing doctoral supervision' for experienced supervisors in a large arts department in a major UK university. During the workshop, participants were given the opportunity to summarise the key points of their approach to doctoral supervision. At the end of the session, the senior professor present was asked to present his points to the group. He started by saying that he had not thought this through explicitly before, but he thought that there were 12 key features of his approach, which he went through one by one. The practice described was exemplary to the extent that his presentation was greeted with a round of applause. The professor's view was that this was what he had been doing for many years, and he didn't think that any one else would be interested. Subsequently, he was asked to expand upon his points and write what became his department's *Handbook for Doctoral Supervisors*.

If, then, there is good practice, the question arises about how it can be unlocked. One way in which a growing number of institutions have decided to do this is by establishing awards for excellence in doctoral supervision.

Examples

The University of Washington has, since 1999, given the Marsha L. Landolt Distinguished Graduate Mentor Awards to members of faculty who have made outstanding contributions to the education and guidance of graduate students. The award is made at a special ceremony, and is worth $5,000.

Criteria used in evaluating nominees for the award are that the nominee:

- Provides intellectual leadership.
- Respects students' goals and helps students to work towards them.
- Is supportive at a personal as well as a professional level, is a good advocate for students.

- Actively guides students' research and training; clearly articulates expectations and holds students to high standards.
- Actively seeks financial support for students' graduate study and research.
- Actively involves students in teaching or research.
- Actively recruits and encourages applications to the unit's graduate program.
- Is accessible for advice and assistance, whether student is in residence, on leave, is or is not 'one of theirs'.
- Actively involves students in professional conferences.

Source: http://www.grad.washington.edu/mentor/criteria.htm

The University of Sydney is one among many Australian universities with awards for excellence in doctoral supervision. Two awards are made every year by the Vice-Chancellor, each to the value of $5,000. The criteria are:
- Essential
  1 Interest in and enthusiasm for supervising, mentoring, guiding and supporting postgraduate research students, including facilitating student access to resources and equipment.
  2 Ability to integrate students into the research community including, where appropriate, encouraging publication and developing professional links with other postgraduate students.
  3 Accessibility to postgraduate students and effective communication with them.
  4 Capacity to establish clear goals and plans for postgraduate research students and to provide effective feedback on their progress.
  5 Ability to manage the supervisory process to achieve timely and successful completion of the thesis.
  6 Use a repertoire of supervisory strategies to take account of the diverse needs of individual students including assisting students from equity groups to achieve success.
- Desirable
  7 Commitment to assisting research students to achieve their career goals.
  8 Professional and systematic approach to the development of effectiveness as a supervisor, including reflective evaluation and participation in professional development activity.
  9 Scholarship in research training and supervision, including impact of research activities on supervision, research and contributions to the literature on effective supervision, and leadership in developing the skills of other supervisors.

Source: http://www.itl.usyd.edu.au/awards/excellence.htm

Usually, it is a condition of the award that winners publish their Statements of Doctoral Supervision on the institution's Web site so that the good practice can be disseminated to colleagues.

Examples

University of Washington award winners
Tom Daniel, Professor of Zoology seeks to:

> ... provide students with considerable intellectual freedom, encourage them to follow their noses in research, give them pride and ownership of their degrees, and most importantly, develop a partnership with students in research and teaching that fosters independence and leads to a win-win situation where they bring to us incredible new perspectives and ideas. What had seemed like a deep secret held by the best mentors is actually simple: surround yourself with excited and energetic students, enjoy the intellectual challenges they put forward, and celebrate the frontiers they conquer. It is so easy it almost seems like cheating.

Judith Howard, Professor of Sociology gives a list of the things that she tries to attend to:

- I ask the student to think about her/his goals and how best to work toward accomplishing them. I also ask the student to reflect on the department's goals, and when the two seem to be in conflict in some respects, we work together to recognize that conflict and make informed choices and decisions.
- I try to be aware of what students do and do not know, and help them find information/have access to resources with which they might be unfamiliar. Examples: alerting students to career opportunities; helping students to 'network' with other relevant professionals and faculty; instructing in norms about publishing and providing assistance and support at each stage in this process; providing information and assistance in teaching support.
- I try to be clear with my students about what I and the department expect – what are reasonable standards for research, for teaching, for general involvement in the graduate program and profession? It seems important to me to have high standards, but also, crucially, individualized expectations. And equally important, I ask my students to think about what they expect from me, and to communicate those expectations.

- A number of students express difficulties in having regular access to the faculty with whom they work. I try to be as accessible as I can. At the same time, it also seems important to model appropriate principles of accessibility. Being eternally accessible probably isn't healthy for either student or faculty; practicing very difficult or inconsistent access poses real problems for the student.
- In general, I try to model behaviors that students would do well to follow, both in negative as well as in positive situations. In other words, I try to encourage students to persevere in the face of adversity and learn from it. For example, it can be very useful to be reminded that every one who is a successful academic has experienced rejection often. The key is developing skills to learn from those experiences and try again.
- I also try to go beyond the strictly academic. Willingness to engage about nonacademic life, or negotiating personal difficulties within the academy, can be extremely valuable.
- One other thought. The norm in the academy is that a student will have one primary mentor. I encourage my students to develop mentoring relationships with a variety of faculty members; I think this deepens the graduate experience and encourages a habit of collaboration and collegiality.
- I also celebrate the changes that take place in my relationships with my students. What may begin as a fairly formal relationship marked by a considerable degree of hierarchical distance can evolve into a mutually supportive and collaborative relationship of peers and colleagues. Some of my most valuable relationships are with former students of mine who have gone on to careers of their own.

David Notkin, Professor of Computer Science and Engineering, says:

'What is it about designing or evolving software that makes you angry?' That is the question that I ask every graduate student who expresses interest in becoming my advisee.

I ask this question for several reasons. First, getting the student engaged immediately is a critical step in developing the give-and-take relationship that I find best for graduate advising. Second, over time – sometimes a few weeks, but often over many months or even a year or two – the students' answers to this question lead to a dissertation project in which they have genuine personal interest; that is, it becomes a problem that they want to solve, rather than one I want them to solve. Finally, it works: I've been able to recruit first-rate students, they've written terrific dissertations and gone on to successful careers, and it has led to the best research I've been involved in.

Of course, mentoring my graduate students goes far beyond attention to their dissertations *per se*. They need to learn a lot about themselves: What problems attract them? What kinds of solutions are they most able and apt to find? What are their strengths and their weaknesses? How do they improve in their weak areas while simultaneously playing to their strengths? What do they want to do after graduation? And what do they need to learn about the discipline of computer science (and the sub-discipline of software engineering)? What problems, when solved, will fundamentally advance the field? What kind of dissertations will be best received by the kinds of organization that they want to work for after graduation? Who are the key people and what are the key organizations in the field? How do they meet these people and get visibility in these organizations? How does one most effectively convey research to the community? This list is by no means exhaustive, but it captures the kinds of topics I cover with my students during their graduate years.

I've developed a set of techniques over the years to gear students up in these dimensions. Perhaps the most important – beyond individual meetings on a regular basis, of course – is taking students, ideally as a small group, to major conferences. I work with them before the conference to understand their responsibilities (e.g. identifying a set of people in the field they'd like to meet), what talks to go to (and not to go to), how to handle expenses, etc. I try to check in with them fairly frequently during the conference, finding out what cool ideas they've heard, introducing them to key people, getting their insights about the conference, etc. Other than the people they meet, the key to going to a conference is learning that they are plenty smart enough to make critical contributions to the field: although the field is populated with really smart people, the students learn that they can compete successfully in the discipline. This confidence, developed first hand, goes far beyond anything I can provide as an adviser and mentor.

Mentoring graduate students has been and continues to be by far the most rewarding and productive aspect of my years in academia. The introspection I've done about mentoring over the past few years has been valuable to me and, I hope, to my current and future graduate students.

Noel Weiss, Professor of Epidemiology:

My philosophy in mentoring graduate students is nothing other than the Golden Rule: Do unto others as you would have them do unto you. And, if

I were a graduate student once again, how is it that I would like to be 'done unto'? I'd like my mentor to:

- Make clear what is expected of me as a graduate student, while at the same time leaving up to me the specific means of achieving those expectations and the pace at which that happens.
- Be available to answer the many questions that arise in a new endeavor of this sort.
- Offer guidance in identifying a topic for my thesis or dissertation research, a topic that is simultaneously instructive, relevant, and feasible.
- Closely scrutinize work I produce, or ideas I develop, and provide input in a timely, constructive, and kind way.
- Make sure I'll have the skills needed to get off to a good start in my post-UW career (recognizing that I'll expect to be learning progressively throughout the whole of my professional life).
- Help me think through career options, including the ways in which these will bear upon my non-professional goals.
- More broadly, be mindful of the fact that I left many potential roads untraveled so that I might journey down this one, and so do everything possible to make my graduate experience as rewarding and enjoyable as possible.

Source: http://www.grad.washington.edu/envision/project_resources/mentor_award.html#

As well as institutional encouragement for the dissemination of good practice, in recent years there has also been the development of inter-institutional networks for this purpose.

Example

In Australia, academic staff in four universities – Deakin, Melbourne, the Victoria University of Technology, and Monash – have established the Studies in Science and Technology in Society Network (SSTSN). The network is open to both candidates and supervisors, and includes opportunities for the latter to meet between 8 and 12 times each year to discuss issues of mutual concern and to share strategies for successful doctoral supervision. See Gilding *et al.* (2002).

Further, and again in the past few years, there has been a growth in national and international forums in which supervisors, staff involved in supporting supervision, and candidates have been able to give papers or presentations on supervision and gain feedback.

Example

The Higher Education Research and Development Society of Australasia (HERSDA) has, in recent years, organised annual conferences on doctoral supervision which have attracted both national participants and international ones drawn from a wide range of countries. The resulting proceedings are published (see, for example, Goody et al. 2002), and constitute a treasure trove of accounts of good practice and as such a major resource for doctoral supervisors.

Interrogating practice

Do you look for opportunities to disseminate your practice and benefit from that of others?

Does your institution have any mechanisms for recognising good practice and disseminating it?

Are there any inter-institutional networks that you could join to share good practice in doctoral supervision?

What national and international opportunities are available for you to share practice?

Conclusions

Part of being an effective supervisor is to reflect upon, and where appropriate improve, practice. In the past, this may have been implicit, but in recent years it has become much more explicit with, as has been seen, the development of questionnaires designed to facilitate discussions between supervisors and candidates and exit questionnaires for doctoral graduates. Such questionnaires may, it has been suggested, be developed to allow for other forms of evaluation, including peer evaluation by co-supervisors and self-evaluation.

Such evaluation, of course, leads to the identification of good practice but, until recently, there were relatively few outlets for it to be disseminated. But now there is a growing number of opportunities to showcase such practice in the context of their institutions, for which award schemes can be a powerful driver, inter-institutional networks and national and international conferences. These, for the first time, give supervisors the chance to receive recognition for their good practice, and to learn from that of others.

At the moment, these developments are still in their infancy, but in the future they offer the potential for a global community of scholarship in relation to doctoral supervision which will benefit both supervisors and candidates alike.

Conclusions

Until comparatively recently, the primary requirement to supervise the research of doctoral candidates was to be a researcher. The belief that underpinned this was that, if one could do research, then by definition one could supervise others to do the same, and the corollary was that supervision was regarded simply as an adjunct of research.

In reality, it is doubtful as to whether being a researcher was ever enough in itself to make for effective supervision, as shown by the evidence uncovered in the 1980s of low completion rates and long completion times of doctoral studies at a time when the candidate population was small and relatively homogenous. But if it ever was, it has certainly become wholly inadequate in view of the changes that have taken place in the last two decades or so and have transformed the doctorate itself, the candidate population, and expectations and requirements of supervisors.

The list of expectations and requirements is a long one. Supervisors have: to be aware of what their institutions expect of them and of candidates and of the sources of support available to both; to be aware of the disciplinary context of doctoral studies, or where appropriate the inter-disciplinary one; to be able to play a role in recruiting applicants for doctoral programmes inside and increasingly outside their institutions; to be able to select candidates on the basis of matching their aptitudes and skills with research projects, resources, and their own expertise as supervisors; to form and maintain professional relationships with candidates; to deploy a repertoire of supervisory styles; to form and maintain professional relationships with co-supervisors; where appropriate, to assist candidates to select topics for research; to help them to develop a research proposal; to give academic guidance as the research develops; to encourage candidates to write often and early; to help them keep the project on track and monitor their progress; to offer personal support and support the development of academic skills, including those relating to networking, publishing, and teaching and learning, and, in many cases, employment-related ones as well; to respond to diversity among the candidate population, domestic and international; to assist candidates with the process of creating a thesis; to advise them on submission and, where appropriate, certify that the thesis is worthy of defence; to help to prepare candidates for examination; in many systems, to act as examiners; and finally to evaluate their performance as supervisors and, where appropriate, disseminate their good practice.

In view of these expectations and requirements, it is no longer realistic to simply regard doctoral supervision as an adjunct of doing research, that is, it has become an area of professional practice in its own right. As such it is one that should take its place alongside personal research, teaching, and administration as the fourth leg of the stool which defines the professional practice of academics.

While full acknowledgement of doctoral supervision as an area of professional practice in its own right is far from universal, in recent years there have been encouraging signs of its emergence, particularly in Australia (from which many of the examples of good practice in this book have been drawn). These include variously: the development of institutional codes of practice for doctoral supervision; the development by academic disciplines of codes for doctorates; the requirement by institutions that prospective supervisors undertake extensive initial professional development in the roles and responsibilities prior to becoming a supervisor; the provision of support for supervisors during their first supervisions in the form of mentors; opportunities or, in a few cases, requirements that experienced supervisors undertake regular continuing professional development; the introduction of time allowances for supervision into workload planning; the use of learning agreements to govern the professional relationship between supervisors and candidates; the use of protocols to regulate co-supervision; the formalisation of the role of monitoring candidates' progress; the expectation that supervisors will evaluate the quality of their supervision; the establishment in a number of institutions of awards for excellence in doctoral supervision; and the growth of opportunities for supervisors to disseminate and to learn from good practice within institutions, between institutions, and at national and international conferences.

If, then, doctoral supervision is in the process of becoming an area of professional practice in its own right, our hope is that the present book will have enabled readers to reflect upon and, where appropriate, consider how to go about improving, their practice. We would be interested to learn what readers made of the book itself and to hear of good practice, whether stimulated by the book or otherwise. For this purpose we have established a web-site at www.freewebs.com/ handbook_for_doctoral_supervisors to which readers are cordially invited to send comments and contributions.

As a final word, we should say that, in writing the book, we have concentrated on the things that supervisors need or are expected to do in order to be effective, which is a fit and proper purpose for a handbook. But we are conscious that, in the process, we have said little about the pleasures of supervision. It is, in many ways, one of the most rewarding parts of academic life to take on a rookie candidate and, over the course of three or four years, work with them as they grow into independent researchers and see them make an original contribution to knowledge and understanding in their subjects. While the tangible reward rightly goes to the candidate who gains the degree and the coveted title of 'Dr', there is an intangible reward of satisfaction to the supervisor who has overseen the process. As a very experienced supervisor once said to one of the authors, 'the best thing is doing path-breaking research in my own right, but the next best is supervising a doctoral candidate to do the same'.

References

Allen, M., Smyth, E. and Walhstrom, M. (2002) Responding to the field and to the academy: Ontario's evolving PhD. *Higher Education Research and Development*, 21(2): 203–14.

Appel, L. and Dahlgren, L. (2003) Swedish doctoral students' experiences on their journey towards a PhD: obstacles and opportunities inside and outside the academic building. *Scandinavian Journal of Educational Research*, 47(1): 89–110.

Aspland, T. (1999) 'You learn round and I learn square': Mei's story. In Y. Ryan and O. Zuber-Skerritt (eds) *Supervising Postgraduates from Non-English Speaking Backgrounds*. Buckingham: Society for Research into Higher Education and Open University Press.

Aspland, T. (2002) Framing graduate supervision and examination in the professional doctorate at QUT. In A. Goody, J. Herrington and M. Northcote (eds) *Proceedings of the 2002 Annual International Conference of the Higher Education Research and Development Society of Australasia*. Perth: Higher Education Research and Development Society of Australasia.

Association of American Universities. Committee on Graduate Education. *Report and Recommendations*. October 1998. Available online at http://www.aau.edu/reports/GradEdRpt.html (accessed 15 June 2004).

Association of Business Schools (1997) *Guidelines for the Doctorate of Business Administration (DBA) Degree*. London: Association of Business Schools.

Atkins, D. (1996) Supervision: a student perspective. Centre for Educational Development and Academic Methods and Graduate School, Australian National University. Available online at http://eprints.anu.edu.au/archive/00001163/ (accessed 14 June 2004).

Austin, A. (2002) Preparing the next generation of faculty: graduate school as socialisation to the academic career. *The Journal of Higher Education*, 73(1): 94–122.

Baldacchino, G. (1995) Reflections on the status of a doctoral defence. *Journal of Graduate Education*, 1(1): 71–6.

Baty, P. (2003) Surrey ordered to compensate PhD student. *Times Higher Educational Supplement*, 5 December.

BBSRC (Biotechnology and Biological Sciences Research Council) (2000) *Outcomes and Underlying Values for the BBSRC Training and Accreditation Programme for Postgraduate Supervisors*. Biotechnology and Biological Sciences Research Council. Available online at http://www.iah.bbsrc.ac.uk/TAPPS/index.html (accessed 10 May 2004).

Becher, T., Henkel, M. and Kogan, M. (1994) *Graduate Education in Britain*. London: Jessica Kingsley.

Blaume, S. and Amsterdamsaka, O. (1987) *Postgraduate Education in the 1980s*. Paris: Organisation for Economic Co-operation and Development.

Blaxter, L., Hughes, C. and Tight, M. (1996) *How to Research*. Buckingham: Open University Press.

Bonnet, A. (2001) *How to Argue*. London: Prentice-Hall.

Bourner, T., Bowden, R. and Laing, S. (1999) A national profile of research degree awards: innovation, clarity and coherence. *Higher Education Quarterly*, 53(3): 264–80.

Bourner, T., Bowden, R. and Laing, S. (2001) Professional doctorates in England. *Studies in Higher Education*, 26(1): 65–83.

Bourner, T., Bowden R. and Laing, S. (2002) Professional Doctorates in England and Australia: not a world of difference. *Higher Education Review*, 35(1): 3–23.

Bowen, W.G. and Rudenstein, N.L. (1992) *In Pursuit of the PhD*. Princeton, NJ: Princeton University Press.

Boxer, M. J. (1998) Remapping the university: the promise of the women's studies PhD. *Feminist Studies*, 24(2): 387–402.

Brew, A. and Pesata, T. (2004) Changing postgraduate supervision practice: a programme to encourage learning through reflection and feedback. *Innovations in Education and Teaching International*, 41(1): 5–22.

British Psychological Society and the Universities and Colleges Staff Development Agency (1996) *Guidelines for the Assessment of the PhD in Psychology and Related Disciplines*. Sheffield: Universities and Colleges Staff Development Agency.

Brown, G. and Atkins, M. (1988) *Effective Teaching in Higher Education*. London: Methuen.

Bruce, C. and Braneld, G. (1999) Encouraging student directed research and critical thinking. In Y. Ryan and O. Zuber-Skerritt (eds) *Supervising Postgraduates from Non-English Speaking Backgrounds*. Buckingham: Society for Research into Higher Education and Open University Press.

Burnham, P. (1997) Surviving the Viva. In P. Burnham (ed.) *Surviving the Research Process in Politics*. London: Pinter.

Cadman, K. (2000) 'Voices in the Air': evaluations of the learning experiences of international postgraduates and their supervisors. *Teaching in Higher Education*, 5(5): 475–91.

Cebrian, S. (2001) Spanish Science Haemorrhages Talent, *Next Wave*. Science magazine and the American Association for the Advancement of Science. 20 September. Available online at http://nextwave.sciencemag.org/cgi/content/full/2001/09/20/1 (accessed 18 March 2003).

Chapman, H. (2002) A tale of graduate supervision and examination in the professional doctorate: a graduate spins her yarn. In A. Goody, J. Herrington and M. Northcote (eds) *Proceedings of the 2002 Annual International Conference of the Higher Education Research and Development Society of Australasia*. Perth: Higher Education Research and Development Society of Australasia.

City University of London. *Research Studies Handbook*. Available online at http://www.city.ac.uk/researchstudies/roles.htm#externally-registered (accessed 14 June 2004).

Clark, B. (1993) *The Research Foundations of Postgraduate Education: Germany, Britain, France, the United States and Japan*. Berkeley: University of California Press.

Clark, B. (1997) The fragmentation of research, teaching and study: university and society. In M. Trow and T. Nyborn (eds) *University and Society*. London: Jessica Kingsley.

Clegg, S. (1997) A case study of accredited training for research awards supervisors through reflective practice. *Higher Education*, 34(4): 483–98.

Colebatch, H. (2002) Through a glass darkly: policy development on higher degree completions in Australia. *Journal of Higher Education Policy and Management*, 24(1): 27–35.

Connelly, J. (2000) *The Sovietization of East German, Czech, and Polish Higher Education 1945–56*. Chapel Hill and London: University of North Carolina Press.

Conrad, L. (1994) Gender and postgraduate supervision. In O. Zuber-Skerritt and Y. Ryan (eds) *Quality in Postgraduate Education*. London: Kogan Page.

Conseil Scientifique de l'Université (1988) *L'habilitation à diriger des recherches*. Available online at: http://guilde.jeunes-chercheurs.org/Textes/Habilit/A881123.html (accessed 18 June 2003).

Council of Graduate Schools (1990) *Research Student and Supervisor: An Approach to Good Practice*, Washington, DC: Council of Graduate Schools. Available online at http://www.cgsnet.org/PublicationsPolicyRes/index.htm#directory (accessed 18 June 2003).

Council of Graduate Schools (1998) *Distance Graduate Education: Opportunities and Challenges for the 21st Century: A Policy Statement*. Washington, DC: Council of Graduate Schools. Available online at http://www.cgsnet.org/pdf/DistanceGraduate Education.pdf (accessed 13 March 2003).

Cryer, P. (2000) *The Research Student's Guide to Success*. Buckingham: Open University Press.

Cryer, P. (2004) Training research supervisors: suggestions from Pat Cryer. Available online at http://www.cryer.freeeserve.co.uk/supervisors.htm (accessed 13 September 2004).

Cryer, P. and Okorocha, E. (1999) Avoiding potential pitfalls in the supervision of NESB students. In Y. Ryan and O. Zuber-Skerritt (eds) *Supervising Postgraduates from Non-English Speaking Backgrounds*. Buckingham: Society for Research into Higher Education and Open University Press.

Cullen, D., Pearson, M., Saha, L. and Spear, R. (1994) *Establishing Effective PhD Supervision*. Canberra: Department for Employment, Education and Training.

Dedrick, R. and Watson, F. (2002) Mentoring needs of female, minority and international graduate students: a content analysis of academic research guides and related print material. *Mentoring and Tutoring*, 10(3): 275–89.

Deem, R. and Brehonm, K. (2000) Doctoral students' access to research cultures; are some more unequal than others? *Studies in Higher Education*, 25(2): 149–65.

Delamont, S., Atkinson, P. and Parry, O. (1997) *Supervising the PhD: A Guide to Success*. Buckingham: Open University Press.

Delamont, S., Atkinson, P. and Parry, O. (2000) *The Doctoral Experience: Success and Failure in Graduate School*. London: Falmer Press.

Department of Education, Training and Youth Affairs (1999) *Knowledge and Innovation: A Policy Statement on Research and Research Training*. Canberra: Department of Education Training and Youth Affairs.

Deutsche Forschungsgemeinshaft (2000) *Graduiertenkollegs*. Bonn: Deutsche Forschungsgemeinschaft.

Dinham, S. and Scott, C. (2001) The experience of disseminating the results of doctoral research. *Journal of Further and Higher Education*, 25(1): 45–55.

Dunleavy, P. (2003) *Authoring a PhD*. Basingstoke: Palgrave Macmillan.

Durling, D. (2002) Discourses on research and the PhD in design. *Quality Assurance in Higher Education*, 10(2): 79–85.

Economic and Social Research Council (2001) *Postgraduate Training Guidelines*. Available online at http://www.esrc.ac.uk/esrccontent/postgradfunding/2000_Guidelines.asp (accessed 21 May 2002).

Evans, T. (2002) Part-time research students: are they producing knowledge where it counts? *Higher Education Research and Development*, 21(2): 155–65.

Eurodoc (2003) *Document on PhD Studies in 14 European Countries*. Available online at www.eurodoc.net/docs/eurodoc03book_country.pdf (accessed 23 May 2004).

Fitzpatrick, J., Secrist, J. and Wright, D. (1998) *Secrets for a Successful Dissertation*. London: Sage.

Flinders University (2002) *Expectations in Research Supervision*. Available online at http://www.flinders.edu.au/teach/research/postgrad/Expectations.pdf (accessed 20 March 2002).

Frame, I. and Allen, L. (2002) A flexible approach to PhD research training. *Quality Assurance in Education*, 12(2): 98–103.

Friedman, S.S. (1998) (Inter)disciplinarity and the question of the women's studies PhD. *Feminist Studies*, 24(2): 301–25.

Frischer, J. and Larsson, K. (2000) Laissez-faire in research education: an inquiry into a Swedish doctoral programme. *Higher Education Policy*, 13(2): 132–55.

Fry, H., Ketteridge, S. and Marshall, S. (1999) *A Handbook for Teaching and Learning in Higher Education*. London: Kogan Page.

Fry, H., Ketteridge, S. and Marshall, S. (2001) *The Effective Academic: A Handbook for Enhanced Academic Practice*. London: Kogan Page.

Galanaki, E. (2002) Greek doctoral students: facing an uncertain future. *Next Wave*. Science magazine and the American Association for the Advancement of Science. 5 March. Available online at http://nextwave.sciencemag.org/cgi/content/full/2002/03/05/7 (accessed 13 March 2003).

Gatfield, T. and Alpert, F. (2002) The supervisory management styles model. In A. Goody, J. Herrington and M. Northcote (eds) *Proceedings of the 2002 Annual International Conference of the Higher Education Research and Development Society of Australasia*. Perth: Higher Education Research and Development Society of Australasia.

Geiger, R. (1997) Doctoral education: the short-term crisis vs. the long-term challenge. *The Review of Higher Education*, 20(3): 239–51.

Genoni, P. and Partridge, J. (2000) Personal research information management: information literacy and the research student. In C. Bruce and P. Candy (eds) *Information Literacy Around the World*. New South Wales: Centre for Information Studies, Charles Sturt University.

Georges, A. (1996) Address to the University of Canberra Postgraduate Students Association, University of Canberra. 15 July 1996. Available online at http://aerg. canberra.edu.au/pub/aerg/eduthes4.htm (accessed 17th May 2004).

Germano, G. (2001) Italy does not value its PhDs. *Next Wave*. Science magazine and the American Association for the Advancement of Science. 6 November. Available online at http://nextwave.sciencemag.org/cgi/content/full/2001/11/06/2 (accessed 18 March 2003).

Gilding, T., Tatnall, A., Arnold, M. and Johanson, G.(2002) Improving the quality of the PhD community: SSTN, an inter-university support network. In A. Goody, J. Herrington and M. Northcote (eds) *Proceedings of the 2002 Annual International Conference of the Higher Education Research and Development Society of Australasia (HERSDA)*. Perth: Higher Education Research and Development Society of Australasia.

Golde, C. (2000) 'Should I stay or should I go?' student descriptions of the doctoral attrition process. *The Review of Higher Education*, 23(2): 199–227.

Goodstein, L. (2003) *The Challenge of Recruiting the Best*. The Graduate School, Penn State University. Available online at http://www.gradsch.psu.edu/gradinit/recruiting. html (accessed 15 September 2003).

Goody, A. and de Vries, J. (2002) Straight talk about queer issues. In A. Goody, J. Herrington and M. Northcote (eds) *Proceedings of the 2002 Annual International Conference of the Higher Education Research and Development Society of Australasia*. Perth: Higher Education Research and Development Society of Australasia.

Goody, A., Herrington, J. Northcote, M. (2002) (eds) *Proceedings of the 2002 Annual International Conference of the Higher Education Research and Development Society of Australasia*. Perth: Higher Education Research and Development Society of Australasia.

Graham, A. and Grant, B. (1997) *Managing More Postgraduate Research Students*. Oxford: Oxford Centre for Staff Development.

Grant, B. and Graham, A. (1994) Guidelines for discussion: a tool for managing postgraduate supervision. In O. Zuber-Skerritt and Y. Ryan (eds) *Quality in Postgraduate Education*. London: Kogan Page.

Green, P. (2002) Coping and completing: the challenge of the professional doctorate in the knowledge economy. In A. Goody, J. Herrington and M. Northcote (eds) *Proceedings of the 2002 Annual International Conference of the Higher Education Research and Development Society of Australasia*. Perth: Higher Education Research and Development Society of Australasia.

Greenfield, T. (2002) (ed.) *Research Methods for Postgraduates*, 2nd edn, London: Arnold.

Gurr, G. (2001) Negotiating the 'Rackety Bridge': a dynamic model for aligning supervisory style with research student development. *Higher Education Research and Development*, 20(1): 81–92.

Hagoel, L. and Kalekin-Fishman, D. (2002) Crossing borders: towards a trans-disciplinary scientific identity. *Studies in Higher Education*, 27(3): 297–9.

Harman, K. (2002) The research training experiences of control students linked to Australian Cooperative Research Centres. *Higher Education*, 44: 469–92.

Hartley, J. and Jory, S. (2000) Lifting the veil on the viva: the experiences of psychology PhD candidates in the UK. *Psychology Teaching Review*, 9(2): 76–90.

Hockey, J. (1997) A complex craft: UK PhD Supervision in the social sciences. *Research in Post-Compulsory Education*, 2(1): 45–70.

Hoddell, S., Street, D. and Wildblood, H. (2001) Doctorates : converging or diverging patterns of provision. *Quality Assurance in Education*, 10(2): 61–70.

Humphrey, F. and McCarthy, P. (1999) Recognising difference: providing for postgraduate students. *Studies in Higher Education*, 24, 371–86.

Huisman, J., de Weert, E. and Bartelse, J. (2002) Academic careers from a European perspective: the declining desirability of the faculty position. *The Journal of Higher Education*, 73(1): 141–60.

Jablonski, A. (2001) Doctoral studies as professional development of educators in the United States. *European Journal of Teacher Education*, 24(2): 215–21.

Jackson, C. and Tinkler, P. (2001) Back to basics: a consideration of the purposes of the PhD viva. *Assessment and Evaluation in Higher Education*, 26(4): 355–66.

Johnson, H. (2001) The PhD student as an adult learner: using reflective practice to find and speak in her own voice. *Reflective Practice*, 2(1): 51–63.

Johnson, L., Alison, L. and Green, B. (2000) The PhD and the autonomous self; gender, rationality and postgraduate pedagogy. *Studies in Higher Education*, 25:135–47.

Joint Funding Councils (2002) *Good Practice and Threshold Standards for Postgraduate Research Degree Programmes*. Bristol: Joint Funding Councils.

Joint Funding Councils (2003) *Improving Standards in Postgraduate Research Degree Programmes*. Bristol: Joint Funding Councils.

Joint Research Councils and Arts and Humanities Research Board (2001) *Skills Training Requirements for Research Students: Joint Statement by the Research Councils and Arts and Humanities Research Board.* Swindon: Joint Research Councils and Arts and Humanities Research Board. Available online at http://www.bbsrc.ac.uk/funding/training/skill_train_req.pdf (accessed 17 May 2004).

Junius, D.J. and Gumport P.J. (2002) Graduate student unionisation: catalysts and consequences. *The Review of Higher Education,* 26(2): 187–216.

Kam, B.H. (1997) Style and quality in research supervision. *Higher Education,* 34(1): 81–103.

Kember, D., Lee, K. and Li, N. (2001) Cultivating a sense of belonging in part-time students. *International Journal of Lifelong Education,* 20(4): 326–41.

Kendall, G. (2002) The crisis in doctoral education: a sociological diagnosis. *Higher Education Research and Development,* 21(2): 131–41.

Kiley, M. (2000) Providing timely and appropriate support for international students. In G. Wisker (ed.) *Good Practice Working with International Students.* Birmingham: Staff and Educational Development Association.

Kiley, M. and Austin, A. (2000) Australian postgraduate students' perspectives, preferences and mobility. *Higher Education Research and Development,* 19(1): 75–88.

Knight, N. (1999) Responsibilities and limits in the supervision of NESB research students in the social sciences and humanities. In Y. Ryan and O. Zuber-Skerritt (eds) *Supervising Postgraduates from Non-English Speaking Backgrounds.* Buckingham: Society for Research into Higher Education and Open University Press.

LaPidus, J. (1997) *Doctoral Education: Preparing for the Future.* Washington, DC: Council of Graduate Schools. Available online at http://www.cgsnet.org/pdf/doctoraled preparing.pdf (accessed 13 March 2003).

Leonard, D. (2000) Transforming doctoral studies: competencies and artistry. *Higher Education in Europe,* XXV(2): 181–92.

Leonard, D. (2001) *A Woman's Guide to Doctoral Studies.* Buckingham: Open University Press.

Loan-Clarke, J. and Preston, D. (2002) Tensions and benefits in collaborative research involving a university and another organisation. *Studies in Higher Education,* 27(2): 170–85.

Macauley, P. (2000) Pedagogic continuity in doctoral supervision: passing on, or passing by, of information skills. In M. Kiley and G. Mullins (eds) *Quality in Postgraduate Research: Making Ends Meet.* Adelaide: Advisory Centre for University Education, the University of Adelaide.

Malfoy, J. and Webb, C. (2000) Congruent and incongruent views of postgraduate supervision. In M. Kiley and G. Mullins (eds) *Quality in Postgraduate Research: Making Ends Meet.* Adelaide: Advisory Centre for University Education, the University of Adelaide.

Marsh, H., Rowe, K. and Marin. A. (2002) PhD students' evaluations of research supervision. *The Journal of Higher Education,* 73(3): 313–48.

Martin, B. (1992) Scientific fraud and the power structure of science. *Prometheus*, 10(1): 83–98.

Massingham, K.R. (1984) Pitfalls along the thesis approach to a higher degree. *The Australian*, 25 July: 15.

May, V. (2002) Disciplinary desires and undisciplined daughters: negotiating the politics of a women's studies doctoral education. *National Women's Studies Association Journal*, 14(1): 134–59.

McAlpine, L. and Weiss, J. (2000) Mostly true confessions: joint meaning making about the thesis journey. *Canadian Journal of Higher Education*, XXX(1): 1–26.

McPhail, J. and Erwee, R. (2000) Developing professional relationships between supervisors and doctoral candidates. *Australian Journal of Management and Organisational Behaviour*, 3(1): 76–99.

McWilliam, E. and James, R. (2002) Doctoral education in a knowledge economy. *Higher Education Research and Development*, 21(2): 117.

McWilliam, E., Singh, P. and Taylor, P. (2002) Doctoral education, danger and risk management. *Higher Education Research and Development*, 21(2): 119–29.

Monash University Research Graduate School (2004) *Supervisor Training Programme*. Available online at http://www.monash.edu.au/phdschol/forms/academic/trainmod. rtf (accessed 16 June 2004).

Morgan, W. and Ryan, M. (2003) Rendering an account: an open state archive in postgraduate supervision. *Higher Education Research and Development*, 22(1): 77–90.

Morley, L., Leonard, D. and David, M. (2002) Variations in vivas; quality and equality in British PhD assessments. *Studies in Higher Education*, 37(3): 263–73.

Morton, M. and Thornley, G. (2001) Experiences of doctoral students in mathematics in New Zealand. *Assessment and Evaluation in Higher Education*, 26(2): 113–26.

Moses, I. (1992) *Supervising Postgraduates*. Cambeltown: Higher Education Research and Development Society of Australasia.

Mullins, G. and Kiley, M. (2002) It's a PhD, not a Nobel Prize: how experienced examiners assess research degrees. *Studies in Higher Education*, 27(4): 369–86.

Murray, R. (1997) *The Viva*. Glasgow: Centre for Academic Practice, University of Strathclyde.

Murray, R. (2002) *How to Write a Thesis*. Buckingham: Open University Press.

Neumann, R. (2002) Diversity, doctoral education and policy. *Higher Education Research and Development*, 21(2): 168–78.

Neumann, R. and Guthrie, J. (2000) Quality enhancement in doctoral education: a case study of MGSM. In M. Kiley and G. Mullins (eds) *Quality in Postgraduate Research: Making Ends Meet*. Adelaide: Advisory Centre for University Education, University of Adelaide.

Noble, K.A. (1994) *Changing Doctoral Degrees*. Buckingham: The Society for Research into Higher Education and the Open University Press.

Nyquist, J.D. and Woodford, B.J. (2000) *Re-envisioning the PhD: What Concerns Do We Have?* Washington, DC: University of Washington.

Oden, B. (1997) Research training and the state: politics and university research in Sweden. In M.Trow and T. Nyborn (eds) *University and Society*. London: Jessica Kingsley.

OECD (Organisation for Economic Co-operation and Development) (1995) *Research Training: Present and Future*. Paris: Organisation for Economic Co-operation and Development.

OECD (Organisation for Economic Co-operation and Development) (1998) *University Research in Transition*. Paris: Organisation for Economic Co-operation and Development.

Office of Science and Technology (1993) *Realising Our Potential*. London: HMSO.

Okorocha, E. (2000) *Supervising International Research Students*. London: Society for Research into Higher Education.

Oliver, M (2003) Oxford don rejects student because he is from Israel. *Guardian*, 30 September. Available online at http://www.guardian.co.uk/uk-news/story/0,,987733,00.html.

Partington, J., Brown, G. and Gordon, G. (1993) *Handbook for External Examiners in Higher Education*. Sheffield: UK Universities and Colleges Staff Development Agency.

Pearson, M. and Brew, A. (2002) Research training and supervision development, *Studies in Higher Education*, 27(2): 138–43.

Peters, R. (1997) *Getting What You Came For: A Smart Student's Guide to Earning a Masters or a PhD*. New York: Noonday Publishing.

Phillips, D. (1994) *The Research Mission and Research Manpower: Universities in the 21st Century*. London: National Commission on Education and Council for Industry and HE.

Phillips, E. (1994) The quality of the PhD. In R. Burgess (ed.) *Postgraduate Education and Training in the Social Sciences*. London: Jessica Kingsley.

Phillips, E. and Pugh, D. (2000) *How to Get a PhD*. 2nd edn. Buckingham: Open University Press.

Powell, S. and McCauley, C. (2002) Research degree examining: common principles and divergent practices. *Quality Assurance in Education*, 12(2): 104–15.

Pruitt-Logan, A.S., Gaff, J.G. and Jentoft, J.E. (2002) *Preparing Future Faculty in the Sciences and Mathematics: A Guide for Change*. Council of Graduate Schools and the Association of American Colleges and Universities. Available online at http://www.preparing-faculty.org/PFFWeb.PFF3Manual.htm (accessed 13 March 2003).

Quality Assurance Agency for Higher Education (1999) *Code of Practice for the Assurance of Academic Quality and Standards in Higher Education: Postgraduate Research Programmes*. Gloucester: Quality Assurance Agency for Higher Education.

Quality Assurance Agency for Higher Education (2001) *Framework for Higher Education Qualifications in England, Wales and Northern Ireland.* Gloucester: Quality Assurance Agency for Higher Education.

Radford, J. (2001) Doctor of what? *Teaching in Higher Education,* 6(4): 527–29.

Repak, N. (2004) *Professor–Grad Relationships: Maximising the Mentoring Potential.* Available online at http://www.gradresources.org/articles/prof_grad.shtml (accessed 18 May 2004).

Rhoades, G. and Rhoads, R. (2002) The public discourse of US graduate employee unions: social movement identities, ideologies and strategies. *The Review of Higher Education,* 26(2): 163–86.

Rowland, S. (2003) Fuzzy skills agenda just dumbs down our PhDs. *Times Higher Education Supplement,* 17 January: 14.

Royal Economic Society (1992) *Code of Practice for the Doctorate in Economics.* London: Royal Economic Society.

Royal Society of Chemistry (1995) *The Chemistry PhD: Enhancement of its Quality.* London: Royal Society of Chemistry.

Royal Society of Chemistry (2002) *Postgraduate Skills Record.* London: Department for Education and Employment. Available online at http://www.rsc.org/lap/educatio/pgskills.htm (accessed 13 September 2004).

Rudd, E. (1975) *The Highest Education: A Study of Graduate Education in Britain.* London: Routledge and Kegan Paul.

Rudd, E. (1985) *A New Look at Postgraduate Failure.* London: Society for Research into Higher Education and National Foundation for Educational Research. London: Nelson.

Ryan, J. (2000) *A Guide to Teaching International Students.* Oxford: Oxford Centre for Staff and Learning Development.

Sheridan, E. (2002) How to make the most of postgraduate open days. *The Guardian,* 26 March. Available online at http://education.guardian.co.uk/specialreports/postgrad/story/0,,674376,00.html.

Simpson, R. (1983) *How the PhD Came to Britain.* Guildford: Society for Research into Higher Education.

Smeby, J.-C. (2000) Disciplinary differences in Norwegian graduate education. *Studies in Higher Education,* 25(1): 54–67.

Strauss, P. and Walton, J. (2002) The language of the thesis: difficulties and expectations of second language students and their supervisors. In A. Goody, J. Herrington and M. Northcote (eds) *Proceedings of the 2002 Annual International Conference of the Higher Education Research and Development Society of Australasia.* Perth: Higher Education Research and Development Society of Australasia.

Syverson, P. (1996) Data sources: the new American graduate student: challenge or opportunity? *The Communicator,* XX1X(8): 7–11. Available online at http://www. cgsnet.org/pdf/cctr610.pdf (accessed 13th March 2003).

Syverson, P. (1997) *It's Not Just Employment/Unemployment Any More: Realities of PhD Labor Market Lead to More Complex Measures of Postgraduation Employment.*

Available online at http://www.cgsnet.org/vcr/cctr704.htm (accessed 12 March 2003).

Tan, R. and Meijer, M.-M. (2001) From Dutch pyramid into Babel's Tower? *Next Wave*. Science Magazine and the American Association for the Advancement of Science. 23 October. Available online at http://nextwave.sciencemag.org/cgi/content/full/2001/10/23/4 (accessed 18 March 2003).

Taylor, S. (2002) Managing postgraduate research degrees. In H. Fry, S. Ketteridge and S. Marshall (eds) *The Effective Academic: A Handbook for Enhanced Academic Practice*. London: Kogan Page.

Tinkler, P. and Jackson,C. (2000) Examining the doctorate: institutional policy and the PhD examination process in Britain. *Studies in Higher Education*, 25(2): 167–80.

Torrance, M. and Thomas, G. (1994) The development of writing skills in doctoral research students. In R. Burgess (ed.) *Postgraduate Education and Training in the Social Sciences*. London: Jessica Kingsley.

Trafford, V.N. (2003) Questions in doctoral vivas: views from the inside. *Quality Assurance in Education*, 11(2): 114–22.

UK Council for Graduate Education (2001) *Research Training in the Creative and Performing Arts and Design*. Dudley: UK Council for Graduate Education.

UK Council for Graduate Education (2002) *Professional Doctorates*. Dudley: UK Council for Graduate Education.

University of Bath (2002) *Code of Practice for Research Degree Students, their Supervisors and Directors of Postgraduate Studies*. Available online at http://www.bath.ac.uk/postgrads/pg-ombudsman.html (accessed 24 June 2003).

University of Birmingham. *Supervision Record*. Available online at http://medweb5.bham.ac.uk/graduateschool/progressreview?o=0 (accessed 10 September 2004).

University of Cambridge Computing Laboratory. *Advice to Research Students*. Available online at http://www.cl.cam.ac.uk/ (accessed 18 May 2004).

University of Essex: Institute for Social and Economic Research (2004) *Postgraduate Research Opportunities*. Available online at http://www.irc.essex.ac.uk/opportunities/postgraduate_opportunities/index.php (accessed 17 June 2004).

University of Leicester (2000) *Code of Practice for the Employment of Part-Time Teaching Assistants*. Available online at http://www.le.ac.uk/personnel/docs/codeofpractice teachingassistants.htm (accessed 9 December 2003).

University of South Australia. *A Checklist for Discussions with Research Degree Candidates*. Available online at http://www.unisanet.unisa.edu.ac/learningconnection/resed/resources/check2.doc (accessed 15 March 2003).

University of South Australia (2003) *Code of Good Practice: Key Responsibilities in Research Degree Management*. Available online at http://www.unisa.edu.au/policies/codes/goodprac/keyresp.asp (accessed 15th March 2003).

University of Sydney (2004) *Vice Chancellor's Awards for Excellence in Research Degree Supervision*. Available online at http://www.itl.usyd.edu.au/awards/excellence.htm (accessed 28 May 2004).

University of Washington (2003) *Marsha L. Landolt Distinguished Graduate Mentor Awards*. Available online at http://www.grad.washington.edu/mentor/criteria.htm (accessed 28 May 2004).

University of Western Australia (2003) *Student Perceptions of Research Supervision*. Centre for the Advancement of Teaching and Learning. Available online at http://www.catl. osds.uwa.edu.au/etu/spors/instructions#TopOfPage (accessed 25 May 2004).

US Department of Education (2003) *Graduate Assistance in Areas of National Need*. Available online at http://www.ed.gov/legislation/FedRegister/announcements/2002–4/100102b.html (accessed 14 June 2004).

Usher, R. (2002) A diversity of doctorates: fitness for the knowledge economy? *Higher Education Research and Development*, 21(2): 143–53.

Voison-Demery, F. (2001) French PhDs need luck as well as talent. *Next Wave*. Science magazine and the American Association for the Advancement of Science. 11 December. Available online at http://nextwave.sciencemag.org/cgi/content/full/2001/12/11/1 (accessed 18 March 2003).

Wakeford, J. (2001) Nowhere to turn. *The Guardian*, 25 September: 3.

Welsh, J. (1979) *The First Year of Postgraduate Research Study*. Guildford: Society for Research into Higher Education.

Williams, B. (2000) Australian universities 1939–1999: how different now? *Higher Education Quarterly*, 54(2): 147–65.

Wilson, K. (2002) Quality assurance issues for a PhD by published work: a case study. *Quality Assurance in Education*, 10(2): 71–78.

Winfield, G. (1987) *The Social Science PhD: The ESRC Enquiry into Submission Rates*. London: Economic and Social Research Council.

Winter, R., Griffiths, M. and Green, K. (2000) The 'academic' qualities of practice: what are the criteria for a practice-based PhD? *Studies in Higher Education*, 25(1): 25–37.

Wisker, G. (ed.) (2000) *Good Practice Working with International Students*. Birmingham: Staff and Educational Developers Association.

Wisker, G. (2001) *The Postgraduate Research Handbook*. Basingstoke: Palgrave.

Wisker, G., Robinson, G., Trafford, V. and Thomas, J. (2000) The effectiveness of PhD support and development programmes for international students: an Israeli case study. In G. Wisker (ed.) *Good Practice Working with International Students*. Birmingham: Staff and Educational Developers Association.

Wisker, G., Robinson, G., Trafford, V., Creighton, M. and Warnes, M. (2003a) Recognising and overcoming dissonance in postgraduate student research. *Studies in Higher Education*, 28(1): 91–105.

Wisker, G., Robinson, G., Trafford, V., Warnes, M. and Creighton, E. (2003b) From supervisory dialogues to successful PhDs: strategies supporting and enabling the learning conversations of staff and students at postgraduate level. *Teaching in Higher Education*, 8(3): 383–97.

Wisker, G., Waller, S., Richter, U., Robinson, G., Trafford, V., Wicks, K. and Warnes, M. (2003c) *On Nurturing Hedgehogs: Developments Online for Distance*

and Offshore Supervision. Available online at http://surveys.canterbury.ac.nz/
herdsa03/pdfsref/Y1199.pdf (accessed 25 May 2004).

Wright, T. and Cochrane, R. (2000) Factors influencing successful submission of
PhD theses. *Studies in Higher Education,* 25(2): 181–93.

Wu, S., Griffiths, S., Wisker, G., Waller, S. and Illes, K. (2001) The learning
experience of postgraduate students: matching methods to aims. *Innovations in
Education and Teaching International,* 38: 292–308.

Younglove-Webb, Y., Gray, B., Abdalla, C. and Thurow, A. (1999) The dynamics
of multidisciplinary research teams in academia. *The Review of Higher Education,*
22: 425–40.

Index

advisor 2, 85
advisory committee 2, 85
Allen, L. 72
Allen, M. 13
Alpert, E. 2, 63, 64, 69, 80, 122
Amsterdamsaka, O. 10
Anglia Polytechnic University 158
Appel, L. 142–3, 148–9
Arts and Humanities Research Board 15, 90–1
Aspland, T. 65, 159, 164
Association of American Universities Committee on Graduate Education 46–7, 135–6
Association of Business Schools 40
Atkins, D. 94
Atkins, M. 1, 65, 102
Austin, A. 46, 135–6
Australia 9, 14, 15, 16, 153, 183, 202, 214, 218

Baldacchino, G. 197
Baty, P. 56, 105
BBSRC (Biotechnology and Biological Sciences Research Council) 26–7, 206–8
Becher, T. 33–4, 51, 53, 94, 102, 111, 113, 125, 148
Blaume, S. 10
Blaxter L. 99, 125, 172
Bonnet, A. 164
Bourner, T. 16, 20
Bowen, W.G. 8–10, 17, 111, 141
Boxer, M.J. 38
Braneld, P. 164
Brenhonm, K. 145
Brew, A. 1, 4, 25, 63, 65
British Psychological Society 34, 184

Brown, G. 1, 65, 102
Bruce, C. 164
Burnham, P. 187

Cadman, K. 66, 158
Canada 8, 15–16
candidates: expectations of in personal research framework 37; expectations of in positional research framework 36; institutional expectations of 23–4; institutional support for 29–30; trends in numbers of 16–17; *see also* domestic candidates, international candidates
Cebrian, S. 17
Chapman, H. 64
Charles Darwin University 23–4, 60–1
China 164
City University of London 78–9
Clark, B. 1, 7
Clegg, S. 1, 25
Cochrane, R. 112
Colebatch, H. 10
completion rates and times 1, 10, 107
Connelly, J. 9
Conrad, L. 17, 141, 144, 148
Conseil Scientifique de l'Université 1
co-supervision 2, 28, 71–81; benefits 71–3; managing 77–81; problems with 73–6
Cryer, P. 3, 59, 76, 110, 111, 113, 114, 123, 127, 155, 157, 160, 161, 162, 171, 173
Cullen, D. 2, 72

Dahlgren, L. 142–3, 148–9
Daniel, T. 211
De Vries, J. 148, 215

eBooks

eBooks – at www.eBookstore.tandf.co.uk

A library at your fingertips!

eBooks are electronic versions of printed books. You can store them on your PC/laptop or browse them online.

They have advantages for anyone needing rapid access to a wide variety of published, copyright information.

eBooks can help your research by enabling you to bookmark chapters, annotate text and use instant searches to find specific words or phrases. Several eBook files would fit on even a small laptop or PDA.

NEW: Save money by eSubscribing: cheap, online access to any eBook for as long as you need it.

Annual subscription packages

We now offer special low-cost bulk subscriptions to packages of eBooks in certain subject areas. These are available to libraries or to individuals.

For more information please contact webmaster.ebooks@tandf.co.uk

We're continually developing the eBook concept, so keep up to date by visiting the website.

www.eBookstore.tandf.co.uk

Learning Resources
Centre